Anita Wohlmann
Aged Young Adults

Aging Studies | Volume 4

Editorial

The series **Aging Studies** is edited by Heike Hartung, Steffen Höhne, Ulla Kriebernegg and Roberta Maierhofer.

Anita Wohlmann (Dr.) graduated from Johannes Gutenberg University Mainz, Germany, with a doctorate in American Studies. Her research interests include age studies, gender studies, North American literature, film and cultural studies.

Anita Wohlmann
Aged Young Adults
Age Readings of Contemporary American Novels and Films

[transcript]

Die vorliegende Arbeit wurde vom Fachbereich 05, Philosophie und Philologie, der Johannes Gutenberg-Universität Mainz im Jahr 2012 als Dissertation zur Erlangung des akademischen Grades eines Doktors der Philosophie (Dr. phil.) angenommen.

This study was accepted in 2012 by the Department 05, Philosophy and Philology, at Johannes Gutenberg University Mainz as a dissertation to graduate as a Doctor of Philosophy (Dr. phil.).

This publication was printed with the financial support of the Gutenberg Academy for Young Researchers at Johannes Gutenberg University Mainz and the University of Graz.

Bibliographic information published by the Deutsche Nationalbibliothek
The Deutsche Nationalbibliothek lists this publication in the Deutsche Nationalbibliografie; detailed bibliographic data are available in the Internet at http://dnb.d-nb.de

© **2014 transcript Verlag, Bielefeld**

All rights reserved. No part of this book may be reprinted or reproduced or utilized in any form or by any electronic, mechanical, or other means, now known or hereafter invented, including photocopying and recording, or in any information storage or retrieval system, without permission in writing from the publisher.

Cover layout: Kordula Röckenhaus, Bielefeld
Cover illustration: ina.mija / photocase.com
Printed by Majuskel Medienproduktion GmbH, Wetzlar
ISBN 978-3-8376-2483-0

Table of Contents

Acknowledgments | 9

Introduction | 13

1   Age and Aging in Theory and Practice | 37
1.1   Positions in Age Studies | 37
1.2   Age as a Metaphoric Practice | 63
1.3   Method: Defining the Age Reading | 72

2   Conflicts of Timing | 79
2.1   Joel Zwick's *My Big Fat Greek Wedding* | 79
2.2   Ageism and the Disciplinary Functions of Age Discourses | 91
2.3   Sam Mendes' *Away We Go* | 101

3   Living Across the Life Course | 113
3.1   Shifting Meanings of Adulthood:
       Perpetual Adolescence and Delayed Adulthood | 113
3.2   Tom Perrotta's *Little Children* | 122
3.3   Normativity and the Life Course | 144
3.4   Jonathan Franzen's *The Corrections* | 157

4   Mental Health and Age | 175
4.1   Positive Thinking and Entrepreneurial Selves | 175
4.2   Benjamin Kunkel's *Indecision* | 186
4.3   Consumer Cycles, Obsolescence, and (Im)Mortality | 200
4.4   Don DeLillo's *Cosmopolis* | 209

**5   Positive Age Metaphors:
     Miranda July's *The Future* and *It Chooses You* | 231**

Conclusion | 251

List of Figures | 259
List of Works Cited | 261

For Ursula and Matthias

Acknowledgments

When the idea for this book was initially conceived in 2009 during the conference "Lebens-Geschichten: Altern im Film" in the Department of Film Studies at Johannes Gutenberg University Mainz, it started out as a quite different project, focusing on characters at or around the age of 30 and examining how they view their thirtieth birthday. Since then, it has undergone many revisions and endless rewrites. Writing this book has been – for the most part – a great joy, and many, many people contributed to its genesis in various ways. These people were attentive readers and patient listeners, who believed in the project and graciously gave their time, energy, and intelligence to help me detect aberrations, flawed logic, and inconsistencies, thereby inspiring the final version of the book. I would like to express my sincerest gratitude and deep appreciation for their help.

In the Department of English and Linguistics at Johannes Gutenberg University Mainz, I am deeply grateful to Prof. Dr. Oliver Scheiding for the many years of his support, his boundless energy, his 6-a.m. emails and, most importantly, his confidence in my work and ideas. Thanks to the department's doctoral college "Life Writing" and its grant, I was able to focus thoroughly on the project and received helpful inspiration in regular colloquiums and doctoral meetings. I also wish to thank Prof. Dr. Alfred Hornung for the many different forms of support, encouraging words, humorous remarks and valuable advice he provided throughout the last years. Prof. Dr. Mita Banerjee was a great inspiration and offered astute and warm-hearted encouragement in many instances on both subject-related and professional levels. With her enthusiasm, Junior Prof. Dr. Birgit Däwes has helped me maintain my own enthusiasm and focus throughout the last third of the project. I am also grateful to Junior Prof. Dr. Antje Kampf for her unstinting support and kind words. Prof. Dr. Susanne Marschall has inspired me to stick to film studies and I am grateful for her guidance, generous support, and trust over so many years. Anette Vollrath has been wonderfully caring and efficient in organizing the many little things that need to be done on the administrative level. Similarly, Elisabeth Bodenstein has been a very supportive and cheerful guide through the bureaucratic jungle.

Many other people and institutions at Johannes Gutenberg University Mainz have supported this project directly and indirectly. The Gutenberg Academy put me in contact with excellent researchers, provided me with a platform in which to present my work, and has generously funded the many conference and study excursions necessary for a dissertation project. In particular, I would like to express my warmest gratitude to Prof. Dr. Ulrich Breuer, who linked his own research to mine and kindly offered himself as a sensible and astute mentor during application processes and other professional decisions. In a similar way, Dr. habil. Anja Hartung has been incredibly kind and helpful as a mentor and offered me honest and encouraging insights into academic life as well as practical support through the GAM network. The Frauenbüro at Johannes Gutenberg University Mainz indirectly supported this book through a grant for "Einzelcoaching," which put me into contact with Dr. Katja Wagner-Westerhausen, who accompanied me for a year with her highly valuable insight and genial advice.

The DAAD has sponsored several activities throughout the past four years, among which were summer schools and a research stay at the University of North Carolina at Chapel Hill, which gave me the opportunity to seek out renowned researchers from sociology and life course studies, including Prof. Dr. Michael J. Shanahan, Prof. Dr. Glen H. Elder, Jr., Prof. Dr. Victor W. Marshall, and Associate Prof. Dr. Lucille B. Bearon, all of whom generously imparted their knowledge and long-time experience to me. During the trinational summer school, colleagues from Georgia State University and Beijing University listened to my project presentations, gave valuable advice and sent books from their private libraries to help me expand my corpus (thanks again, Prof. Dr. Glenn T. Eskew).

Many people in colloquiums, in the American Studies division in Mainz, or at conferences abroad have listened to presentations and have read exposés, chapters, or articles related to this book, and I am incredibly thankful and appreciative to them (in alphabetic order): Junior Prof. Dr. Sibylle Baumbach, Dr. Rada Bieberstein, Dr. Margaret Morganroth Gullette,

Christian Knöppler, Prof. Dr. Rüdiger Kunow, Assistant Prof. Dr. Shauna Morgan Kirlew, Dr. Thomas Küpper, Dr. Frank Obenland, Junior Prof. Dr. Clemens Spahr, Prof. Dr. Nicole Waller as well as those kind readers I have already mentioned. I also want to express my appreciation for Annie McWhertor's meticulous and incredibly astute proofreading.

A big "thank you" goes to my dear colleagues in the Life Writing doctoral group, Pascale Cicolelli, Yvonne Gutenberger, Dr. des. Katja Kurz, and Pan Shan. You were a wonderful PhD support group.

There are many people who have read large excerpts of this book and/or supported me morally, financially, or through their invaluable friendship and love over the last years. My warmest gratitude and deepest appreciation to Tanja Budde, Johanna Gather, Axel Henke, Ralf Münch, Alice Roth, Martina Stöppel, Dr. des. Meike Uhrig, Susanne Wagner, Annette Wincowski, Kathrin Zeitz, and Ursula and Matthias Wohlmann.

I am also very thankful to Prof. Dr. Roberta Maierhofer and Assistant Prof. Dr. Ulla Kriebernegg, who have not only welcomed my research within the Aging Studies series at transcript Verlag but have also been extremely supportive and encouraging over the last few years. Thank you for introducing me to your network of so many wonderful people, for sharing ideas, and for your incredible energy and compassionate encouragement.

This publication was printed with the financial support of the Gutenberg Academy for Young Researchers at Johannes Gutenberg University Mainz and the University of Graz.

Introduction

A young woman with gray hair, as on the cover of this book, is an odd sight. Gray hair is testament to the passing of time and caused by a waning of pigment production. It is thus often considered a marker of chronological and biological old age. In 2010, a trend emerged in the fashion industry and among British and American socialites which showed twenty-year old women in a "silver rush," dyeing their hair gray and parading this edgy look on runways or red carpets (Hermanson 2010, La Ferla 2010).[1] According to Rose Weitz,[2] gray hair on young women has become a fashion statement, which "flout[s] one of fashion's last taboos" and is comparable to the subversive, individualistic aura of piercings or tattoos (qtd. in La Ferla n. pag.). This fashion trend appears ironic in light of the concerns voiced by scholars from age and gender studies, who warn against the all-pervasive youth cult and ageism in Western cultures and its detrimental effects (particularly) on aging women. Are age scholars wrong? Has old age become fashionable? Or do young women wear gray hair precisely *because* they are still young? How can we understand the "silver rush" of twenty-somethings?

Researchers in age studies do not ask these particular questions because young people are typically of little concern to age scholars who start their investigations with later age stages, such as middle-age, which starts around

---

1   Powdered white hair or white wigs were also fashionable in the eighteenth century, of course.
2   Weitz is the author of *Rapunzel's Daughters: What Women's Hair Tells Us About Their Lives*. New York: Farrar, Straus and Giroux, 2004.

age forty (e.g. Gullette 1988). Upon a closer look, however, there are many examples that suggest a relation between young people and age awareness. Take for instance the anti-aging skin cream market. For some time, anti-aging products have no longer been restricted to consumers whose skin shows actual signs of aging. Increasingly, the cosmetics industry is advertising anti-aging products to people in their twenties as a measure of prevention and protection of their youthful looks (cf. Wright 2008, Penning 2012). Walmart, for example, released an anti-aging beauty line aimed at 8- to 12-year-olds (cf. "Retailer Launches" 2011). It seems that the relentless agenda of the youth cult not only discriminates against old(er) people but also sends out warning messages to the young.

A second example is the term delayed adulthood (also called Peter Pandemic), which has become a research field for social scientists and life course scholars who investigate the lives of people in their twenties or thirties whose lifestyles resemble those of teenagers (Côté 2000, Blatterer 2007, Arnett 2007, Settersten & Ray 2010). Here, the topic of age appears as a chronological issue of poor timing for the so-called kidults, boomerang kids, or adultescents who are stuck between childhood and adulthood (Tierney 2004, Furman 2005, Hunter 2009, Henig 2010), indicating a conflict between chronological age, an expected age-appropriate social behavior, and a person's actual age-inappropriate conduct.

This conflict reappears in a different form in self-help books that are aimed at readers in their late twenties who seem to experience a life crisis upon turning thirty. Lia Macko's and Kerry Rubin's *Midlife Crisis at 30: How the Stakes Have Changed for a New Generation – And What to Do About It* (2004) is such a case in point. Similarly, Colette Petersen's book title *30 Isn't Old* (2007) suggests that a thirtieth birthday triggers an (age) crisis. These books insinuate that age is a conflictual topic for young people.

Age awareness is also thematized in contemporary novels. When the protagonist of Don DeLillo's novel *Cosmopolis* (2003), Eric Packer, aged 28, compares himself to a young dancing crowd he observes during a rave, he has an epiphany: "He felt old," the reader is told, because "[a]n era had come and gone without him" (127). In the course of the novel, DeLillo repeatedly refers to obsolescence or mortality when he describes his character's life crisis. In the Hollywood blockbuster *My Big Fat Greek Wedding* (2002), it is also a reference to age that sparks the life crisis of 30-year-old

Toula Portokalos, who is told by her father: "You'd better get married soon. You're starting to look ... old." With these first lines of Joel Zwick's romantic comedy, the movie sets the tone for a distinct sense of the finitude of time. A story unfolds in which the protagonist repeatedly struggles with her age-inappropriate situation and appearance before she symbolically rejuvenates and meets the man of her dreams.

These exemplary observations suggest that there is a conflictual relation between young people or characters and notions of age or aging. The cover picture and the "silver rush" fashion trend indicate that there might also be a playful, ironic, or resisting connotation to this age awareness. These preliminary observations raise several questions:

- Where does the apprehension of age and aging in twenty-somethings come from? How can we understand this phenomenon? What is the nature of age experiences in young people or characters? What does a phrase like "I feel old" stand for?
- What is the *cultural meaning* behind the seeming contradiction of chronologically young people or characters and their subjective age awareness? What does it mean to be (chronologically) young? Is there a standard or a specific age that marks people as young? If so, who determines this standard? And when does the change between 'young' and 'old' occur? Is it at 30, 35, or 40? Does aging unfold between polar opposites of young and old? Or should we rather speak of a spectrum, in which the markers of young and old are flexible and situational?
- If we keep the idea of a spectrum in mind, which *function* does a reference to age have in specific contexts? What does Toula's father, for example, imply when he calls his daughter old? Do references to age have a *symbolic meaning* that expresses something else? Assuming that fictional works are not simply mimetic representations of a social reality but complex negotiations of cultural knowledge, what kind of meaning do fictional negotiations add to the phenomenon of age awareness in young adult characters?

These research questions touch upon two distinct disciplinary areas: (a) the cultural background and the social realities of age or aging and (b) the function and meaning of age or aging in fictional narratives, such as films or novels. The first area inspires investigations into social practices, interpersonal relationships, and social institutions. It asks for the cultural notions and values connected with age or aging, such as 'youthfulness equals attractiveness.' The second area is of interest to literary critics and film scholars who analyze the fictional negotiations of a zeitgeist.

This study approaches the phenomenon of young characters' age awareness from the point of view of literature and film studies. Taking my cue from the early literary gerontologist Janice Sokoloff and her study *The Margin That Remains* (1987), I concentrate on novels because

> [l]iterature [...] appears to be the richest source we have for representations of aging, and for the effort to understand the contradictory and complex ways in which the human psyche's experience of time shapes character. Such a subjective experience of time is frequently in a state of negotiation or conflict with society's more objective and chronological measure of time. Furthermore, each century perceives time, and therefore the relation of years to 'maturity,' differently. (129-130)

Hence, if literature constitutes a rich source of knowledge, experiences, and negotiations, as Sokoloff claims, it makes sense to look to novels to investigate the meanings and functions of age or aging. Sokoloff examines British canonical novels from the nineteenth and twentieth centuries. While her pioneer study is inspiring in its approach, it needs further development and an expansion. My study attempts to update Sokoloff's research by focusing on very recent American novels that were published in the first decade of the new millennium. In view of the observations I made on anti-aging products, delayed adulthood, and self-help books, it seems that the topic of age has assumed a new urgency in the last decade. Moreover, I would like to open up the corpus of Sokoloff's study by integrating films into the analysis.

This cross-media approach, which is based on an extensive definition of text, appears mandatory in light of the observations made by one of the most prominent figures in the field of age studies. The age critic Margaret Morganroth Gullette examines the ways in which people are aged by culture, and, in doing so, she works with the notion of "age narratives," which she defines as "vehicles for organizing" cultural knowledge about aging (*Aged by Culture* 15). According to Gullette, age narratives (or narratives of aging) are "our virtual realities" and they "make a fundamental difference to the quality of our lives, starting with our willingness or reluctance, at any age, to grow older" (11). Gullette's age narratives take many shapes: They can be autobiographical interviews, childhood experiences, novels, cultural myths, or visualizations used by scientists. In *Aged by Culture* (2004), Gullette gives an example of such a visual age narrative when she describes how the Boston Museum of Science (during a "Secrets of Aging" show in 2000) used photographs of children to show them how they will look as they age. "This is the way all faces age," the title of the exhibit implied (4). The movie-like sequence of their own aging appalled the children, who learned, as Gullette argues, that they will invariably become ugly upon growing older. Gullette finds "that even without text, visual sequences always have life narratives secretively embedded in them. Such narratives declare the meaning of the passing of life time, not day by day but on a big scale" (10). The message that the children at the exhibition received was one about loss and decline.

Gullette's age narratives also permeate films, as the analyses by Karen M. Stoddard (1983), Robert E. Yahnke (2000), Amir Cohen-Shalev (2009), and Thomas Küpper (2010) demonstrate. In Stoddard's analysis of the representation of aged women in American popular film, she argues that

[p]opular media images[3] relate to what a culture believes, wants to believe, and wishes to legitimize – these images are part truth, part myth, and part wishful thinking – and an examination of the evolving images allows speculation on their possible relationships to cultural needs and realities. A cycle exists in which the media give the audience what they feel the public wants [...], while the public is often highly accepting of what passes before them, the psychological strength of the media form lending instant credibility to its products. (6-7)

Following Gullette's definition of age narratives and Stoddard's reasoning on the mutual exchange between film and culture, I understand films and novels as *fictional age narratives* or *fictional narratives*,[4] which feed from the culture from which they emerge and simultaneously send out messages about age and aging to their viewers and readers. In order to grasp and understand these embedded messages present in fictional (age) narratives that

---

3   Stoddard defines "popular media images" as "images in advertising, television and film" (6).
4   Also see page 73.

feature young adults, I suggest that a distinction between media- and genre-specific differences of film and novel is no longer necessary – even though the discrepancies regarding aesthetic and representational techniques are duly noted.

Examples that document the dissolving boundaries between genres or media forms abound. *Little Children* (2004), for instance, one of the fictional narratives I will discuss, was first a novel written by Tom Perrotta and then adapted to the screen by Todd Field two years later. *Little Children* illustrates that Perrotta's story functions within different media forms.[5] Similarly, Julie Powell's cross-media success of *The Julie/Julia Project*, which started out as a blog in 2002, was then published as a novel in 2005 and eventually became a Hollywood movie in 2009, justifies an approach that leaves aside generic and genre-specific differences for the sake of understanding the cultural meanings of age and aging embedded in fictional narratives.

In order to denaturalize the cultural meanings of age and aging, Gullette calls for an inventory of the invisible practices, metaphors, narratives, and genres that shape a culture's imaginaries of age or aging ("From Life Storytelling" 107). Gullette's inventory is meant to "elevate subtextual matters into explicitness and contextualize spotty evidence" (107). This book would like to contribute to such an inventory by focusing on the age awareness of characters whom one would not automatically consider to be candidates for age experiences. The oddness of this phenomenon might explain why there is little theoretical research on young adults in age studies. This lack of attention to young adults, that is adults in their twenties and thirties,[6] is unsat-

---

5 Also consider the following film adaptations made or currently being made. DeLillo's novel *Cosmopolis* was filmed in the summer of 2011 and released in 2012. Andrew Bujalski wrote a screenplay of Kunkel's novel *Indecision* in 2007, and Noah Baumbach will be the director of Franzen's *The Corrections*, which is currently in the casting process.

6 The term "young adults" is defined differently in various contexts. Young-adult fiction, for instance, refers to teenage readers (cf. Halverson 20). The British "Transition to Adulthood Network" defines young adults as aged 18 to 24 (cf. <http://www.t2a.org.uk>, accessed on 13 September 2012). Other scholars, such as Robert J. Havighurst or Erik Erikson, define early or young adulthood between age 19 and 29 or between age 19 and 40. According to the *Oxford English*

isfactory given that, as Gullette argues, people of all ages are aged by culture[7] (cf. *Aged by Culture* 18, 118). Similarly, Kathleen Woodward acknowledges that "old age and middle age are part of the larger continuum of a discourse on age itself, a system of age that includes infancy, childhood, adolescence, and young adulthood" („Introduction" x). However, Woodward's focus lies on old age and middle age because „at this point in time it is critical that research in cultural studies and the arts focus on the later years precisely because this time of life has been largely ignored" (x). In establishing age studies as an interdisciplinary and international field of research, age scholars like Woodward and Gullette have produced a substantial body of theories and concepts which provide the basis for this book.

Research Field

Age Studies or gerontology encompasses a multi-disciplinary field, spanning medicine, biology, neuroscience, social science, cultural studies, and literature or film studies. Terminologically speaking, gerontology is the older designation for this vast area of research, coined by Elie Metchnikoff in 1904 (cf. Cole 195). Age studies was introduced in 1993 by Gullette (cf. "Creativity, Gender, Aging" 45-6). She envisions age studies as a "combination of critical gerontology and cultural studies" (cf. Cole et al. xvii). Or, in Gullette's own words:

Age studies is my term for a large interdisciplinary zone whose practitioners are becoming increasingly aware of age as a category and increasingly skillful at using it

---

Dictionary, young adulthood is preceded by adolescence and followed by middle age, with middle age being defined as age 45 to 65. When I speak of young adult characters, I refer to characters in their twenties and thirties.

7   To speak of a single American culture evokes an essentialist notion of culture. While I am very much aware of this problem and want to emphasize that I do not suggest that there is one unified American culture but rather multiple different cultures within American society, I am nevertheless using the singular form of culture in this study. On the one hand, the singular facilitates the use of Gullette's terminology, which is central to my study. On the other hand, the social demography of the characters in my corpus is surprisingly alike: All characters (with the exception of Toula) come from white, middle-class American families.

in their very different kinds of work. The zone includes women's studies, gender studies, literary gerontology, life-course studies in developmental psychology, sociology, family and social history, and anthropology. ("Creativity, Gender, Aging" 45)

Gullette prefers the designation age studies over literary gerontology because she sees a need to expand the field of gerontology beyond studies that consider the elderly through literature or film, positioning age studies as "an interdisciplinary study of culture" ("Age (Aging)" 11).[8] I share Gullette's preference for the term age studies. Even though my approach is geared towards an understanding of young characters and their age experiences in novels and film, I consider the cultural influences on age and aging vital to the analysis of my subject. By combining theories from cultural studies and age studies, the concept of age or aging becomes more fluid, more open and situational.

It is only since the 1970s that scholars of the humanities showed an interest in the topic of age or aging. Anne Wyatt-Brown considers the "Conference on Human Values and Aging" in 1975 at Case Western Reserve University as the first incentive to venture into this new field of research, which was received rather hesitantly in the academic community, given that literary gerontology not only demanded that scholars familiarize themselves with the terminologies and methodologies of other disciplines; these pioneers also had difficulties in convincing natural scientists of the value of their qualitative research findings. Nevertheless, literary gerontology gradually emerged as an avenue of research and began to explore the following areas:

(1) analyses of literary attitudes towards aging;
(2) humanistic approaches to literature and aging;
(3) psychoanalytic explorations of literary works and their authors;
(4) applications of gerontological theories about autobiography, life review, and midlife transitions; and
(5) psychoanalytically informed studies of the creative process. (Wyatt-Brown, "Coming of Age" 300)

---

8   Likewise, Woodward prefers „age studies" over „a study of aging" because „age studies" is more comprehensive in scope, including the „system of age" and thus all age groups („Introduction" x).

In their comprehensive *Handbook of the Humanities and Aging*, Thomas Cole et al. suggest that any study of age and aging "both promotes and necessitates interdisciplinary thinking" (xii). Social sciences, demography, public policy, literary and visual representations, cultural studies, philosophy, bioethics, clinical care, theology, end-of-life-care, and multiculturalism represent only some of the vantage points used by the authors of the *Handbook*. Relevant to social scientists, physicians, policy makers, and care takers, as Cole et al. argue, research into age and aging borders on a variety of different themes, such as cultural meanings of age, intergenerational relations, philosophical and ethical concerns, religiosity and spirituality, creativity, alternative representations of age, or issues about death and dying (cf. xx). Constance Rooke lists the following recurring themes as central topics in age studies:

[i]ntergenerational conflicts, societal change, disengagement, the life review, poverty, loneliness, sexuality, body image, frailty, memory loss, illness, loss of independence, loss of friends and family, stereotypical reduction and marginalization, the motivation and behavior of caregivers, the terrors and possible benefits of institutionalization, attitudes toward religion and death. (254)

The narrative representations of older characters have inspired studies, which investigate an older character's development in terms of a decline plot (Gullette 1997) or, in more positive terms, in the form of a "Reifungsroman" or "Vollendungsroman," a novel of ripening or "winding up" (cf. Rooke 1992, Waxman 1990). Some studies apply psychological or psychoanalytic vantage points or use a gender perspective (e.g. Waxman 1990; Woodward 1991). Creativity in old age and the literary development of authors throughout the life course is of interest to scholars who consider aging to be a creative process that influences the "late style" of an author (e.g. Wyatt-Brown 1988).

Acclaimed feminist authors also became interested in the topics of age and aging and published pertinent studies, such as Simone de Beauvoir's *La Vieillesse* (1970), Susan Sontag's essay "The Double Standard of Aging" (1972), Germaine Greer's *The Change: Women, Aging and the Menopause* (1993), or Betty Friedan's *The Fountain of Age* (1993). These studies focus on the youth cult and its social, psychological, and individual consequences for women. Second-Wave Feminism, just as theories of multiculturalism or post-structuralism, contributed significantly to the field of age studies with theories and approaches regarding "cultural differences, notions of representation, displacement, diaspora, models of margin-center[, or] hegemony-difference relations" (Kunow "The Coming of Age" 304).

Scholars of American literature and culture have also focused on the topic of age and aging and found age studies to be an intriguing lens through which to view American novels and films. Roberta Maierhofer suggests, for instance, that we consider female aging a paradigm of American culture because, as she maintains, aging puts questions of personal identity into the center of attention and forces individuals to negotiate possibilities and constraints in terms of social structures and individual experiences (cf. 17, 35). According to Maierhofer, the topic of aging as a vantage point of American literature is particularly conducive to themes that are often treated in American literature, such as individuality, personal identity, difference, race, class or gender (cf. 35). In like manner, Kunow suggests that we consider age and aging central themes in American culture. A complex treatment of the topic of age or aging might challenge "the 'monogenerational myth' of U.S.-America" and thus of a nation that conceptualizes itself as "forever young" (Kunow, "Chronologically Gifted" 26).

Most age scholars disregard the possibility that young adults might have age experiences and use this age group as a mere reference group in their studies on midlife or old age.[9] This observation is particularly true for empirical studies by scholars with a medical, neurological, or psychological background who assume that age experiences originate exclusively in material, biological, and physical changes of the body or brain (e.g. Anguera et

---

9 The studies by Sinikka Aapola, Janice Sokoloff, and Lisa Niles are an exception to the rule. Aapola is one of the few sociologists who applies gerontological research to the phase of youth. The literary scholar Sokoloff focuses on the representations of aging across a character's life course, and Niles analyzes the nineteenth century novel *Armadale* by Wilkie Collins and discusses the relations between cosmetics and a 35-year-old criminal woman whose age is experienced as a threat.

al. 2013).[10] As a consequence, since young adults have young bodies, it is assumed that they do not have age experiences. Therefore, Phoenix et al. contend that there is almost no systematic research on the aging experiences of young adults and that "to date we have little comprehension of the ways in which growing older may be anticipated by young people" ("Young Athletic" 110). Thus, according to the Finnish sociologist Sinikka Aapola, a chronological approach to age is "unidimensional" and must be expanded with other dimensions in order to acknowledge the multi-faceted discourses of age (296, 299).

In my attempt to open up the field of age studies to younger people or characters, Gullette's work is central. On the one hand, Gullette herself has expanded the scope of age studies towards midlife and has thus examined an age group that was previously ignored in earlier research on age or aging.[11] In doing so, Gullette has started to establish a critical field of age studies that "should be as comfortable dealing with 'the midlife' as with 'youth' or 'old age'" and thus should engage in research that tries to understand age *"across the life course"* ("Age Studies as Cultural Studies" 217-8; original emphasis). On the other hand, Gullette has introduced and coined several terms, from which I have taken a cue for the terminology I apply in this book. In conceptualizing the intricate and often invisible ways in which people are aged by culture, Gullette was inspirational for what I call *aged young adults*. This term designates characters in their twenties and thirties who have internalized the cultural meanings of age or aging (also see pages 74-5). Similarly, when I speak of *cultural imaginaries about age and aging*, Gullette provided a terminological point of departure with her concept of life course imaginaries (cf. "From Life Storytelling" 102), which helped me to frame cultural imaginaries associated with age and aging as a body of knowledge about what it means to grow old(er) in a particular cultural context. A more detailed definition of these terms will follow in the next chapter (see pages 72-3).

---

10 The study by Anguera et al. actually demonstrates that cognitive impairment due to old age is a not a one-way street as the capacity to multitask of elderly participants could be improved with training.

11 Consider, for instance, Gullette's studies *Safe at Last in the Middle Years: The Invention of the Midlife Progress Novel* (1988) or *Declining to Decline: Cultural Combat and the Politics of the Midlife* (1997).

There are further age scholars who have laid the groundwork for the approach used in this study. A handful of sociologists have conducted qualitative interviews with high school students and twenty-somethings and found empirical evidence that confirms my observations on the importance of age in the lives of young adults (cf. Rambo 1992, Aapola 2002, Phoenix & Sparkes 2005, Wainwright & Turner 2006). These studies undermine the simplistic union of body and mind, which presupposes that only an old body can cause age awareness or feelings of being old. The researchers found that the respondents (who are students, athletes, ballet dancers, and table dancers) rely on a youthful, strong, and attractive body. Their feelings of being aged or old have, however, emerged from quite different situations.

Cassandra Phoenix and Andrew C. Sparkes find in their study on young athletes that "gerontophobic images" play a major role in people's imaginations of their future selves (117). There also seems to be a discrepancy between looking old and feeling old, as ballet dancers (or other top athletes) are considered (or can start to feel) old in their mid-twenties. One of the dancers who Steven P. Wainwright and Bryan S. Turner interviewed admits:

25 is the verge of getting old. It sounds awful but it's true. You can take your pension at 35. [...] But your body does change as you get older. What I've noticed, even at 24, 25, is that I can still do anything I always could but just not as easily. I'd have to warm up a bit more, or I'd have to think about it. Before I'd just do something without thinking. I can still do it, but it just hurts to do it. It's not like agony, but it hurts. (245)

Wainwright and Turner summarize that, "[i]n the social world of ballet, as in many athletic sports, a thirty-year old is perceived as 'old'" (245). Wainwright and Turner challenge simplistic constructivist views of aging: Instead of assuming that age is only dependent on an aging body or only a social construct, they advocate an 'intermediate constructionist stance [which] contends that the body is socially moderated, not simply invented by society" (245). The ballet dancers are considered old because their bodies have become old (in terms of less efficient) in comparison to younger, more flexible or resilient bodies.

Carol Rambo's study on table dancers substantiates the importance of the socio-cultural context on the meaning of age or aging for younger people. In the world of table dance, aging is significant regarding the ideal of an attractive, youthful body. The peak of perceived youthfulness – which is around age 26 for ballet dancers (cf. Wainwright and Turner, 246) – occurs even earlier in the careers of table dancers. Rambo finds that the average age of dancers is 19 or 20 (cf. 307). Table dancers in their mid-twenties are considered old for two reasons: On the one hand, the customers in strip bars are often very young and are looking for women who are younger than themselves (cf. 307); on the other hand, Rambo remarks that, with aging, table dancers are considered less desirable (because they might get heavier, for example) which negatively affects their sexual appeal (cf. 313). Hence, regardless of how chronologically young table dancers might be, they can be considered old at an early age (cf. 315). Therefore, for dancers, "the definition of old is both bodily and socially contingent" (308). Even though Rambo's study is problematic in some aspects,[12] her research is crucial because she shows that feeling or being old is situational. Hence, age or aging in young adults is subjectively experienced, culturally shaped, and socially moderated. But it also has a biological or physical dimension. Consequently, the meanings connected with age or aging – such as loss of attractiveness, employability, loss of physical resilience, or pain – are highly contingent.

---

12 Rambo's observations on the working conditions of table dancer seem to uncritically reproduce stereotypical notions of aging as decline. Rambo observes, for instance: „While she [the 'older' table dancer] still may be an adept dancer, her body loses appeal as a sexual object. Sustaining the resources she formerly possessed – youth and beauty – becomes strained and in the eyes of customers has diminished sexual utility, that is, a form of aging" (309). Similarly questionable is Rambo's terminology in this respect. In speaking of „managed utility," she evokes a sense of agency and active managing on the side of the aging table dancers, which I find problematic. After all, Rambo's descriptions of the work options for older table dancers illustrate that the dancers' strategy of „carving out a niche" is invariably connected with a loss of status and harsher working conditions. These 'managing' women seem to have no alternative to this downward spiral because "no one just quits" (311-2, 315).

Aapola maintains in her analysis of 88 autobiographical essays written by fifteen- and sixteen-year-old students that one of the dimensions or discourses of age is symbolic age, which "refers to expectations attached to various life-phases regarding a person's appropriate behavior, skills and dress styles" (307). A particular age, adulthood in the case of Aapola's teenagers, is thus associated with symbolic meaning, such as "freedom of movement," "autonomy," "independence," or "agency," all of which are indicative of the social status of a young person (308). Which other meanings of age or aging become apparent through age experiences?

The decline narrative that is imagined as a universal trajectory of the aging process (Gullette 1997, 2004, 2011), for instance, represents a prejudiced (or ageist) cultural concept of what it means to age because it suggests that growing into old age inevitably entails a loss of health, vitality, social power, beauty, or sexuality. Such a cultural imaginary about age and aging can result in young people's feelings of repulsion and fear when they think about growing older (Phoenix & Sparkes 2006, Gullette 2011). Generally speaking, age scholars critically observe that old age – in Western cultures at least – predominantly involves unfavorable, stereotypical, and even discriminatory images and narratives.

The field of age studies provides important concepts for investigating how cultural imaginaries about age and aging are used in social interaction. Kathleen Woodward's concept of age as a movable marker is crucial in this respect (*Aging and Its Discontents* 6). According to Woodward, individuals develop different "age-selves" over time between which they oscillate (cf. "Performing Age" 166, 173). Simon Biggs considers age as a signifier, which can be applied as desired or as necessary (cf. "Age" 48). Susan Sontag's concept of age as a movable, recurring doom also turns out to be highly significant in an analysis of contemporary young adult characters (cf. "The Double Standard" 32-33). Claiming that aging is "a crisis of the imagination rather than 'real life,'" Sontag's feminist analysis expands the idea of age experiences and age crises beyond the realm of the body and its biological contingency (33). The subjective and cultural dimensions of age imaginaries thus take center stage. And, eventually, since age or aging is not only experienced by the individual but also observed by others, ascriptions of being young or old also influence a person's age awareness because ascriptions imply value judgments and expectations. Therefore, Cheryl Laz claims that age is a performative social practice and thus actively and interactively constituted. The cultural meanings upon which people "act their age" or are "doing age" remain invisible, however, and it is the aim of this study to render them visible.

Approaching Aged Young Adults

Departing from the abovementioned theoretical and methodological concepts on age and aging, which I will discuss in more depth in the next chapter, this study hypothesizes that the cultural imaginaries associated with age or aging circulate in fictional narratives but are often unnoticed, invisible, or naturalized. When a character's age is mentioned in a novel or film, a reader or viewer tends to consider this information as a simple, descriptive feature with no further meaning or function. A closer look into the fictional narratives of this study will reveal, however, that the mentioning of a character's age often has a metaphoric function. Thus, when we are informed about a character's age, we are not dealing with a simple description of a chronological fact but with a metaphor that points to a more complex meaning. Therefore, a character like Toula Portokalos in *My Big Fat Greek Wedding* is not actually old in a chronological or biological sense. Rather, her father's ascription of Toula's old looks marks her as deviant from what he expects to be normal and appropriate for a woman her age. Hence, when Toula's father uses references to age, he actually talks about something else, such as female roles, 'normal' life courses, and Toula's nonconformity to his expectations. He also seems to reprimand his daughter for her status, which indicates a disciplinary function that references to age involve. Moreover, it is conspicuous that references to age typically coincide with conflictual moments or life crises and that they are common in the beginning of a plot, when a crisis triggers the ensuing action, which suggests that references to age also have a function within the plot structure.

I understand *references to age* as any kind of evocation that refers to a character's age, to a character's feelings regarding his or her age (e.g. feeling old), or to a description of a character's appearance or conduct that is framed in terms of age (e.g. behaving childishly). Age or aging do not constitute the dominant or obvious themes in the fictional narratives. They are rather smaller textual, dialogical, or visual elements, which recur throughout the narratives. In this sense, I will suggest that we consider such age references to be *metaphoric practices*, borrowing the term from Susan Sontag's analysis of cancer and AIDS metaphors (cf. *Illness as Metaphor* 92). The metaphoric practice of age does not take references to age literally but metaphorically. Age references thus insinuate feelings or associations that may but need not be linked with age or aging.

The normative framework that surfaces in age metaphors manifests itself in the characters' sensitivities regarding social position, achievements, or timing and finds expression in a range of 'symptoms,' such as a sense of failure, depression, or apathy. Moreover, references to a character's age seem to work within binaries of young and old, good or bad, successful or unsuccessful, healthy or sick. Despite these rigid binaries and in accordance with Woodward's concept of age as a movable marker, the functions and meanings of age or aging are flexible and thus operate within a spectrum. With a focus on the textual and visual strategies and devices used by authors and filmmakers when they evoke age or aging, this study examines the multiple and situational functions and meanings of age metaphors.

Age Readings

I selected seven fictional narratives that feature young adult characters in their twenties and thirties who have a conflictual relationship to their age. This conflict either surfaces in the form of age-inappropriate behavior or in a crisis that is somehow connected to age. I used the following selection criteria to establish a well-balanced variety of narratives that are comparable: The narratives all feature characters in their mid-twenties to mid-thirties as central characters.[13] More specifically, the characters' ages range from 28 to 35. The plots describe a conflict, discomfort, or crisis of the central characters, which is linked repeatedly to age, age-related behavior, or a sense of temporality. I decided to focus on novels and films – and not on television series, short stories, poetry, or songs for example – because nov-

---

13 The character of Denise Lambert in Jonathan Franzen's *The Corrections* constitutes an exception because she is not a central character. I decided to include *The Corrections* into my corpus because of the novel's particular metaphoric use of age and because the topic of age pervades the characterization of Denise Lambert's parents and her older brother Gary.

els and films have a similar narrative structure.[14] For reasons of comparability, I also chose very contemporary films and novels, which were published or released in the United States within a time period of ten years (between 2001 and 2011). Therefore, all of the fictional narratives are written or directed by Americans in an American context. Only the British director Sam Mendes is an exception to the rule (*Away We Go*). *My Big Fat Greek Wedding* is set in an intercultural, Greek-American context and was written by a Canadian-American, Nia Vardalos. The film is set in Chicago.

The resulting corpus of fictional narratives comprises three films – *My Big Fat Greek Wedding* (2002), *Away We Go* (2009), and *The Future* (2011) – and four novels – Jonathan Franzen's *The Corrections* (2001), Don DeLillo's *Cosmopolis* (2003), Tom Perrotta's *Little Children* (2004), and Benjamin Kunkel's *Indecision* (2005). This corpus represents a balanced selection on several levels. The narratives are set across the North American continent – three take place on the East coast (*Indecision, Cosmopolis, Little Children*), two are set in the Midwest (*The Corrections, My Big Fat Greek Wedding*), and one movie is set on the West Coast (*The Future*). *Away We Go* is a road movie and features the West (Arizona), Midwest (Wisconsin), Canada (Toronto), and the South (Florida). The fictional narratives include small independent productions (e.g. *The Future*) and blockbusters (e.g. *My Big Fat Greek Wedding*) as well as debut novels (e.g. Kunkel's *Indecision*) and novels by well-established authors (e.g. DeLillo's *Cosmopolis*). Some of the fictional narratives were highly praised and awarded several prizes (e.g. *The Corrections*), while others received critical reviews (e.g. *Away We Go, Cosmopolis*). Since this study does not pursue a particular focus on gender,[15] the protagonists' gender is equally distributed

---

14 When I speak of a similar narrative structure, I mean that the story is typically told within 90 minutes or within a finite amount of pages. The stories do not have the open structure of a television series, yet they allow enough time for character development. In this sense, novels and films are easier to compare than a feature film would be with a short story or a novel with a television series.

15 Gender and age are closely related, of course. In *The Corrections* and in *The Future*, for instance, age figures as a problematic topic for the female characters when it comes to pregnancy and fertility. For reasons of conciseness, this study does not fan out the complexities of age for women and men. Moreover, Susan

with five female characters (Verona, Toula, Sarah, Denise, Sophie) and five male characters (Burt, Todd, Dwight, Eric, Jason).

As I have noted earlier, the age crises of young adult characters have not been discussed from a cultural age studies perspective so far. Life crises of young adults, however, have interested scholars from various disciplines. Sociologists and journalists have thematized the quarter-life crisis and have tried to define new generations of Millennials or Generation Y. The figure of the perpetual adolescent or delayed adult has been theorized by developmental psychologists and sociologists. And, of course, for literary scholars, the genre of the *Bildungsroman* imposes itself as an expectable point of departure for investigating typical crises of young characters. *Aged Young Adults* does not aim at a generational portrait nor does it try to inscribe itself within the genre of the (late-) coming-of-age story. On the contrary, this study asks whether these approaches and labels might actually oversimplify or misunderstand the meanings and functions of age awareness in contemporary fictional narratives. After all, one might wonder how fitting it is to speak of coming of age when a character feels old or is considered to look old: Such an ascription implies that the character has already matured and is about to transition into (symbolic) old age.

A note on the methodology of this study, the age reading. Following Stoddard's claim on the reciprocal relationship between film and its audience, I assume that fictional narratives respond to the socio-cultural environment from which they emerge and, conversely, they incorporate cultural knowledge about narrative genres or conventions, life crises, generations, and transitions into adulthood. Instead of reading the fictional narratives through either a purely literary or a purely socio-cultural lens, I will try to juxtapose these perspectives and their ensuing topics, explanatory models, and narrative conventions in order to find out how the novels and films negotiate public discourses and narrative conventions but also how they criticize, satirize, transform, or dismiss them. This juxtaposition is based on the assumption that novels and films are rarely direct mirrors of a social reality.

Sontag, for example, concedes in "The Double Standard of Aging" that her argument regarding age or aging is applicable to both genders, though in different ways and with different consequences. For a more gendered approach to fictional narratives dealing with female young adults, see my article "Junge Altersbilder in den Medien" (2013).

While they incorporate and respond to a social reality and a recognizable cultural context, novels and films create their own fictional universes and semantic associations. A juxtaposition of fictional and sociological approaches unveils the creative usage and intrinsic value of metaphors of age or aging in fiction and clarifies whether or not the use of age in fictional narratives is realistic, exaggerated or even distorted. Taking my cue from Woodward's example in *Aging and Its Discontents* (1991), in which she juxtaposes Freudian concepts with twentieth-century American fiction, an age reading is a close reading of fictional (age) narratives that has its main focus on the topic of age or aging and that consults studies from other disciplines or fields in order to better understand the functions and meanings of age in the corpus of fictional narratives. An age reading thus suggests a dialogic structure, in which fictional narratives and pertinent scientific studies respond to each other and pose new questions, which are passed along to the next chapter, fictional narrative, or study.

The Structure of an Age Reading: Chapter Organization

Ensuing from the methodological approach of an age reading, the organization of this study reflects a dialogic nature. In the following chapters, I will first establish the theoretical background and work out the method of an age reading from an in-depth discussion of existing theories and concepts. It will become clear how my approach positions itself within the research field of age studies (Chapter 1.1). I will then define the concept of age as a metaphoric practice (Chapter 1.2) and the method of an age reading (Chapter 1.3). *My Big Fat Greek Wedding* will serve as an entry door into my analysis. This movie is particularly well-suited as a departure point because it appears as an innocuous romantic comedy. Even though it starts out with an obvious reference to the protagonist's age and her conflictual relation to age, most viewers will focus on the apparent themes of love, self-realization, and intercultural relationships. The movie's invisible messages about age and aging, however, as I will show in Chapter 2.1, are very problematic because of the ageist, i.e. age-discriminatory agenda of the film.

My age reading of *My Big Fat Greek Wedding* raises several questions: How do age scholars conceptualize age discrimination? What are the meanings of being old in Western cultures? And how can ageism be a disciplinary strategy or mechanism of control? In Chapter 2.2, I will elaborate on these questions by discussing how, according to gerontological research, age and aging constitute a moral enterprise and how old age is predominantly perceived as a social problem. It will become clear that age is often envisioned as a binary of young and old. The meanings associated with age are therefore binary as well. Youth is stereotypically linked with health, productivity, resilience, or attractiveness while old age is generally imagined as the loss of all such qualities. Within such a binary logic, control mechanisms and disciplinary practices have emerged that label old, unproductive people as losers. The workings of these mechanisms can be observed in the characters of Sam Mendes' movie *Away We Go* (Chapter 2.3). Burt and Verona consider themselves losers because they are of a certain age (33 and 34) and have not achieved what they expected to have achieved. In *Away We Go*, 'feeling old' functions as a form of self-marginalization and as a concession of being unsuccessful and a failure. This crisis triggers the characters' journey in the movie, which is accompanied by references to age and an acute sense of temporality or timing. The male protagonist Burt is repeatedly described as a perpetual adolescent and thus as someone who is stuck in the transition between two age stages and who does not behave appropriately for his age.

The term 'perpetual adolescent' feeds from a phenomenon that is profusely discussed by developmental psychologists and life course sociologists who wonder: Why do so many adults in their twenties and thirties behave like teenagers? What is the larger socio-cultural context of the perpetual adolescent? What is delayed adulthood symptomatic of? And what are the theoretical repercussions of kidults or adultescents on the definition and meaning of life stages? As sociologists and psychologists have shown, the perpetual adolescent is symptomatic of a particular cultural and economic context, in which the meanings of life stages and moralities associated with adult behavior have become fluid and unstable (Chapter 3.1). In *Little Children*, we can see how the figure of the perpetual adolescent is used to undermine the norms and moralities of a smug, white, middle-class suburban community, in which Todd, the protagonist, longs for his earlier life as a teenager (Chapter 3.2). In the novel, age-inappropriate behavior is metaphorically linked with inappropriate relationships and improper sexual desire. By blurring the boundaries between morally correct and incorrect behavior, the metaphoric practices of age used in *Little Children* challenge the norms and meanings of transgressions.

Norms and expectations also shape the background against which life course imaginaries project predictable patterns of living through time. Life course theorists have conceptualized what (allegedly) standard or default life courses look like and examined the often quite visual trajectories associated with living through time (Chapter 3.3). The consequences of nonconformity with the default version can become a pungent device of social control and devaluation. Denise Lambert, the youngest daughter in Jonathan Franzen's fictitious family in *The Corrections*, experiences the powerful consequences of her transgressions in terms of timing and age-appropriate behavior (Chapter 3.4). Denise has a tendency to date much older men, which profoundly upsets her family and which functions as an indicator of a deeply conflicted personality and family. Age and mental health, that is depression, coalesce in Franzen's fictional universe on several interconnected levels.

What is the nature of this semantic connection between age and mental health? Do references to depression imply mechanisms of control and marginalization similar to the cultural imaginaries associated with age or aging? Why does Franzen evoke economy when he speaks about depression? Like age metaphors, mental health is, as suggested in Chapter 4.1, an interesting gauge in terms of ascertaining conformity or non-conformity to the expectations of a particular culture. The normative background against which mental conditions are categorized as healthy or unhealthy is informed by the compliance of an individual with values, such as self-responsibility, self-observation, agency, and entrepreneurialism. These values also surface in the studies of age scholars who critically discuss the dogma of positive aging. Hence, there seem to be semantic and functional similarities between depression and old age or aging.

In *Indecision*, Benjamin Kunkel negotiates this association (Chapter 4.2). His protagonist Dwight Wilmerding is introduced as a character who has failed on several dimensions: He is aimless, (soon) unemployed and homeless, financially dependent on his father, and he suffers from a mental disability, abulia, which means that he is unable to make decisions. Dwight associates his many problems with his age. Instead of reading Dwight Wilmerding as a perpetual adolescent, I will focus on how Kunkel uses irony and satire to mock the pharmaceutical industry as well as academic discourses that try to explain contemporary American culture through consumer cycles or entrepreneurial concepts of the self.

Economic thought patterns, as some philosophers and age critics contend, are applicable to life cycles, lifestyles, youthfulness as symbolic capital, and concepts of the self (Chapter 4.3). Like Kunkel, Don DeLillo portrays the consequences of this coalescence of economy and life cycles (Chapter 4.4). But in his novel *Cosmopolis*, he casts an entirely different tone over the story of his protagonist Eric Packer. It is a bleak and lethal atmosphere, in which Eric, aged 28, senses that his time is up. Not only does he surmise the imminence of his own death, he also sees himself and the world around him become obsolete.

Miranda July creates an alternative response to the entanglements of age and aging, consumer culture, life course imaginaries, and living in contemporary American culture (Chapter 5). Her fictional characters Sophie and Jason in *The Future* as well as her semi-autobiographical account *It Chooses You* portray aged young adults who have internalized the meanings of age and aging and who struggle to come to terms with the consequences. By combining fictional and non-fictional approaches, July offers an optimistic and creative alternative to the stereotypical cultural imaginaries of age and aging. July's recent work completes the previous age readings because it widens the scope of age readings considerably. *The Future* blends fictional and (auto)biographical as well as magical and realistic elements and provides a transition into my conclusion, in which I suggest that the metaphoric practice of age is not only a device in fictional narratives but, coming back to Gullette's concept of age narratives, imbues all kinds of narratives.

Following Carol Rambo, I agree that the "separation of aging from old age" may "add an important dimension to formulating a general processural approach to aging as an experience across the life course" (308). After all, as Sara Munson Deats and Lagretta Tallent Lenker remind us:

From birth to death we all age, and from womb to tomb our chronological progress is obsessively and meticulously recorded: on our driver's licenses, on our passports, in the newspapers (if we are unfortunate enough to be celebrities), on the end papers of our books, and at our birthday parties. (9)

In bringing together and elaborating on the few isolated attempts to study younger age groups from an age perspective, this study suggests that the inclusion of *aged young adults* is a necessary next step in the field of age studies.

1 Age and Aging in Theory and Practice

1.1 POSITIONS IN AGE STUDIES

In 1989, the American historian Howard Chudacoff wrote a book whose title seems to speak directly to the concern of this study: *How Old Are You? Age Consciousness in American Culture.* The publisher's blurb reads: "Most Americans take it for granted that a thirteen-year-old in the fifth grade is 'behind schedule,' that teenagers who marry 'too early' are in for trouble, and that a seventy-five-year-old will be pleased at being told, 'You look young for your age.'"[1] This form of age awareness, as Chudacoff sets out to prove, did not always dominate American everyday life. Cultural, social, and economic developments since the nineteenth century led to particular concepts of time and age that most Americans take for granted today without truly understanding that

age has come to represent more than a chronological, biological phenomenon. It has acquired social meaning, affecting attitudes, behavior, and the ways in which individuals relate to each other. (4)[2]

---

1 See the full blurb on <http://press.princeton.edu/titles/4418.html>, accessed on 9 September 2013.
2 In a similar manner, Sinikka Aapola suggests a differentiation between four main discourses of age: (1) the discourse of chronological age; (2) the discourse of physical age; (3) the discourse of experiential or subjective age; and (4) the discourse of symbolic age (299). Also consider Amei Koll-Stobbe (cf. 239) or Peter Laslett (cf. 24ff.).

Throughout the nineteenth and early twentieth century, as Chudacoff argues, industrial and scientific virtues – such as rationalization, precision, numerical measurement, or scheduling – were transferred to the human life course (cf. 5, 49, 91). Distinct life stages, such as childhood or adolescence, emerged which made American society into an age-graded (or age-segregated) society (cf. 91, 107).[3] Age became a formal measurement for institutionalized forms of care: Compulsory education, the emergence of pediatrics, and many other pedagogical, medical, and legal endeavors established childhood as a sensitive stage of life (cf. 22, 44-5, 64). Kindergartens, (grade) schools, and other forms of institutionalized supervision established formal age norms and categories to measure development (cf. 49ff., 81). The institutionalization of life stages in terms of education, marriage, or retirement helped to manage the increasing individualization in industrialized societies by providing more formal guidelines for transitional moments in the life course (cf. Kohli 2007). As a result, age increasingly functioned as "an organizing principle" and became "a prime distinguishing feature in American culture and social policy" (Chudacoff 5, 159). Age was "an ascriptive trait" with a set of expectations of 'normal' behavior behind each ascription (184). Even though, as most age scholars concur, age or aging are not stable categories but constantly changing processes, aging through the life course, as Chudacoff argues, was increasingly categorized into ordered sequences and was thus fashioned into a

handy framework for representing social and cultural expectations for individual experiences and roles. Thus, although one's accomplishments cannot change his or her age, one's age has become a gauge by which to assess his or her accomplishments. (184)

Here, Chudacoff provides an important insight into the connections between age and people's sensitivities regarding "social and cultural expectations" (184). As I will show in this chapter, Chudacoff's gauge function of age in social interaction is informed by cultural imaginaries, and these im-

---

3   Chudacoff also differentiates between "formal age, which is determined by an event, usually a birthday," and "functional age, which is determined by ability or change in ability" (189). According to Chudacoff, formal age has replaced functional age (cf. 189).

aginaries can, in part, be retraced to the ideals of measurement and scheduling that industrialization furthered.

Heike Hartung and Rüdiger Kunow expand on the consequences of age as a gauge and its impact on identities and social interaction. They argue that a chronocentric view of development through life has assumed a central rationale in "our social and cultural agendas," which "means that the number of years lived so far becomes the definite feature and the limiting condition for what kind of life a certain person is living" (18). Therefore, as Hartung and Kunow find, "'old age' is an index pointing to a set of biological, social, and cultural norms. The interpellation 'old' then marks the essential and irreversible deviation of a given person and his or her body from a norm" (19). Following Hartung and Kunow's reasoning, age is thus inevitably connected to a set or norms and agendas, which define proper behavior and limit or sanction deviance from cultural or social expectations. Hence, the concept of age as a gauge implies moral, authoritative, and punitive dynamics, and I will come back to this function shortly.

Chudacoff traces and contextualizes an assemblage of cultural manifestations that indicate and spur age consciousness. In doing so, he exposes the many interconnections between cultural practices and cultural knowledge about age or aging. Birthdays, for instance, came to play a vital role in the increasingly age-stratified organization of individual lives because they represent official rituals that grant a set of legal rights (cf. 126-37, 189). Historically speaking, the commemoration of birthdays, which celebrates the individual and renders people even more age conscious, is a relatively new practice (cf. 126-30). Before the emergence of birthday celebrations, people imagined their age in terms of life stages or in terms of "functional age" (cf. 126-7, 189). Therefore, until the Reformation, birthdays as such, if the exact date of one's birth was known at all, were not considered important events in a person's life (cf. 127-8). Instead, people celebrated their name days.[4] In the early twentieth century, birthdays emerged as a crucial celebration of the individual and birthday cards and other birthday rituals (such

---

4   According to Christian Marchetti, the practice of name days is a Christian, particularly a Catholic, tradition. Name days celebrate a patron saint and his or her virtues. With the baptism of a child, a saint becomes the guardian of this child. The yearly commemoration of the saint is thus not a celebration of the individual but of a communal and abstract figure, the saint (cf. 46-50).

as birthday cakes) became popular and celebrated the processes of growing up during childhood (cf. 132-7). Birthday parties became more and more elaborate and families began to commemorate (and romanticize) childhood as a special phase in life (cf. 130). "By the middle of the twentieth century," Chudacoff summarizes, "age and age norms had come to occupy a prominent place in the public consciousness" (137).

With individualization and industrialization, Chudacoff argues, two major social developments can be observed: On the one hand, birthdays in modern times became commodified events accompanied by an industry that produced commercial products, such as birthday cards, cake manufacturers, or party planners that artificially heightened the significance of a birthday for an individual (cf. 133-4). On the other hand, the new (industrial) conception of time in terms of efficiency, punctuality, and timetables also affected age specificity, which became increasingly important in the self-concept of an individual (cf. 5, 49ff., 144). Instead of long-range life stages or time-neutral name days, a person's chronological age became a specific and precise marker of his or her identity. Therefore, according to Bill Bytheway, teaching children their age represents a social practice that generates age awareness early on in the life course.

> The practice of numbering and celebrating birthdays ensures that, as children, we learn not just to think of them as exciting occasions, but also that the number is part of our identity: 'I'm four!' The candles on the cake are carefully counted before being blown out. Through number, children obtain an acute sense of being the *same* age or a *different* age to other children. (365; original emphasis)

Hence, through social comparison and a search for sameness and difference, children learn to use practices of quantification as a measurement of their identity (cf. Bytheway 365). In doing so, children internalize and apply the social practices of age. Under such circumstances, as Chudacoff and Bytheway point out, age and aging must be understood as culturally contingent concepts that have evolved over centuries and now form the foundation of many naturalized social practices, which are used unconsciously in everyday life but which, upon closer inspection, reveal a cultural setting informed by specific rules and norms.

Apart from birthday celebrations and institutionalized forms of age-grading, age has become a dominant topic in Western media. Kathleen Woodward observes that

> age is reported everywhere in the media. News stories typically begin with the name of the person followed by his or her age. We know the precise ages of our politicians and of politicians around the world, of celebrities, of the people who are getting married in our towns, of the people who are arrested, and of the people who have died. [...] The deep structure of the story is: name and age. (*Aging and Its Discontents* 5)

Age is thus a lens through which we have learned to assess people. It has become a crucial social category, similar to class, race, and gender, which classifies and describes individuals. The comparison of age with categories such as race or gender is a problematic one because the category of age lacks stability. I will come back to this aspect. For now, Woodward's argument is enlightening because, as she rightfully observes, the casualness with which the media use age in their stories suggests that age is a natural, self-evident feature of a person, just as his or her name. To Woodward, this observation is peculiar but not hazardous because she believes that there are "remarkably few meanings [attached] to different ages across the life course" (5). Instead, as Woodward argues, our culture operates with a single binary: youth and old age (cf. 6).

The Meanings of Age: Language and Narrative

The age critic Margaret Morganroth Gullette is convinced of the opposite: While she agrees that age is everywhere, she argues that the meanings of age are often stereotypical and ageist and are derived from cultural imaginaries about age and aging. Gullette has made it her prime endeavor to investigate this body of cultural knowledge in order to uncover its detrimental effects on people of all ages. According to Gullette, age socialization and thus the internalization of what it means to grow old begins early in a person's life and tends to occur under the radar (cf. *Agewise* 6). Gullette is one of the few age scholars who emphasizes that "Americans at all ages" are affected by ageist notions and who criticizes the "age-related language" associated with, for instance, branding generations into "Boomers" or "Xers," which increases the conflictual relationship between generations and establishes a "contrived war" (cf. Chapter 3 in *Aged by Culture*). Linked with this detrimental language are cultural narratives that cast the "Xers" as slackers or oppressed and the elderly as "greedy geezers," who are unwilling to make room for the next generation (cf. 215-6). Gullette retraces the Baby Boomers' and Generation Xers' narratives of intergenerational conflict to the Bush recession and describes several scenarios that emerged from economic fears in terms of unemployment or Social Security (cf. "Age Studies" 215, 226). The pattern seems to be similar in these scenarios: The young are set against the older generation, creating a hostility in which "[e]conomic history [is] disguised as generational rivalry" (226). The elderly are, however, not always the discriminated or disadvantaged party in this rivalry. Gerontocratic structures, in which the elderly (whose number is steadily increasing) are imagined as the age group that rules over younger, diminishing generations, represent an alternative scenario that sets the generations against each other as opponents who are fighting over authority and control (Wilinska and Cedersund 2010, Blasberg 2013). Whether this intergenerational conflict in terms of a gerontocratic social structure actually exists has been questioned (Rosenmayr 1987, Gullette 2011). After all, as research in Germany shows, parents and their children get along with each other better now than ever before (Spiewak 2013). Moreover, when old people try to stay young as long as possible and when young people feel old in their twenties, it is questionable if intergenerational conflict which features generations as opposing rivals is still an issue. I will address this aspect in the following age readings (see particularly Chapter 2.3).

At the basis of the competing intergenerational relations, Gullette finds an ageist culture of social practices and cultural imaginaries that has harrowing effects on the elderly. The disproportionally high number of elderly victims who died during Hurricane Katrina is a case in point (cf. *Agewise* 78). In a similar way, Gullette puts her finger on cultural imaginaries such as "the Eskimo on the ice floe," which (falsely) assumes that the Inuit have their elders die alone on an ice floe, or the duty-to-die injunctions, which posit the elderly as a burden who had better commit suicide if they impose on the young (*Aged by Culture* 45; cf. *Agewise* 21-41). In short, the idea of age as ugly, as burdensome, or as decline "leads to shunning behavior, illegal discrimination in hiring, elder abuse, funding cuts (violence by budget), and even death dealing" (*Agewise* 37).

Being "aged by culture" is the term Gullette uses to describe the internalization of the meanings of aging and old age. In her eponymous book *Aged by Culture* (2004), she puts forth a forceful call for action against the detrimental and often invisible mechanisms of this internalization. Gullette's activist claims and the empirical evidence she provides have been crucial for the field of age studies and are very enlightening and convincing when, for instance, she unveils that the fears of menopause or the apprehension of a declining sexuality in old age are exaggerated, unjustified, or simply wrong. Gullette fights for alternative cultural imaginaries about old age and "aging-past-youth" that are optimistic and enabling (*Aged by Culture* 19). Her studies are passionate deconstructions of social practices, metaphors, and cultural narratives that serve to bring internal, unvoiced, and often unconscious meanings to light.

Decline narratives, for instance, constitute a central case in point in Gullette's argument. From childhood on, she maintains, everyone has "seen a prior self fade and a new one emerge" and has thus experienced a form of aging (*Aged by Culture* 149). Until adulthood, early developments tend to be told as progress narratives, whereas later changes in life are imagined as decline narratives. A typical progress narrative is the American Dream ("From Life Storytelling" 103). Coming-of-age stories or the *Bildungsroman* also tell the story of a positive maturation of a young character into a full member of society. But when does the progress narrative change into one of decline? Gullette does not specify a universal transitional moment, but she gives several examples, which point to the fact that the decline pattern is learned early in life. Gullette mentions a 20-year-old Brandeis intern, for instance. The woman, a junior in college, noticed that senior men were often more interested in freshman students than in juniors and replied "I am still young" as a "counter-assertion to imposed decline" (107). According to Gullette, this young woman experienced how she was "superannuated prematurely" (107-8). Employees in midlife, who fear to remain unemployed due to their age once they are laid off, represent another example for the ways in which people are affected by an internalized decline narrative (*Agewise* 1-2). Even a seemingly innocent practice such as bodybuilding, Gullette claims, is based on a decline narrative because it "promises a staving-off of decline but no exit from the cycle" and thus a "continuous awareness of the shortfall, a kind of 'slow death'" ("Fashion Cycle" 52).

This fear of old age and the warning messages about the detrimental consequences of aging are circulated by scientists and journalists who argue that the body's decline starts early and is a 'natural' fact of life. Gullette cites an article from the *New York Review of Books* in which a physician argues that "the body starts 'its long preparation for death,' a 'relentless physical and mental attrition,' as early as 'the twenties and thirties'" (qtd. in *Agewise* 34).[5] Gullette observes that the warning has sunken in: College students expect a decline in sexual activity to start at age thirty (cf. 126).[6] Consequently, she argues: "The assumption of our culture is not just ageist but middle-ageist, that bodily decline starts not in old age but every younger: for women and even some men, as early as thirty" (33). And, "aging-past-youth (which seems to start between thirty and forty for urban middle-class European Americans)" is therefore a threat to both men and women and is not necessarily connected with the looming biological clock that women in their twenties and thirties often evoke as a matter-of-fact destiny of their physical bodies (33). One might find fault in Gullette's way of playing down the physical contingencies of biological and physical aging, but Gullette makes a crucial point here: She argues for an approach towards age and aging that encompasses both male and female experiences. I follow Gullette's assessment on this point and the fictional narratives that I have selected reflect her approach.

Aging-Past-Youth and the Coming-of-Age Genre

The aging-past-youth narrative that Gullette locates in middle-class European Americans is reminiscent of the genre of the *Bildungsroman* and its middle class background, in which typically white, male, middle-class heroes come of age. According to G. Robert Stange, the traditional *Bildungsroman* "is almost an image of the life of the middle class" because it functions as "a guide to the good life" and describes the ideals of social mobility and individual self-development (qtd. in Alden 2). Particularly in the re-

---

5   For the original article, see Diane Johnson and John F. Murray. "The Patient Talks Back." *New York Review of Books*. (23 October 2008): 24-27.
6   Also see Freud's lecture on „Femininity," in which he observes that age thirty marks the beginning of old age for women (qtd. in Woodward, *Aging and Its Discontents* 192-3).

views of *Indecision*, critics have used the label *Bildungsroman* or "late-coming-of-age story" to describe the larger genre-specific framework within which they believe the novel needs to be understood (cf. Kakutani 2005, McInerney 2005, Schäfer 2011). But also *Away We Go, My Big Fat Greek Wedding*, and *The Corrections* bear resemblance to the *Bildungsroman*. This literary genre, which falls into Gullette's inventory of invisible narrative practices that naturalize age seems to shape the expectations and conventions that underlie stories told about aged young adults.

In her article "The Limits of Development," Heike Hartung uses the *Bildungsroman* genre to analyze the meanings of age and aging in a selection of contemporary American novels. She argues that "the *Bildungsroman* and its transformations or rewritings may serve as an exemplary literary genre in which to explore age difference" (49). She finds that several core ideas of the *Bildungsroman* are negotiated in contemporary novels about longevity and dementia, such as in Kazuo Ishiguro's *Never Let Me Go* (2005) or in Ian McEwan's *Atonement* (2001): The "humanist value of the progress narrative," "the dialog between generations," or the "possibility of growing old" are challenged or simply denied in these stories (63). Hartung places age at the center of her analysis of contemporary transformations in the *Bildungsroman* genre. She defines age, on the one hand, in terms of aging as a universal process and a synonym of development through time (cf. 46). On the other hand, she conceptualizes age as a binary construction of youth versus old age (cf. 46), which constitutes one of the themes of the *Bildungsroman*, namely generational conflict. This binary also points to another premise of the *Bildungsroman*: the youthfulness of the adolescent hero. In this sense, Hartung's approach to the *Bildungsroman* from a perspective of age studies is exemplary for my investigations.

Resting on a male paradigm of education and experience, the "traditional *Bildungsroman* describes the journey of a sensitive boy from childhood through his coming of age as an adult. Schooling is often depicted as a stifling form of education in contrast to the value of educative experiences in the wider world" (Rishoi 59). Being orphaned or separated from his parents, the hero embarks on a journey, which is typically a journey from a rural home into the city, where he experiences disillusionment or alienation and, with the help of a mentor, learns to integrate into society (cf. Kohl 17, Rishoi 64). According to Smith and Watson, the "*Bildungsroman* culminates in the acceptance of one's constrained social role in the bourgeois social order, usually requiring the renunciation of some ideal or passion and the embrace of heteronormative social arrangements" (189; my emphasis). Initiation plays a central part in the maturation of the hero, who has his first life-changing encounters and experiences with sexuality, love, the working world, drugs, or death (cf. Freese). Hence, the hero develops from one stage (adolescence) into the next (adulthood) and in doing so, he finds his role and place in society. Often, a *Bildungsroman* has an autobiographical or confessional dimension that relates the story of the hero to the life of the author (cf. Freese 85, Kohl 22, Millard 3, Rishoi 61). This autobiographical dimension will surface in my discussion of Miranda July's work.

With Goethe's *Wilhelm Meisters Lehrjahre* (1795/1796) as the prototype of the *Bildungsroman*, the term *Bildung* is historically grounded in humanist philosophy and an Enlightenment context, which – as some critics argue – is not transferable to other cultures (cf. Millard 3). Nevertheless, the term *Bildungsroman* has travelled internationally and keeps appearing in literary criticism on contemporary novels of adolescence. The term, however, has undergone many transformations with regard to its core characteristics. Female and ethnic writers, for instance, have revised the definition of the *Bildungsroman* arguing that the "European male modernist tradition [...] of integrated universal selfhood" and the "one-size-fits-all journey of development" do not match the experiences of women and minority writers (Rishoi 60-1). From this critical reflection on the cultural heritage of the *Bildungsroman*, more inclusive terminologies emerged, such as the novel of education, the novel of apprenticeship, or the coming-of-age story.

In order to acknowledge the contemporary, American, and non-gendered diversity of the fictional narratives I analyze in this study, I will use the term coming-of-age narrative. The term has the advantage that it can also be applied to films.[7] However, it is a term that is equally problematic as the *Bildungsroman* because coming of age implies a transition between life stages and means "to reach full legal adult status" (Millard 4). This adult status is, however, not only culturally contingent, it is also a status difficult to define because the concept of maturity, which is generally

---

7 See, for instance, Karen R. Tolchin's *Part Blood, Part Ketchup: Coming of Age in American Literature and Film* (2007), Sarah Hentges' *Pictures of Girlhood: Modern Female Adolescence on Film* (2006), or Dennis Maciuszek's *Erzählstrukturen im Coming-of-Age-Film* (2010).

used to define adulthood (cf. *OED*), does not specify which kinds of social experiences or psychological dispositions mark a successful transition into adulthood (cf. Millard 5). In addition, the typical coming-of-age story features adolescent characters between twelve and nineteen (cf. 4). According to Millard, however, the age of a character is "not the best guide to that teleological process which is the proper focus of the coming-of-age narrative" (5). After all, the characters in Douglas Coupland's coming-of-age novel *Generation X* (1991), for example, are in their twenties.

In recent discussions of the coming-of-age narrative, transformations have been observed that tie in with the fictional narratives of this study. According to Rishoi, who suggests a female coming-of-age narrative,[8] the genre describes "the quintessential outsider's genre:"

rather than valorizing a social integration that requires the partial denial or repression of the subject's identity, these narratives avoid the teleology of a unified self by constructing subjectivity as provisional. The subjects of coming-of-age narratives [...] construct themselves as outsiders, but unlike them, they choose to remain marginalized at the end of their texts. (63-4)

Rishoi's contemporary redefinition of the traditional maturation story includes failed, unsuccessful, or only party achieved maturation (cf. Rishoi 71, Millard 4). Curnutt traces these developments in coming-of-age novels from the 1980s and the 1990s. While J.D. Salinger's *The Catcher in the Rye* (1951) or Sylvia Plath's *The Bell Jar* (1963) were informed by a rebellion "against the stifling conformity, empty materialism, and false piety of the bourgeois home" which continued in the 1970s novels with a resistance to authority and a struggle for autonomy, "[i]n contemporary novels, however, youth's disaffected disposition is credited not to the oppressiveness of adult authority but to a lack of it" (Curnutt 94). Quoting the film historian Thomas Doherty, Curnutt suggests that "parents today 'are more likely to be condemned for being self-centered, weak, and uncertain than for being overbearing, intrusive, or present.' If the cry of the teenager in the 1950s and 1960s was 'You're tearing me apart!' the cry of the modern teen is 'You're

---

8 Rishoi defines women's coming-of-age narratives as descendants from the novel of development, the slave narrative, and the traditional autobiography, privileging "the autonomous individual who feels at odds with society" (63).

leaving me alone!'" (cf. 101).⁹ According to Curnutt, the intergenerational conflict of the *Bildungsroman* has changed into a nostalgic and idealized vision of family life, in which the home stands for security and settledness, which adolescents long for or hope to perpetuate in their own adult lives.

Curnutt's characterization of a transformed generational conflict in the 1980s and 1990s sheds a new light on Gullette's assertion of widespread hostilities against older generations, which she sees as an ageist form of pitting generations against each other (cf. *Aged by Culture* 53). According to Gullette, the gap between generations is thus widening instead of closing. The accusation (and fear) of gerontocractic hegemony, which sometimes resonates in reports on the demographic changes in the Western hemisphere, is yet another characterization of future transformations in generational interaction (or the lack thereof), characterizing young people as overwhelmed, insecure, and aimless (cf. Blasberg 2013, Jessen 2013). Curnutt's findings on intergenerational conflict due to nostalgia and a longing for stable families resonates in some of the fictional narratives I will analyze in the following chapters.

Against this background, the coming-of age genre appears as an intriguing site to study intergenerational conflict as well as the conditions of and social imaginaries associated with young people. Yet, I agree with Curnutt's assessment that "the genre risks oversimplifying" the situation of young adults (105). While Curnutt argues for a redefinition of the coming-of-age genre (cf. 106), I would like to suggest that using this genre as an analytic frame may risk misunderstanding or overlooking the meanings and functions of references to age and aging because this approach either forces the narratives into a generic formula of teleological development and progress or implicitly aims at a generational portrait. Moreover, it is difficult to bring together the intergenerational conflict in *Away We Go* (where the parents abandon their children) and *The Corrections* (where the parents overwhelm their children) without risking overlooking how the topic of age and aging is used to express meanings that are not aimed at a standard transitional movement through time in terms of a gradual coming of age. Instead, as I will suggest in the following chapters, when age is mentioned in my corpus of fictional age narratives, a sense of stasis, delay, or regression is

---

9   Thomas Doherty. *Teenagers and Teenpics: The Juvenilization of American Movies in the 1950s.* Boston: Unwin Hyman, 1988.

invoked, which contradicts the teleological development that underlies standard coming-of-age stories.

Therefore, I would like to adapt Hartung's approach and suggest that age and aging be placed at the center of an analysis of (aged) young adults. From such a perspective, the mentioning of a character's age appears more multi-faceted than being a simple description of a chronological fact. At the same time, I do not want to discard the coming-of-age narrative and the themes it contains because coming of age is one of Gullette's "invisible practices" of thinking about young adult characters in fictional narratives ("From Life Storytelling" 107). Moreover, some of the themes typical of the coming-of-age narrative resonate in the fictional age narratives in this book and offer a potential platform for contention:

- The **insider/outsider problem** is a crucial aspect for the aged young adults, who feel at odds with their situations as well as the norms and expectations they feel (or fear) to have failed.
- The **intergenerational conflict** is present as well but in quite different ways: Sometimes the parent generation is experienced as overwhelming (*My Big Fat Greek Wedding, The Corrections*); at other times, the parent generation is considered to be weak or self-centered (*Away We Go, Indecision*). But there are also examples in which a conflict with an older generation is missing altogether either because there are no older characters in the plot or because older characters are considered as friends and mentors (*Cosmopolis, Little Children, The Future*).
- The **concept of development through time**, which underlies the coming-of-age narrative in terms of a teleological and linear transition from one stage to the next, is challenged by the so-called perpetual adolescents and delayed adults, who seem to be stuck in the present or directed towards the past. At the same time, the cultural ideal of progress and development represents the normative background.

These three dimensions of the coming-of-age narrative correspond with the concept of age as a metaphoric practice (which I define in Chapter 1.2) and are part of the subtle cultural knowledge about age and aging, which – following Gullette – is diffused through narrative patterns. Gullette believes that "[n]arratives may have the most power over us when they are most invisible: that is, infinitely repeatable but unnoticed and unanalyzed" (*Aged*

By Culture 143). It is the task of age studies to render these implicit narrative conventions visible.

In a similar way, language represents a practice, "another powerful zone of loss," through which age knowledge is diffused ("Fashion Cycle" 37). On the one hand, expressions can become kitsch, for example; thus, people learn that language can undergo a similar life cycle of decline. This effect is described in Don DeLillo's *Cosmopolis* (see Chapter 4.4). On the other hand, "simple statements about time" can carry "implicit messages about aging," Gullette argues in *Agewise* (148). Paying close attention to the ways in which people refer to temporality and timing is therefore crucial for understanding how these references can carry connotations that point to cultural meanings of age or aging. For this reason, Gullette suggests that age scholars should establish an inventory of invisible practices in order to enable a more critical handling of age in everyday life. The fact that a person speaks about age and thus displays some form of age consciousness does not do the trick for Gullette: "[S]elf-description involving age and aging [...] is an obstacle to true age consciousness. We can be *too* conscious of age, too prompt to fall into decline's scripts" ("From Life Storytelling" 108; original emphasis). Therefore, terms like "*being young, being a Generation X-er, being no-longer-young,* or *being old-old* [...] have little age critique" (107; original emphasis). Hence, the patterns behind the socialization processes through which people are aged by culture need to be carefully reconstructed and made conscious. Gullette's claims function as guiding principles for this study: With the age readings that I will present in the subsequent chapters, I hope to contribute to expanding Gullette's inventory by de-naturalizing the functions and meanings behind seemingly factual or descriptive references to age. Central to such an understanding of age references is the semantic and functional diversity of age.

Age as a Movable Marker

The feminist critic Susan Sontag made an eminent contribution to age studies with her essay "The Double Standard of Aging" (1972), in which she illustrates that age functions as an intersectional category, meaning that it operates on many interconnected levels and is therefore inseparable from issues of gender, class, or race.[10] Even though Sontag mainly focuses on the psychological damages of the age ideology on the psyches of women, she also indicts its detrimental effects on men. Like Gullette, Sontag links age awareness with class, specifically with middle-class, and argues that

> [m]iddle-class men feel diminished by aging, even while still young, if they have not yet shown distinction in their careers or made a lot of money. (And any tendencies they have toward hypochondria will get worse in middle age, focusing with particular nervousness on the specter of heart attacks and loss of virility.) Their aging crisis is linked to that terrible pressure on men to be "successful" that precisely defines their membership in the middle class. (31)

Even though Sontag has been criticized throughout her career for not providing enough empirical evidence for her claims,[11] her argument here is intriguing: Success, career, and wealth as the hallmarks of economic thinking appear as directly connected to age and self-esteem. If success or wealth are not available at a particular age in a man's life, an aging crisis can occur.

Sontag's main argument, however, is dedicated to the double standard of aging and to the particularly harmful effects that age and aging have on women. While men age with regret and melancholy, women associate a strong feeling of shame and vulnerability with their aging.

> [F]or most women, aging means a humiliating process of gradual sexual disqualification. Since women are considered maximally eligible in early youth, after which their sexual value drops steadily, even young women feel themselves in a desperate race against the calendar. They are old as soon as they are no longer very young. (32)

If one follows Sontag's argument, female aging implies loss of attractiveness and femininity; it causes feelings of shame and worthlessness (cf. 29, 33). Whether this gender bias regarding age actually exists can be and has

---

10 Gullette also argues in *Agewise*, that ageism cannot be separated from other -*isms* such as racism, sexism, classism, or ableism (cf. 82).
11 See for instance Denis Donoghue's critical review of Sontag's study *Illness as Metaphor* (1978).

been contested (cf. Teuscher & Teuscher 2007). Nevertheless, Sontag's observations on the social function of age and the psychological effects of ageism seem as relevant today as they were in the 1970s. One of the ways in which Sontag's claim still rings true today is the threat of the biological clock that haunts women's psyches regarding their reproductive capabilities and which shapes their sense of finitude.[12]

Sontag's claims become highly topical in the context of age awareness in young adults when she elaborates on the crisis of aging that birthdays can cause. The intriguing feature of Sontag's argument is the flexibility and fictionality she ascribes to this age crisis (cf. 32). She observes that birthdays radiate "a poignant apprehension of unremitting loss," which is of a "fictional nature" (31-2). Describing an incident with a female friend from college, who turned twenty-one and lamented that the best part of her life was over and that she was no longer young, Sontag concedes that this birthday crisis and distress may appear absurd, but that it reveals a vital aspect of American age culture: It is only because this crisis is largely fictive and seems inauthentic that it can become "a poison in the imagination" (33).

> Aging is a movable doom. It is a crisis that never exhausts itself, because the anxiety is never really used up. Being a crisis of the imagination rather than of 'real life,' it has the habit of repeating itself again and again. The territory of aging (as opposed to actual old age) has no fixed boundaries. (33)

This movable doom or "apprehension of unremitting loss" (31, 33) recurs on the thirtieth birthday of the college friend, and Sontag recounts: "But thirty, she [the friend] said ruefully, that really is the end" (33). Clearly, the boundaries of age experiences are movable. Sontag acknowledges a form of fluidity in the ways in which age awareness is a subjective reaction to an assumed threat that is both a cognitive negotiation and an observable, behavioral response to cultural imaginaries associated with age or aging.

---

12 In her study *Why Love Hurts* (2012), the sociologist Eva Illouz states a similar observation and claims that the biological clock is not only a biological fact but also a cognitive and emotional mechanism that powerfully shapes women's conceptualization of time as biological time and gives them the impression of a declining range of options in life (cf. 149-50).

Sontag's conceptualization of the age crisis as a movable doom recurs in Woodward's idea of age as a movable marker. Woodward observes that Western cultures divide the life course into a strict and single binary of young and old, even though "[a]ge is a subtle continuum (*Aging and Its Discontents* 6). Woodward echoes some of Sontag's ideas about mobility and malleability when she claims that

youth is, subjectively speaking, a remarkably fluid and seemingly almost infinitely expandable category. Youth is a point which in our psychic economy is not fixed. Youth – 'being young' – is a moveable marker. Young and old may frame the continuum of the life course. But as people grow older, most of them – of *us* – take youth with them, as if it were a precious possession not to be left behind. Concomitantly, age – meaning 'old age' – is pushed ahead [...] youth comes to occupy the vast proportion of the continuum of the life course. Old age is relegated to the very end. (6)

This paradox – growing older but staying young – raises the question: What does youthfulness actually represent? According to Susan Sontag, "the most popular metaphor for happiness is 'youth'" (cf. 31) and, with this interpretation in mind, it is understandable that people, as Woodward observes, want to 'take youth with them.' What other meanings may be implied in the idea of youth? And, how can one achieve the nearly impossible – to be young (and happy) across the life course? Vice versa, does unhappiness imply that a person is no longer young or youthful?

Woodward argues that even though age is "a subtle continuum", it is organized into "polar opposites" (6) between which youth functions as a flexible marker. This flexibility is culturally contingent: "In the West youth is the valued term, the point of reference for defining who is old" (6). Hence, the marker (or gauge in Chudacoff's terminology) is one that measures the degree of (or compliance with) a culture-specific norm, that is youthfulness, which is linked with a sense of morality, in which youth equals 'good' and old age equals 'bad' (cf. 7). Within such a cultural context, it appears logical that people cling to youthfulness as long as possible.

Woodward elaborates on the malleability of age in an essay on the performance of age and gender from 2006. She uses the term "psychic age," as opposed to age that becomes visible through the body, and defines it as "a continually fluctuating oscillation between our older selves and younger selves" ("Performing Age" 173). From such a performative perspective, youth and age, even though they constitute two ends of a binary, are not "irreconcilable opposites; rather they are intertwined" (166). For this reason, "at virtually any age and as we grow older we all contain different age-selves" (166). With this definition, Woodward's idea of age performance emerges as a versatile tool with multifaceted social and cultural functions. Woodward's conceptualization of age allows people to use their age (or age performance) in resourceful ways: Depending on the situation, the culture, the expectations or mood, a person can assume different age-selves. People can thus not only be young and old at the same time, they can also influence to some extent how they are perceived in terms of their age performance.[13]

In this respect, age is a "different kind of difference" because the difference "out there" (i.e. old age), as Kunow calls it, will gradually turn into a difference "in here" ("The Coming of Age" 305). Featherstone and Wernick agree with this problematic aspect of age as a category of difference. They acknowledge that gender, of course, can also change throughout the life course, as in cross-dressing, gender bending, or medical sex transformation. These changes of status, however, are a matter of choice and effort. Aging occurs involuntarily (cf. Featherstone & Wernick, "Introduction" 8). Woodward's concept of age-selves puts a playful twist on this involuntary nature of aging. Furthermore, in contrast to cross-dressing, for instance, age is "the one difference we are all likely to live into" (Woodward, "Introduction" x). One may never change one's race or gender; the changes related to aging, however, affect everybody across the life course (cf. Kunow, "The Coming of Age" 305).

Despite this universal dimension of aging, a person's age-self and the meanings attached to it are situational. Taking my cue from Kunow's assessment that "'old age' is not an ontogenetic state" but an "*attribution* that produces action and reactions," I would like to stress that, in thinking about

---

13 Stephen Katz makes a similar observation: "[C]hildren are all kinds of ages now. Being a child can happen at various ages. Being a 'mature person' can happen at various times" (*Cultural Aging* 24). Katz attributes this phenomenon to the de-differentiation of life stages, which implies that the segments of the life course are no longer strictly separated; therefore, people can perform any age and their behavior is thus (theoretically) independent of their chronological age.

being young or old, we are not dealing with a simple chronological reference or with a biological fact but with an attribute that people can ascribe to themselves or that others can ascribe to them depending on a specific situation and a particular meaning, that is an attitude or feeling they want to express (Kunow 23-4; original emphasis). Simon Biggs' conceptualization of age in terms of a postmodern signifier supports this (self-)ascriptive feature of age references. Applying Baudrillard's ideas on signs, images, and signifiers that are detached from concrete objects, Biggs argues that

[a]n implication for signifiers of age would be that identifying statements, such as 'youthful,' 'old,' or 'mature' may no longer refer back to particular positions or attributes that are part of a fixed life course pattern. They can be swapped around as desired, or as circumstance dictates. ("Age" 48)

Biggs suggests here that age references in terms of young, old, or otherwise can lose their referential quality to chronological age and can be employed freely in specific contexts. This versatility of age is an intriguing concept that explains how, for example, a teenager can say that he or she feels old. Nevertheless, as Woodward contends, these signifiers of age are not empty (cf. *Aging and Its Discontents* 19). Instead, age-related self-ascriptions or attributes are often morally tinged and normatively shaped. Hence, 'young' or 'old' are references that are imbued with a particular function and meaning. Being old, for instance, i.e. behaving like an old person or being considered old (regardless of one's chronological or biological age), can marginalize or sanction a person and designate a failure to conform to a particular morality or norm. I will elaborate on these particular meanings and functions in the next subchapters.

If age is situation-specific and part of social interaction, there also needs to be an agent who participates in the construction and dissemination of the cultural meanings of age. Rüdiger Kunow understands age not only as a "property of individuals but as a *relation* between people" ("Chronologically Gifted" 24; original emphasis). Similarly, scholars such as Cheryl Laz and Simon Biggs theorize age in terms of a situation-specific, context-dependent performance and thus as a mechanism of identity management. Age thus requires active construction and permanent negotiation by and between individuals. This process defines age as an interactive, mutual exchange, which draws on and is shaped by cultural resources, norms and value judgments (cf. Chudacoff 3). The call to "act your age" represents a request to act according to cultural rules and, at the same time, illustrates the interactive quality of age performance:

> 'Act your age. You're a big kid now,' we say to children to encourage independence (or obedience). 'Act your age. Stop being so childish,' we say to other adults when we think they are being irresponsible [...] When we say 'act your age' we press for behavior that conforms to norms. However, the saying also expresses a common-sense understanding that age is not natural or fixed, and it implies that age requires work, i.e., physical or mental effort. (Laz, "Act Your Age" 86)

The sociologist Cheryl Laz understands age performance in terms of an invisible, unconscious, and culturally shaped concept as well as a verbal, performative, and relational social practice. These features are interdependent and feed off of each other. Age is thus actively and interactively constituted, both individually and collectively (cf. Laz, "Age Embodied" 505-6). Therefore, "age is something we do" and doing age is linked with "agency, choice, and action" (506).

Laz differentiates between age as something that is performed and age as something that is accomplished. Preferring accomplished over performed, she argues that age accomplishment is not an artificial performance or something that can be stopped because it is deliberate or purposeful. Instead, people "do age" continually.[14] Laz also claims that doing age has an effect on the body. The corporeal aspects of age have an effect on how people perceive themselves and how they use their bodies to accomplish a certain age.

For example, a teen trying to present herself as mature and 'grown-up' might adopt straight posture and an assertive stride. Similarly, a grandparent who leaves the vigorous recreation to the grandkids might find himself with reduced stamina and flexibility and extra pounds. ("Age Embodied" 508)

---

14 Laz theoretically anchors these observations in the concept of "doing gender," which Candace West and Don Zimmerman have developed (cf. "Act Your Age" 106).

The concept of age-as-accomplished thus presents an intriguing shift in perspective that diversifies Gullette's constructivist view: Laz implies that people can skillfully and creatively make use of cultural norms and expectations through their bodies, conduct, speech, and social interaction. Conversely, age-as-accomplished is imbued with existing norms, social roles, and cultural expectations. Thus, according to Laz, it is not only the norms that shape people's knowledge about age but the interactive and creative use of cultural resources and their individual enactment. For this reason, Laz speaks of age as a proxy, arguing that age or the accomplishment of age is "often mediated through mechanisms like competence, dependence, or maturity without awareness of the way these function as proxies for age" (506).[15] Laz observes the proxies for age in everyday interaction, when, for instance, "elementary school students and nursing home residents, each in their own way, act their age by demonstrating [...] their 'competence' (i.e., their ability to do the things that someone 'of that age' should be able to do" ("Act Your Age" 106). Due to the proxyship that age or doing age entails, Laz can claim that age is "potentially relevant to people of all (chronological) ages" (108-9) because age is a "reciprocal relationship between actors acting and structural factors constraining and enabling action" (101). Evidently, the accomplishment of age is dependent on many different factors.[16]

Age performance, as Simon Biggs argues, can assume a voluntary and playful nature, when it is used in terms of a willful masquerade. To Biggs, a masquerade is an identity "put on [...] in a particular context and for a specific audience, even if that audience exists in the inner world of the self" (46). Biggs defines his concept of masquerade as a vital tool of identity management because it bridges several binary opposites, such as fixity vs. flux (47), the binaries of "surface appearance and hidden depth" as well as

---

15 Gullette also mentions that "age or aging might be a proxy for" something else ("What Exactly" 194). The similarities with metaphors are quite obvious here, given that metaphors are also said to stand for something else (see page 61-3).

16 Laz gives an interesting example that clarifies the interactive and relational qualities of doing age. An individual might be more candid regarding frailties and fears with an older (or same-aged) counterpart while, with a younger counterpart, the person might rather stress his or her competence and well-functioning in everyday life (cf. "Age Embodied" 517).

the connection between internal and external worlds (53). The masque balances these binaries and allows for an identity that is free to maneuver within coercive social forces, marginalization, and idealization (cf. 53). Thus, age masquerade represents a "tactical manoeuvre," a means of protection and a "Machiavellian vehicle for self-expression" (53). The masquerade becomes visible in particular moments (often a crisis):

> Whilst social masking and active story-making[17] are common to all people, they may appear at their most pronounced when a group or individual becomes socially excluded from a dominant sources [sic] of value and esteem. (48)

In a similar way, Miriam Haller also highlights the performative aspect of age over chronological (or calendric) age. If the social behavior of a person does not match his or her calendric age, Haller speaks of "ageing trouble," borrowing Judith Butler's idea of gender trouble (cf. 60-1). Ageing trouble implies that age performance and particularly age-inappropriate behavior has the potential to make underlying norms visible and undermine their socio-cultural influence (cf. 60-1). Thus, deviance from the expectations of age-appropriate behavior challenges the order established by calendric age.

Following Haller's and Bigg's ideas on the significance of age-inappropriateness, I would like to shift attention to the normative and moral background against which age and aging must be understood. Instead of speaking of ageing trouble, I prefer the term deviance, even though it implies yet another binary conceptualization of social conduct between the poles of normal and abnormal. This choice of words will prove to be adequate, however, and the following age readings of contemporary fictional narratives will emphasize how a conflictual relation to age is connected to marginalization, sanctioning, and the idea of failure.

---

17 Biggs compares masquerade and narrative in his article, identifying the differences between these two strategies of individual identity management and resistance to stereotypes. According to Biggs, narrative includes the aspect of time (which masquerade is missing) and allows for closure (cf. 54). Masquerade, on the other hand, enables a "conceptual tension between what can and cannot be expressed" (54).

Intersections between Age and Norms

Clary Krekula's concept of "age coding" describes the intersection of age and norms and designates "practices of distinction that are based on and preserve representations of actions, phenomena, and characteristics as associated with and applicable to demarcated ages" (8). Similarly to what I will suggest in the next chapter regarding the metaphoric practice, Krekula approaches the topic of age in terms of its function and identifies four functions of age codes: (1) they work as age norms, (2) they correlate with symbolic and material resources, (3) they are a resource in interactions, and (4) they create age-based norms and deviance (cf. 15). These functions make clear that, for Krekula, age coding is not a materialization or a simple reproduction of age norms; it is rather an important toolkit or strategy that is used in social interaction and that adds a creative and subversive quality to the practices related to age or aging. At the same time, age coding also plays a role in "doing identities" because it interacts with the normative background against which people define themselves (cf. 17). Krekula's concept of age coding is particularly informative in the context of this study because, even though she does not equate age coding with age norms, she acknowledges the significance of the normative background and fields of power that influence practices of age coding (cf. 25). Thus, while age coding has a dynamic and (inter)active quality, it also functions within parameters of control and sanctioning. Age coding is thus informative about age categories and their endowed qualities (cf. 10), which are often not only "conceptions of how something *is*" but also how it "*should be*" (13; original emphasis). Krekula uses the concept of "othering" to maintain that practices of age coding unfold within a field of power: "Someone commandeers the power to define the relationship and the situational manuscript, deeming him or herself as the subject and perceiving the counterpart as 'the Other'" (25).[18]

I will refer to these processes of othering as 'disciplining' (see Chapter 2.2). Discipline and coercion, as (Foucauldian) age scholars suggest, play a

---

18 The first age reading that I will do of *My Big Fat Greek Wedding* in Chapter 2.1 is a perfect example of such a field of power, in which the protagonist turns into an object while her family takes over and defines the (anti-)heroine as 'the Other,' the failed spinster, the 'old' woman.

crucial role in understanding the intersection of age and norms. Kathleen Woodward, for instance, speaks of a "normative youthful and male structure of the look," which functions like a filter through which the old body appears as "taboo, as grotesque and naked" ("Performing Age" 172-3, 176). In her essay, Woodward highlights alternative ways of performing age and analyzes several art projects, in which older bodies are displayed as "publicly, playfully, theatrically, flamboyantly, sardonically, ironically, and pensively, self-consciously performing age" (167). These artistic examples stand out even more forcefully when they are compared with everyday performances of age. Particularly when these everyday performances occur in a culture in which old age is typically associated with negative stereotypes. As a response to this cultural setting, people want to pass as younger and perpetuate their youthfulness (cf. Woodward 163, 185). In doing so, they try to conform to the cult of youth by evading or tricking the "youthful structure of the look" (163). In Woodward's concept of the look, youthfulness is equated with the norm.

Combined with a similar concept suggested by the youth scholar Charles Acland, Woodward's notion of the look becomes applicable to younger characters because the structure of the look also works in the opposite direction. In *Youth, Murder, Spectacle: The Politics of Youth In Crisis* (1995), Acland studies the representation of dangerous, troubled, or deviant teenagers in Hollywood teenpics and argues that deviant youth is often presented through the "disciplinary gaze of the adult" (118). The adult gaze then becomes the normative gaze that determines the boundaries between normal and deviant or inappropriate behavior. In combination, Acland's and Woodward's concepts of normative gazes looks[19] offer an intriguing approach towards a study of aged young adults in films and novels. If, as Acland and Woodward argue, youth and old age can become foci of normative looks, both youthful and elderly conduct can be considered deviant, depending on the situation and the 'looker.' This normative look on age-inappropriate behavior is thus bi-directional.

---

19 Woodward makes a distinction between look and gaze. In her terminology, the 'look' is disfiguring while the 'gaze' may be benevolent (*Aging and Its Discontents* 16). I will use the Woodward's disfiguring concept of the look unless I directly address Acland's concept.

The intersections of age and norms are also negotiated via the notion of accountability, which suggests that people are usually expected to explain or excuse their behavior. Laz maintains that

> we act with an eye toward accountability; that is we anticipate how our actions may be characterized, understood or misunderstood, excused, condemned, etc., and act in ways that will minimize the need for accounting (since accounting holds the possibilities of being misunderstood, discounted, or contradicted). As a result, we often conform to dominant norms and conceptualizations, including those related to age and gender, even if we question or reject those norms. (Laz, "Act Your Age" 99)

According to Laz, "age-clicks" compel people to review and evaluate their lives because the meaning of age "cannot be taken for granted" and must be actively constructed ("Act Your Age" 100-1).

> Perhaps the click comes from realizing that we are not acting our age or from noticing how effectively and unconsciously we have been acting our age. Or maybe we realize that we are 'ahead of' or 'behind time' [...] 'Clicks' often require us to offer accounts to others or to ourselves, and accountability is social and interactional. (101)

These clicks – and thus the deviances from what is conceived to be normal or natural – are central, informative moments because it is in these moments that the accomplishment and the naturalization of age become visible (cf. 100). The naturalization of age is, according to Laz, the result of people continually accomplishing age in predictable ways. Hence, most of the time, people usually act their age in appropriate ways. The clicks or reminders in life – which can be caused by birthdays, anniversaries, High School reunions, death of parents, and many other events (cf. Sontag, Montepare) – reverse the invisibility of age and make individuals aware of their age. Laz states that these reminders might become more frequent the older a person is; younger people, however, "are not exempt" and my age readings of aged young adults will prove Laz right (101).

Accountability thus begins to play a vital role as soon as the meaning of age must be actively constructed upon a reminder of age,. A birthday, for instance, can challenge a person's capacities of providing accounts that justify and legitimize his or her personal status in life. Chudacoff locates the beginning of this surge of account-taking at the onset of birthday celebrations in the nineteenth century.

Individuals used the occasion of a birthday to take stock of themselves, assessing their past and present careers, and to peek at an uncertain future. Personal timetables, comparisons with peers, and, above all, age norms pervaded these reflections. (131)

Personal narratives and narratives in general thus take a central place in the negotiation of age awareness and cultural imaginaries about age. Fictional narratives, as I will show in the following age readings, use similar allusions to timetables, comparisons, evaluations, and stock-taking, which are either displayed openly or are suggested as an expected strategy of which the protagonists should but fail to make use (see my discussion of *Indecision*, *The Corrections*, *The Future,* or *Cosmopolis*).

Hence, age awareness can point to some form of deviance and can trigger an agentic negotiation of cultural norms and expectations. Fear in the face of an impending birthday or a significant turning point in a person's life (such as the birth of a child in *Away We Go* or the adoption of a cat in *The Future*) thus not only implies a fear of aging as such, but also indicates a fear of agentic failure to provide coherent and meaningful narratives of the self. Shimshon M. Neikrug discusses this agentic perspective. He locates the origins of the fear of age and accountability in socio-economic changes and a specific cultural background.

'Today [...] personal fear of aging – of what will happen to me when I grow old – coincides with a massive loss of confidence in those institutions that might protect us from the vicissitudes of time and old age.'[20] [...] Persons require a strong sense of their ability to cope and find meaning in their present life, in order to believe in a positive and meaningful future. (328)

Hence, sense-making becomes an essential technique of dealing with age awareness. When strategies of sense-making fail, a breakpoint rips open and 'ageing trouble' or deviance becomes visible.

---

20 Neikrug quotes Harry R. Moody's *Abundance of Life* (1988).

In the fictional narratives of this study, the 'ageing trouble' is framed in terms of conflicts or crises which trigger the plot. These conflictual points render the naturalized age of a character visible and point to a form of deviance or inappropriateness. Thus, when a character feels old or is said to look old, we can assume that the character does not act his or her age and does not conform to age-related expectations or norms. Moreover, following Woodward, Sontag, Biggs, and Laz who argue that age is a flexible, situational, and interactional marker, age awareness can signify meanings which may but need not be related to one's chronological age and which can evoke a sense of an impending doom, dependence, incompetence, failure, or shame. Hence, age awareness or age attributions can indicate a meaning beyond the direct and literal denotation. In negotiating their age awareness, as I want to suggest in the following subchapters, the young characters of the selected novels and films participate in a metaphoric practice, in which they use age as a metaphor for feelings or states of mind that insinuate inappropriateness or failure.

1.2 AGE AS A METAPHORIC PRACTICE

When Susan Sontag analyzes the metaphors that surround AIDS, she explains that "one cannot think without metaphors" (*Illness as Metaphor* 91). The metaphors that are used for diseases like AIDS, cancer, or tuberculosis ascribe a particular meaning to an illness of the body which reflects social, political, cultural, and didactic concerns. The "metaphoric practice" (92) of imagining the body as a metaphor of social conflict is at the center of Sontag's argument in *Illness as Metaphor* (1977) and *AIDS and Its Metaphors* (1988). Similarly, in her essay the "Double Standard of Aging," Sontag discusses a metaphoric practice – though in a much more condensed fashion: When she argues that "the most popular metaphor for happiness is 'youth,'" Sontag insists "that it is a metaphor, not a literal description" and thus stands for "energy, restless mobility, appetite: for the state of 'wanting'" (31). Sontag challenges the equation of youth with happiness by highlighting the fact that youth is culturally construed as happiness. Adapting Aristotle's definition of metaphor, which Sontag uses in *Aids and Its Metaphors*, one could say that happiness is given a name ("youth") that belongs to something else and thus is not necessarily related to happiness (cf. 91).[21] Sontag's concept of metaphoric practice also resonates in many age scholars' approaches to the multi-dimensional aspects of age and aging, as I will show shortly.

Metaphors are traditionally perceived to be a matter of poetic language, but they are also increasingly studied in prose texts, speeches, scientific models, or ordinary language. Some scholars argue that all language is metaphorical (cf. Preminger 137), while others extend the meaning of metaphor to unconscious cognitive processes of everyday thought and action, such as Lakoff and Johnson and their theory of conceptual metaphor. Therefore, the definition of metaphor is expectedly vague. Typically, metaphor is defined as a figure of speech or, more generally, as a "condensed verbal relation in which an idea, image, or symbol may, by the presence of one or more other ideas, images, or symbols, be enhanced of vividness, complexity, or breadth of implication" (Preminger 136). Quinn uses the following definition: "In its narrow sense, a figure of speech in which something (A) is identified with something else (B) in order to attribute to A a quality associated with B [...] In its broader sense, the term serves as a general category for all figures of speech, such as SIMILE, METONOMY, and SYNECHDOCHE" (257; original emphasis). The intersections between metaphor and other figures of speech or rhetorical devices – Quinn's list can be extended by symbol, analogy, and trope – is characteristic of the many existing attempts to define the term metaphor (cf. Steen 1992, Preminger 1986). This terminological vagueness is also due to the many different disciplines or fields involved in defining metaphor, such as philosophy, semiotics, cognitive linguistics, and rhetorical or literary studies. Moreover, film scholars frequently speak of cinematic metaphors, though this usage is debated (cf. Whittock 1-2).

I would like to use a more general definition of metaphor that speaks to the puzzling association of 'young' bodies and (self-)ascriptions of being 'old,' which are the focus of this study. To Elyse Sommer and Dorrie Weiss, "a metaphor compares two unlike objects or ideas and illuminates the similarities between them. It accomplishes in a word or phrase what could otherwise be expressed only in many words, if at all" (vii). Conse-

---

21 According to Aristotle, "metaphor consists in giving the thing a name that belongs to something else" (qtd. in Preminger 136).

quently, the function of metaphors is "to peel away layers of camouflaged meaning" (vii). In a similar manner, Roger M. White argues that "in metaphor, by combining words in an unusual way, we can do something highly creative, and succeed in saying something that we could not say without recourse to metaphor" (2). Following I.A. Richards' definition of metaphor, in which a metaphor consists of two parts – a vehicle and a tenor –, we can understand the paradoxical combination of a young character saying 'I feel old' in terms of 'old' as a vehicle that defines (and alters the meaning of) the tenor 'I.'

Suggesting that a phrase like 'I feel old' is a metaphoric practice when it is used by a young character (or person), I would argue that insinuations of old age and aging may be used to express complex feelings or ideas that would otherwise be difficult to put into words. This metaphoric practice is implicitly understood by others because age has been used as a metaphor for a long time.

Metaphors of Age

According to Diana Wallace, "English literature has always, of course, offered representations of ageing and old age, but criticism has tended to focus on them as a motif, metaphor or symbol of something else: love, time, creativity, memory, mortality" (391). King Lear's old age, for example, is interpreted as a symbol of grief, rejection, exclusion, and loneliness (cf. Wallace 391). Gray hair is often regarded as a sign of wisdom and distinction, particularly in men (cf. Davidson 241). Yet old men are also associated with impotence or lechery (Classen 79-80). Thomas Küpper's chronologically old protagonists in film and television represent features that are, sometimes stereotypically, attributed to old age, such as maturity, experience, finitude, being an outsider, or being considered unproductive, "anti-digital," or outdated (40). Seasonal metaphors represent another well-known case, in which unrelated objects or events, such as the natural life cycle of death and rebirth, are compared to aging through the life course. Winter as a metaphor of decay and death is firmly established in how people in Western cultures describe old age (cf. Sokoloff 1987, Waxman 1990, Classen 2007). According to Woodward, "[t]he metaphor of old age as a foreign territory or new country is widely used" (cf. "Against Wisdom" 213). A similar spatial metaphor, namely the journey metaphor, casts aging through life stages in terms of a journey, as in the paintings by Thomas Cole (cf. 210).[22]

Metaphors in age studies are not only discussed in literary works but also in ordinary expressions or narratives. L. Eugene Thomas et al., for instance, analyzed the use of metaphors in conversations of older English and Indian men on their experiences with old age. When Thomas and his colleagues speak about metaphors of old age, they use the term metaphor for "connotations and nuances" that transcend the literal meaning of a word or phrase (3). In doing so, they categorize connotations of old age in terms of recurring major themes, such as dissatisfaction, stoic acceptance, concern for health, sadness of life, or desire to be active and independent (cf. 7). Some of the more implicit metaphors that they find refer to images of "building or erecting structures" or nature metaphors (8, 9). In understanding metaphors as "a unique way of looking at psychological states and underlying assumptions" (13), Thomas et al. represent a typical approach to metaphors of age in age studies. Similar to Thomas et al., the age critic Margaret Morganroth Gullette believes that metaphors of old age and aging are representative of entrenched cultural imaginaries. The developmental metaphor of aging as decline is a central concern in Gullette's work, as I already mentioned. Other metaphors that she discusses are metaphors of "gravitas – 'weight' of age, 'pull' of death" (*Aged by Culture* 107). Likewise, Gullette argues that "[v]isual images of men and women clinging to 'past' styles are still a metaphor for not keeping up" ("Fashion Cycle" 47).

When Gullette suggests that the concept of discarding is "a practice and a metaphor for the slide that 'aging' has become" ("What Exactly" 192), she conceptualizes the use of metaphor not as a strictly textual or verbal concept but as a meaningful social practice. This approach echoes Sontag's notion of metaphoric practices as well as Lakoff and Johnson's definition of metaphor as a pervasive phenomenon in everyday thought and action (cf. 3). Similarly, Laz understands metaphor as a form of language but also as a cognitive and conceptual category (cf. "Act Your Age" 104). In doing so, she follows Bryan Turner in his suggestion that "bodily practices are metaphors for larger social structures" (qtd. in "Age Embodied" 504).[23] Biggs

---

22 For a discussion of Thomas Cole's paintings, see page 146.
23 Laz quotes from Bryan S. Turner. *Regulating Bodies: Essays in Medical Sociology*. New York: Routledge, 1992.

also understands age masquerade as a "mask metaphor" and thus as a form of identity performance (53). Laz and Biggs use an extensive definition of metaphor, which functions as a conceptual framework for analyzing how social structures and discourses influence ideas about age or aging and how these discourses are voiced and enacted.

Discourse is fundamental to metaphors because, as Lakoff and Johnson argue, discourse forms structure our use of metaphors. The metaphor of argument as war, for instance, is influenced by a culture-specific discourse form, which influences our understanding of argument in terms of a battle (cf. Lakoff and Johnson 5). In similar ways, discourses of age, as the Finish sociologist Sinikka Aapola argues, are "more or less systematically organized ways of speaking, based on interrelated concepts, ideas and practices, and often linked to social institutions" (296). Even though Aapola does not speak of metaphors, I suggest that her definition of discourses of age as "conceptual repertoires" is comparable to metaphors of age. After all, metaphors are also informed by the concepts and practices prevalent in a society, its institutions, texts, and social interactions (cf. 297-8). Discourses of age (as well as metaphors of age) involve multidimensional and polyvalent concepts and imaginaries, and Aapola makes a convincing case for four major and several adjacent discourses of age that partly reflect the meanings or themes that age scholars have related to age and aging. In Aapola's categorization, age as a measure of the passing of time corresponds with the 'chronological discourse of age' (cf. 300). 'Institutional age' and 'developmental age' (cf. 301, 302) reflect an understanding of aging (or coming of age) as a natural and universal course (similar to seasonal metaphors of age). Age as a contextual and experiential discourse (cf. 305, 306) speaks to the various meanings of age that can be activated depending on a given context (see for example the themes in the metaphors of age detected by Thomas et al.). And 'symbolic age' uncovers the norms and expectations that are typically linked with a particular age stage and which are also reflected in metaphors of age that signify authority, maturity, or wisdom (cf. 307).

Despite the similarities between discourses of age and metaphors of age, the conceptualization of age as a metaphor has advantages in the context of this study. Aapola uses autobiographical essays written by adolescent boys and girls, and Thomas et al. have looked at conversations of older men. Fictional contexts, in contrast, can unfold semantic dimensions through metaphors that go beyond Lakoff and Johnson's intuitive meanings of conceptual metaphors[24] and can therefore be used for exaggeration, irony, or playfulness. Gerard Steen's differentiation of literary and scientific metaphors is based on a similar assumption: Departing from Dedre Gentner's approach, which he partly reformulates, Steen argues that literary metaphors are "typically richer" and more expressive compared to scientific (or journalistic) metaphors, which are clearer due to their explanatory function (cf. 688). The aesthetic quality and polyvalent dimensions of metaphors in literary texts are thus different from metaphors in other textual (or conversational) forms, in which metaphors are more direct and factual (cf. 688-9). Steen highlights the "macro-conventions and contextual motivations" that also play a role in understanding the polyvalence of metaphors in a literary text, which "has its own intricate rules and regulations" (700, 702). In her analysis of the metaphors of cancer, Sontag also acknowledges the narrative conventions in particular genres, such as science-fiction, which add a new semantic layer to cancer metaphors. She expands her analysis of the military metaphors surrounding cancer by looking into a "standard science-fiction plot" (69). She finds that cancer metaphors draw on mutation, conquest, or demonic possession, and thus on a "science-fiction scenario" which imagines cancer as an alien invader that changes its host and destroys an organism from within (69). In a similar vein, we can assume that the standard plot of the coming-of-age story, with which some of the novels and films of this study are associated, involves metaphors of age that draw on age as initiation or aging as growth or progress.

Even though Sontag's essays on metaphors, particularly her first essay on *Illness as Metaphor* from 1978, have brought in their wake numerous

---

24 To Lakoff and Johnson, metaphors are largely unconscious and intuitive products of language or knowledge. This approach reduces the innovative and creative power attributed to metaphors in poetic contexts. Hart, therefore, contradicts Lakoff and Johnson, arguing that "metaphors are [...] chosen by speakers to achieve particular communication goals within particular contexts rather than being *predetermined* by bodily experience" (Charteris-Black qtd. in Hart 5; original emphasis).

critiques,[25] Sontag's study is inspiring as an analysis of metaphors of age because it juxtaposes novels, autobiographical notes, obituaries, and health campaigns. Sontag examines literary, journalistic, scientific, and ordinary metaphors and carves out their punitive and shaming functions as well as their potentially lethal consequences (cf. *Illness as Metaphor* 3, 59, 131). From her manifold textual examples, Sontag draws a complex genealogy of the semantic dimensions of illness metaphors and unveils how these metaphors have seeped into the cultural unconscious. Age metaphors, as I argue in this study, function in a similar way to the metaphoric practices involved in illness metaphors.

Age as Deviance

An age metaphor, as I will use the term in the following analyses, is the comparison of two unrelated concepts or ideas in such a way that a new meaning is created. Age metaphors are based on references to age, which can be differentiated into five types:

- the evocation of a character's chronological age, e.g. in *Away We Go*: "We're 34."
- the description of an external appearance that is related to age, e.g. in *My Big Fat Greek Wedding*: "You look so old."
- the mentioning of age awareness, e.g. in *Cosmopolis*: "He felt old."
- the description of age-inappropriate behavior, e.g. in *Little Children*: "It was like suddenly being a teenager again."
- the evocation of the passing of time or a sense of temporality (being premature or belated), e.g. in *Away We Go*: "Maybe it's just late coming to me."

Assuming that age is a movable marker and can be used as a metaphoric practice, a reference to age is not understood as a simple description or mere factual information about a character's age, emotional state, or conduct. Instead, age references are a complex practice of negotiating dis-

---

25 Sontag was criticized for not providing respectable evidence for her claims (cf. Donoghue n. pag.), for a too negative view of (the silenced) cancer patients, and for her naive belief in the power of scientific progress (cf. Clow 2001).

courses that circulate in a given culture and that revolve around norms, ideals, and expectations. Age reference, such as 'young,' 'old,' or specifically citing the number of years a person has lived, are thus not simply to be taken literally but also metaphorically. Hence, they do not only express what is typically considered to be a description of a character's chronological age but also indicate a meaning beyond the literal denotation. There are nuances, of course. When twenty-eight year old Eric Packer says that he feels old, the metaphoric insinuation is more obvious because it is paradoxical that a young person expresses such a feeling. When Verona states that she is 34, however, the metaphoric implication is less obvious and one might simply take this reference to age as a literal description of her chronological age. However, the repetitive nature of age references in the movie and the moment in the plot in which the reference to age occurs indicate a metaphorical dimension, as I will argue in Chapter 2.3.

Age metaphors, as I want to hypothesize, associate a character with a particular age and create a meaning that indicates deviance or failure. Age metaphors are used to voice complex feelings of discontent, doubt, or inadequacy and point to a status of being different from what is otherwise considered to be normal. Thus, age references are part of an expressive repertoire onto which other meanings are transferred. These semantic implications can be derived both from the immediate context in which an age metaphor occurs, such as a moment of crisis, as well as from the cultural meanings of old age and aging, as we can find them in Western cultures. Therefore, age metaphors are contingent on the narrative and cultural context, in which they appear, and these two fields – i.e. the narrative and cultural contexts – must be taken into account in order to understand the full potential of age metaphors in terms of their functions and meanings. At the same time, like figures of speech in poetic language, age metaphors carry an innovative potential and, therefore, they can be used flexibly and creatively – similarly to age performances (cf. Biggs, Laz, Woodward).

According to Sontag, metaphors that rely on a vehicle that is mysterious, complex, and multi-determined – such as age – "have the widest possibilities as metaphors for what is felt to be socially or morally wrong" (*Illness as Metaphor* 62). Moreover, successful metaphors are rich enough to provide for contradictory applications (cf. 26). Age or aging is certainly a multifaceted, polyvalent, and ambiguous fact of life, and the metaphors of age or aging can indicate such disparate meanings as wisdom or foolishness, progress (maturation) or decline (into old age). When I consider the fictional narratives of this study in the light of age metaphors that cast age-as-deviance, deviance implies a life that is different from what is considered to be normal. 'Deviance' can also be used in a more positive sense to denote an opportunity to be different from what is believed to be a stifling, malfunctioning norm. Similarly, in analogy to Sontag's concept of cancer and AIDS narratives, the metaphoric practice of age can function as a didactic or punitive strategy to shame a character. And it can be used in a playful, ironical sense to challenge conventions, labels, and thought patterns. It is thus important to distinguish between these different dimensions of the age metaphor and to determine its different functions and semantic implications.

As a guideline for the following analyses, I want to suggest a differentiation into four dimensions of age metaphors.

1. *The descriptive dimension.* The mentioning of age or temporality is not automatically an indication of a metaphoric practice. After all, as Woodward maintains, age is a ubiquitous social category (cf. *Aging and Its Discontents* 5). Nevertheless, the mentioning of a character's must be understood within its cultural context and its function as a category of difference.
2. *The ascriptive dimension.* When age is used as a (self-)ascriptive trait, it can point to a meaning beyond a mere chronological or biological fact. References to age usually imply norms or expectations (e.g. Chudacoff 184, Aapola 302, 307). Against this background, the metaphor can function as an affective, punitive, ironical, playful, or sociocritical strategy within a fictional narrative.
3. *The narrative dimension.* Age metaphors are embedded in fictional narratives, which typically follow conventions and allude to genres or plot patterns. The timing of the occurrence of an age metaphor, for example in the moment of an emotional breakdown, is vital to its functional and semantic implications.
4. *The contextual dimension.* The meanings associated with age are not only influenced by a narrative situation but are also culturally contingent and thus point to discourses outside of the fictional world. Age metaphors reflect imaginaries, concepts, and ideals regarding the meanings of being of a certain age in a particular culture, decade, or century.

These four dimensions are interrelated and intersect frequently. For instance, the punitive function of an age metaphor is conditioned by the contextual dimension of age since age – in Western cultures at least – often has negative connotations. Similarly, the narrative dimension is linked with the affective function of age metaphors because age metaphors typically appear in a moment of crisis and thus emphasize or amplify particular feelings.

A few additional notes need to be made on the use of metaphoric practices of age in this study. Age metaphors involve related concepts, such as life stages, temporality, obsolescence, or mortality. According to Gullette, references to temporality, for example, carry implicit messages about age or aging (cf. *Agewise* 148). Thus, characters might consider themselves to be belated or ahead of time or feel that their life style is outdated. These insinuations add important layers to the semantic implications of age-as-deviance and will therefore also be discussed in what will constitute a more extensive definition of age or aging in the following age readings.

I have decided to speak of metaphors of age and not metaphors of aging because the selected stories in which references to age occur do not primarily focus on the process of a character's gradual maturation or growing into a new life stage. Instead, when age is mentioned, it primarily seems to imply temporary conditions in the sense of a status report. Kunow's differentiation between temporal and temporary aspects of age is helpful here (cf. "Coming of Age" 305): While temporality implies the passing of time and thus the notion of aging, the young adult characters of my corpus are predominantly concerned with their present age and thus with their position within their life course. Transitions do play a role, particularly the transition between life stages, but again, these transitions are significant because they involve a change of status and less a gradual, long-term development through time.

1.3 Method: Defining the Age Reading

The four dimensions of the metaphoric practice of age require textual, intertextual, interdisciplinary, and socio-cultural approaches. The analytic approach of an age reading that I will use in the following analyses addresses and combines the multi-dimensional aspects of age metaphors. Simply put, an age reading is a hermeneutical endeavor interested in understanding the functions and meanings of age metaphors in their many dimensions and forms.

A precursor of the age reading, which I understand as a juxtaposition of fictional and non-fictional texts in a reciprocal cross-fertilization, has been undertaken by Kathleen Woodward in her study *Aging and Its Discontents* (1991), in which she reads twentieth-century American fiction against Freudian psychoanalysis in order to show how anxiety, fear, denial, and repression are feelings associated with aging and old age (cf. 4). Woodward's aim is to reveal the complicity between Freudian psychoanalysis and "our culture's repression of aging" (192). Her approach is methodologically akin to an age reading: Woodward reads "literary texts and psychoanalytic texts in a reciprocal fashion, asking what the two together can suggest to us about aging" (8). This is a framework that I would like to expand.

An age reading, therefore, is conceived as a critical method of analysis that, on the one hand, tries to understand metaphors of age by focusing on fictional age narratives. On the other hand, an age reading juxtaposes these narratives with discourses, theories, and concepts from sociology, psychology, or cultural studies. By reading these different narratives, concepts, and theories against each other, a dialogic or reciprocal reading emerges that understands cultural imaginaries about age and aging as a body of cultural knowledge, shared meanings, and discourses that circulate in a particular culture and that are negotiated by novelists, filmmakers, academic researchers, and journalists. In other words, to understand the ways in which Gullette's age narratives feed from and cater to cultural knowledge about age and aging, it is essential to pay attention to both the fictional age narratives themselves and the contemporary discourses that surround them.

Similarly to Roberta Maierhofer's concept of "anocriticism," which she defines as an analytic approach to a specific female culture of aging that analyzes the meanings of being aged by culture for women (cf. 26), I also understand an age reading as a critical and analytic approach without, however, focusing on a gendered perspective. An age reading challenges the notion of age or aging as a mere natural fact of life and understands it as a culturally contingent, situational, and fluid marker that unfolds particular functions and meanings in specific contexts. In addressing the guiding questions of this study (see page 13), the approach of an age reading illustrates that age awareness of young adult characters in contemporary American fictional narratives is a response to and a negotiation of cultural imaginaries associated with age and aging.

Instead of following Maierhofer's gendered perspective, I have decided to include both male and female characters because the fictional narratives of this study involve metaphoric practices of age in similar ways or to similar ends, regardless of a character's gender. When the female protagonist in *My Big Fat Greek Wedding*, for instance, is associated with old age, it is the lack of a husband and children that makes her appear as a loser and outsider. In the case of Benjamin Kunkel's male hero in *Indecision*, age awareness indicates Dwight's lack of financial and professional success, which also results in his self-awareness as a loser and outsider. The non-gendered approach of this study does not wish to downplay, however, that there are indeed significant differences in the perceptions and meanings of age for men and women.

In defining the age reading, I need to explain additional terms that play into my understanding of this approach. *Cultural imaginaries*, for instance, constitute a central concept. The idea of imaginaries in the context of age or aging follows Gullette's notion of "life-course imaginaries," which she defines as "naturalized narratives" about aging ("From Life Storytelling" 102). Instead of speaking about cultural constructs or bodies of knowledge, I prefer the term cultural imaginaries because it evokes useful associations: Imaginaries imply a visual dimension of cultural knowledge and since films play a central role in my analysis, it stands to reason to use a term that indicates a pictorial quality. Furthermore, some of the concepts I will discuss in the following chapters, such as the graphic illustrations of the staircase of life, the U-bend, or the circle of life, are visual imaginations of the life course. Susan Sontag also describes aging as a "crisis of the imagination" to which she ascribes a fictional nature ("The Double Standard" 32-3). This imaginary quality is an important feature in understanding how aged young adult characters have processed their knowledge about age and aging into (imagined) perceptions and beliefs that need not necessarily be reasonable, justified, or verifiable in order to be perceived as real. In contrast to the term bodies of knowledge, which suggests facticity and provability, the term cultural imaginaries indicates a form of knowledge in which one needs to *believe*. In short, cultural imaginaries about age and aging are characterized by their double-sidedness: They are nurtured by common ideas and meanings, which are specific to a particular culture and which are comprehensible to those who share the same cultural (and, as will become clear in this study, the same class-related) background; at the same time, these imaginaries also have "intensely personal" repercussions for the individual (Gullette, "From Life Storytelling" 102).

A second fundamental term within the concept of age readings – and also closely connected to the idea of imaginaries – are *fictional (age) narratives*, which is a term I use as an umbrella term to encompass both novels and films. To Gullette, age narratives, from which I derive the concept of fictional (age) narratives, are "vehicles for organizing" cultural knowledge about aging (*Aged by Culture*, 15). These age narratives are "secretively embedded" in all kinds of cultural artifacts. Gullette examines these age narratives in visual sequences, social practices, autobiographies, interviews, and novels (*Aged by Culture* 10). In speaking of fictional age narratives, I use an extended definition of text and, following Gullette's use of age narratives, I regard both films and novels as fictional age narratives that constitute manifestations of cultural imaginaries about age and aging. These cultural imaginaries are naturalized in cultural artifacts and my age reading is an attempt to locate and denaturalize cultural imaginaries about age and aging.

Doing an Age Reading

An age reading operates on several levels. At a very basic level, it functions like a search mask in that it collects manifest as well as less discernible age metaphors. Locating a reference to a character's chronological age or a character's sense of temporality constitutes the microscopic lens that I use for fictional (age) narratives. (Also see the five types of age references on page 67).

On a second level, an age reading unfolds its analytic potential when it contextualizes the age metaphors in the immediate narrative situations in which they occur. Age references usually appear early in the selected fictional narratives, and they are often grouped around a character's conflict or crisis. Doing an age reading then raises a set of questions:

- What is the function of a particular age reference in the moment of its occurrence in a fictional narrative?
- What does it mean? How is the age metaphor related to the character (or object) that is described?
- How does the age metaphor contribute to the atmosphere or tone of the fictional narrative?

Finally, on the third level, an age reading is a critical approach that presupposes an exchange between literary (or cinematographic) topics and cultural discourses. The dialogic organization of the chapters in this study is a logical consequence of this assumption. It arranges the fictional narratives and studies on cultural discourses in such a way that they respond to each other and, at the same time, raise new questions that are carried forward to the next chapters. Therefore, depending on the focus of the age reading and the guiding research questions, an age reading can potentially take any direction. In this study, which tries to investigate the age awareness of young adult characters, the dialog occurs between my analyses of the fictional narratives and excursions into the areas of life course theory, developmental psychology, sociology and cultural studies. The academic research approaches are treated as alternative negotiations of topics or ideas that circulate in the fictional narratives, such as delayed adulthood, life course imaginaries, mental health, mortality, and consumer culture. My investigations into sociology, developmental psychology, and cultural studies thus identify issues that are also present in the films and novels. In juxtaposing these topics, the meanings of old age and agings become visible and intelligible.

One of the results of the age reading in this study is the understanding of the characters in the fictional narratives as *aged young adults*. The term aged young adult might appear lengthy, but it is a meaningful name to indicate a crucial ambivalence in the characters. The chronological age of the characters who are between 28 and 35 years of age clearly designates them as *adult* characters. The term young adult is typically used for slightly younger age groups (see footnote 6 on page 16). Despite this ambiguity, I decided to speak of young adults because the adjective *young* indicates that the boundaries of a life stage such as adulthood are not stable or fixed. Adulthood is a contested field (see e.g. Raby in Chapter 3.1). The term young adult then points to the flexibility and instability that age as a marker adds to social categories such as adulthood. The term *aged* young adults signifies the cultural component of age and is a term I borrow from Gullette's notion of being 'aged by culture.' The term *aged young adults* therefore mirrors the many different layers that impact the characters that I analyze in the following chapters: unstable life stages, flexible age markers, and internalized meanings of age that are culturally specific, situational, and flexible.

An age reading, as I would like to use it in this study, also has its limits. Being primarily a thematic analysis, it looks specifically for evocations of the topic of age or aging and, therefore, an age reading does not aim at a comprehensive examination of a given film or novel in all its respects. Furthermore, the age reading as it is used in this study departs from particular assumptions. It does not consider fictional narratives to be mimetic representations of a social reality, even though the novels and films are juxtaposed and are read against analyses from social or cultural studies. The fictional narratives are understood as autonomous pieces of art that can launch new ideas, insights, and visions and that respond to literary and cinematographic conventions. An age reading thus traces the many ways in which cultural imaginaries associated with age and aging become manifest in metaphoric practices and are negotiated, resisted, confirmed, or instrumentalized in creative, imaginative, practical, and scientific ways.

2 Conflicts of Timing

2.1 JOEL ZWICK'S *MY BIG FAT GREEK WEDDING*

Most people know *My Big Fat Greek Wedding* (2002) as a Greek-American romantic comedy "about ethnic identity and last-chance romance" (Kehr n. pag.). Set in Chicago, *My Big Fat Greek Wedding* narrates how 30-year-old Toula Portokalos falls in love with Ian Miller, an American upper middle-class university teacher, who is willing to put up with Toula's exuberant Greek family and teaches her the value of her cultural heritage. Besides the underlying story of culture clash between Greek and American middle-class families and their dissimilar ideals and values, which, as Ebert bemoans, "has been played out countless times as America's immigrants have intermarried" (n. pag.), the film tells the story of Toula's emancipation from the position of a subordinate and belittled waitress in the family restaurant to a self-confident and successful businesswoman. Toula learns to realize her own dreams while simultaneously accepting and appreciating her cultural heritage and ethnic identity. There is also a makeover storyline or "Cinderella-like transformation" of the heroine that first presents Toula as an ordinary caterpillar who gradually emerges from her cocoon and becomes a "radiant Hellenic butterfly" (Kehr n. pag.).

According to Rick Lyman from the *New York Times*, *My Big Fat Greek Wedding* is "the biggest independent film in history" and "the most financially successful romantic comedy" (n. pag.).[1] Joel Zwick directed the movie, which is based on a screenplay by Nia Vardalos, who plays the lead role of Toula Portokalos. Much of the story is based on Vardalos' autobiographical background as a Greek-Canadian woman, who married a non-Greek to the chagrin of her overbearing, very traditional Greek family. Similar to the character Toula, Vardalos married at the age of 31, after her fiancé agreed to be baptized in the Greek Orthodox Church. All of these aspects of Vardalos life were integrated into a one-woman show that Vardalos had written and performed before she adapted her story for the big screen.

An Old Woman at Age 30: Constructing Old Looks

In *My Big Fat Greek Wedding*, the topic of age and aging is generally overlooked, even though it is fundamental to the story. In the first quarter of the movie, the topic of age surfaces explicitly and repeatedly. In the very first scene, Toula sits in the car with her father. It is five o'clock in the morning and it is raining. Toula yawns and her father eyes her up and remarks in a heavy Greek accent: "You'd better get married soon. You're starting to look ... old." Toula, who is also the narrator of the movie, comments her father's statement as follows:

My dad has been saying that to me since I was 15 'cause nice Greek girls are supposed to do three things in life: marry Greek boys, make Greek babies and feed everyone until the day we die.

With this assessment of supposedly typical Greek expectations regarding the roles of females, the movie establishes the seemingly central themes of the movie – culture clash, oppressive cultural customs, and gender roles. These themes are triggered by the father's comment on his daughter's old looks, specifically her age-inappropriate status as an unmarried woman. It is thus the reference to (old) age that indicates the actual conflict in the nar-

---

1   According to the Internet Movie Database, the film had an estimated budget of $5 million and grossed $240 million in the United States alone (<www.imdb.com>, accessed on 20 May 2013).

rative: Toula does not fulfill the age-related expectations of her family and thus breaches her parents' beliefs regarding appropriate female behavior.[2]

It is important to recognize that Toula's father does not actually say that his daughter *is* becoming too old to get married. Hence he does *not* relate to age as a chronological marker, to a limited window in time and thus a physical inability to get married. Instead, he claims that she is starting to *look* old. If he had said that Toula is starting to look old*er*, he would have referred to the factual process of aging, which is undeniable and which applies to all stages in life. Claiming, however, that Toula *looks old*, her father insinuates an important nuance, which allows for a differentiation between surface and essence, and literal and metaphoric meaning. Toula's old looks are based on a subjective impression and not on a biological or physical fact. This differentiation is crucial to the metaphoric practice of age. Visually and thematically, the film characterizes Toula as old and stages her as a 'problem' and as an object of pity and concern. With thick glasses, ugly clothes, fuzzy hair, and no make-up, Toula appears as the black sheep of the family, or, seen through the lens of age, as an old spinster.[3]

In a second scene, the age references recur and the cultural constructedness of Toula's looks is emphasized again. When Toula asks her father for his permission to go to college, the following dialog unfolds:

Father (whining): Why do you want to leave me?
Toula: I'm not leaving you. Don't you want me to do something with my life?
Father: Yes, get married, make babies. You look so old.

---

[2] Toula's gender, of course, plays a crucial role with regard to her age. As I am not pursuing a gendered approach to the topic of age, I will not elaborate on this issue. But, to illustrate why my neglect of gender is justified, I want to give a short example. If one compares Toula's relation to age with that of her adult brother Nick, it becomes clear that his relation to age is equally conflictual. Like Toula, Nick is strongly patronized and denigrated by the family. He is treated as a little child, who is allowed to fool around with his nephews but who fails to receive the desired acknowledgement from his father for his artistic talents.

[3] For a more elaborate analysis of the spinster figure in romantic comedies, such as *Bridget Jones's Diary*, see my article "Junge Altersbilder in den Medien: Stereotype über das Alter(n) in zeitgenössischen romantischen Komödien" (2013).

Again, the age reference "You look so old" signifies that Toula's actions are contradictory to her father's expectations of normal behavior. The reference to Toula's age functions as a disciplinary measure that is supposed to make her comply with her father's rules.

In a third scene, Toula's father consults with her uncle and aunt, discussing his plans to send Toula to Greece to find a husband. The age reference is used again. Toula's uncle asks: "Is she not too old?" Toula's father replies: "She is okay." The uncle advises: "In Greece, don't tell anyone how old she is." All agree. In this scene, the chronological aspect of age is highlighted in order to complicate Toula's (allegedly) precarious situation. Interestingly, her chronological age, as all concur, can be concealed. The chronological pressure is thus relativized because Toula is actually "okay." In this scene, the metaphoric practice of age emphasizes that Toula represents a problem and burden to the family. Her problematic situation is not so much due to the chronological dimension of her age, but rather to her outsider position in the family. The family members indicate this difference by referring to Toula's age.

In a fourth scene, the reference to age comes from Toula herself as she describes herself and her situation in a voiceover: "Nice Greek girls who don't find a husband, work in the family restaurant. So here I am. Day after day, year after year. Thirty, and way past my expiration date." Here, the reference to age amplifies the protagonist's desperate situation. Her association of being thirty and "past her expiration date" signifies a notion of decline and worthlessness. As age scholars contend, a loss of value and social recognition is stereotypically associated with old age (e.g. Butler 1969, Gullette 2004). In *My Big Fat Greek Wedding*, the cinematographic choices emphasize this impression: Shortly after Toula speaks of her expiration date, she is filmed in the backyard, near the garbage cans (see fig 6). The setting and the camera angle insinuate that Toula feels worthless, useless and unrecognized in her desires and talents. The camera slowly moves from a bird's-eye perspective to her eye level and the initial wide shot emphasizes her smallness and insignificance. The camera movement towards a medium shot and an eye level angle foreshadows that a transformation of the protagonist and her social status can be expected in the course of the movie.

In all four of these scenes, which occur in the first quarter of the movie, the use of age metaphors indicates a breach of expectations and highlights Toula's conflictual situation. The age metaphors establish Toula's behavior as different from those around her and function as disciplinary devices that emphasize her misdemeanors. The cinematographic devices employed in the film support this disciplinary function and verbal reprobation of Toula: The image composition and mise-en-scène in the first part of the movie consistently present Toula as an outsider. She is often spatially removed from the rest of the family and the camera typically singles her out (see fig. 3 and 4). While the family is shown sitting together, Toula stands somewhere else in the background or alone. She is presented as a distant observer of the hubbub created by the others. Toula's mocking tone from the voiceover further amplifies her remoteness.

A Metaphoric Rejuvenation

The central conflict within the film, namely the age-inappropriate behavior of Toula in terms of (allegedly) female duties in Greek families, is established in the first half hour of the film. Over the course of the movie, this conflict is gradually resolved and the happy ending shows Toula married, with a child, and reconciled with her intercultural background. Several symbolic plot strands are woven together and indicate Toula's transformation: She develops from an ugly spinster to an attractive woman, from a dependent and unappreciated help in the family restaurant to a successful and emancipated businesswoman in the tourism industry, from a cultural outsider to an integrated member of an intercultural American middle-class. These developments fit with the coming-of-age plot since Toula becomes more independent from her family and finds her place in life. Furthermore, typical of the coming-of-age genre, the movie features intergenerational conflict and presents the protagonist as an outsider. Toula's transformation might also be interpreted in terms of an emancipation or feminization story, in which Toula develops from a helpless, asexual daughter to an independent and sensual woman. And then, of course, the film is also a story of cultural integration.

I want to suggest that, besides these quite common interpretations of the story, there is also a plot in *My Big Fat Greek Wedding* that relates to aging, or rather a reverse-aging plot, which frames the character's transformation in terms of a metaphoric rejuvenation of her lifestyle, appearance, and behavior. This metaphoric rejuvenation is accompanied by references to age. In the first part of the movie, these references mark Toula as old (and deviant). As the film progresses, Toula is increasingly associated with features of youthfulness. This development from 'old' to 'young' constitutes the rejuvenation plot, which gradually reduces Toula's deviance and lets her assume an age-appropriate role. The movie thus unfolds within the binaries of young and old and normal and deviant, which contribute significantly to the ageist tendency of the story, as I will explain later.

Toula's rejuvenation unfolds as follows. In the beginning of the movie, Toula wears oversized, old-fashioned eyeglasses and ill-fitting, brown- and grey-colored clothes (see fig. 1 and 4); she does not use makeup or have any recognizable hairstyle. She is marked as ugly and shows neither interest in fashion nor makes any effort to look attractive. Later in the movie, Toula uses the expression "frump girl" as a description of who she was, implying that she used to be a "cross, old-fashioned, dowdily-dressed woman" (*OED*). While "frump" as such is not age specific, it is "frequently associated with the elderly," as Frank H. Nuessel argues (274). Fittingly, Toula's body posture appears limp, chubby, and weak – the stereotypical body language of an old person. At the same time, Toula calls herself a frump *girl*, which reinforces the ambiguity of her situation as an old-looking but chronologically young woman. Nonetheless, the aged Toula seems to lack vitality, energy, or physical strength, all of which are typical markers of youthfulness (see Chapter 2.2). Instead, Toula moves slowly, drags her feet, and seems to be worn down by a life filled with toil and little pleasure. Compared to her sister, who storms into the restaurant with her three children and who – despite the obvious strain – has an energetic, dominant, and dynamic attitude, Toula's lack of these qualities becomes even more conspicuous.

Later, after Toula has started working in the travel agency, the viewer observes a dynamic and energetic woman who moves self-confidently in the office and who emphasizes her lively sales conversations with vigorous gestures and a self-assured attitude. This rejuvenation of Toula's body language also plays into the feminization of her character. Toula develops from a grey and mousy spinster into a radiant, attractive, and sensuous woman. Her transformation is celebrated in a humorous makeover sequence, in which Toula puts on make-up and tries on contact lenses. She begins to wear bright, flowery dresses and sheds the shapeless, colorless, and dull clothes she wore in the restaurant. We observe a transformation: The age-inappropriate and bland spinster turns into an attractive and sensual woman. Clearly, Toula has undergone a Cinderella-like transformation, as Kehr argues, but what he misses in his interpretation is the fact that another transformation is completed as well: Toula has been symbolically rejuvenated. The stereotypes often associated with old age – such as lack of beauty, attractiveness, or sexuality (see Chapter 2.2) – have vanished and Toula is associated with youthful attributes.

Fig. 1: 'Old' Toula in the family restaurant

Fig. 2: 'Young' Toula on a date with Ian

Cinematographic devices also contribute to this story of rejuvenation. Before Toula's transformation, the lighting, for instance, makes the heroine's face look darker than the other faces – as if she were living in the shadows.

Sometimes the light is direct and harsh and creates noticeable lines and shadows on Toula's face (see fig. 1). At other times, the light is pallid and makes Toula's face look pasty. In short, in the first part of the movie, the lighting is always unfavorable and unflattering. With Toula's metaphoric rejuvenation, the lighting changes: When she goes out on dates with Ian, for instance, she is shown as a glowing and radiating woman with shining hair and sparkling eyes (see fig. 2). The light is set indirectly, so that her face looks softer and more delicate. The main light comes from behind her and highlights her shiny curls.

The image composition also reflects Toula's transformation. While in the first part of the movie the image composition was used to distance Toula visually and spatially from the community of her family, after her metaphoric rejuvenation, Toula moves to the foreground and the camera frames her as part of her family (see fig. 5). In addition, after the rejuvenation, the mis-en-scène has changed: In figure 7, we see Toula with a headset and a computer, which signify her advancement on the social ladder. She is now a productive and successful member of the service society, which gives her confidence and independence.

Fig. 3: The Portokalos family from Toula's point of view

Fig. 4: 'Old' Toula is singled out

Fig. 5: 'Young' Toula is part of the family

The rejuvenation plot is also intertwined with the emancipation theme in the movie. In the beginning of the film, Toula appears to be a burden to her family, even though the family business profits greatly from her work. Yet Toula is not in the position to save or spend any money according to her own desires or to participate in consumer culture. This assumed lack of productivity, dependence, and incapacitation is often associated with old age (see chapter 2.2), as the elderly are often considered a burden to their families or to the welfare state in general – a situation that is not dissimilar to Toula's.

Over the course of the movie, Toula's status changes due to her metaphoric rejuvenation: Toula enrolls at a college and specializes in tourism.

We watch her excelling in class, making friends with fellow students, and, eventually, working in her aunt's travel agency in which she has set up a modern computer system, which she operates successfully. Toula has managed to modernize her aunt's business and has emancipated herself from the family restaurant. She has traded her apron and menus for a headset and a computer. Toula now appears to be a thriving businesswoman who brings profit to the agency and is thus a productive member of the working world. In contrast to Toula's previous work in the old-fashioned family restaurant, she now participates in the modern world of high-skilled labor, computer work, and the service industry. Toula skillfully manages transactions between customers, hotels, and airlines, which are clearly more complex than food orders. Toula has thus developed from a seemingly slow-witted, uncreative, and averagely competent waitress into an efficient, skilled, and productive travel agent. She is fit for the demands of contemporary society and the information technologies within it. By zeroing in on age, an age reading unfolds new dimensions to what initially appeared to be a typical emancipation story. In doing so, it focuses on the ways in which the cultural meanings of age are interwoven with a young woman's story about intergenerational conflict, a sense of worthlessness, failure and marginalization.

An age reading of *My Big Fat Greek Wedding* also puts into perspective the interpretation of the movie as a coming-of-age story. *My Big Fat Greek Wedding* does indeed describe a progress, particularly in social terms, but the meanings of age stages and maturation become more difficult to pin down against the background of the heroine's rejuvenation. Toula does not mature from adolescence to adulthood but regresses from a state of premature old age to (age-appropriate) adulthood. The chronologically young Toula has been aged before her time – by her family and by the cinematographic decisions made by the film team. This metaphoric practice of age marks Toula as deviant and age-inappropriate. Despite her chronological age (which is not a problem as such, as her father admits), the references to age used to describe Toula imply a semantic dimension beyond the literal meaning of 'you look old:' Toula is not acting according to her family's expectations; she is a disappointment, an outsider. This outsider status fits the contemporary coming-of-age plot, yet *My Big Fat Greek Wedding* inverts the timeline of maturation into adulthood and symbolically inverts the character's passing through time.

Age references fulfill several functions in *My Big Fat Greek Wedding*. They describe the conflict of the main character, they insinuate a disciplinary or moral dimension, and they categorize Toula as different. The references to age also coincide with the transformation of the protagonist and thus trigger the rejuvenation plot.

Fig. 6: 'Old' Toula at work in the family restaurant

Fig. 7: 'Young' Toula at work in the travel agency

Finally 'Young' And 'Normal:' Ageist Messages

Toula's transformation involves her becoming 'normal.' At the end of the movie, she looks and acts more age-appropriately, both of which imply a more youthful appearance. This age-appropriateness coincides with the fulfillment of other expectations: She is finally married, lives in her own house, and has given birth to a daughter, thus giving her a family of her own. By marrying an American man, Toula has also managed to merge two of her own most eager wishes: to become 'normal' in a cultural sense and in the sense of being a woman of a certain age. Toula is no longer labeled as old but is presented as a normal, adult woman who is independent, responsible, productive, active, energetic, self-determined, and a full member of society.

Robert N. Butler, who coined the term ageism in 1969, defines it as a "form of bigotry" that discriminates the elderly and that values "pragmatism, action, power, and the vigor of youth" as core values of American ideology (243). It seems that *My Big Fat Greek Wedding* praises and rewards exactly these cultural values and, in doing so, it contributes to reinforcing the binary between youth and old age and thus puts out an ageist message. This ageist agenda is interwoven with a seemingly naive romantic comedy plot and it might be exactly this elusive and unexpected nature of the ageist messages that contributes to its efficiency: After all, the main character Toula is not chronologically old; therefore no viewer would suspect that ageist stereotypes would be applied to this character.

The ageism in *My Big Fat Greek Wedding* does not only refer to the presentation of the main character. It can also be found in the ways in which secondary characters, like Toula's father and her grandmother, are characterized. As Kirk Combe and Kenneth Schmader demonstrate, the comedy genre powerfully contributes to the exaggeration and misrepresentation of old age by using ageist notions to mark old characters as asexual, senile, and the like (cf. 93). Gus, Toula's father, is described as a man of senile stubbornness who is attributed whimsical features that are instrumentalized for running gags. Gus believes that every word has a Greek origin and that he can heal any skin ailment with Windex. He appears to be reactionary and ignorant. When he refuses Toula's education and marriage plans, he is presented as the typical "grumpy old man" and stubborn "curmudgeon" (Bearon n. pag.). He is old-fashioned and naive and devotedly clings to obsolete ideas. Similarly, Toula's grandmother is presented as the stereotypical old "bat" or "witch:" a demented, hunched, and wrinkly woman who behaves strangely, even aggressively, for no apparent reason. The grandmother is an object of ridicule that adds to the humor of the movie.

She mistakes her son for "an ugly Turk," sleeps with a knife under her pillow (because she ignores or refuses to believe that the war between Turks and Greeks is over), and repeatedly tries to escape from her new home. These stereotypical cultural imaginaries associated with old age are exploited for comic purposes in *My Big Fat Greek Wedding*. Chronologically old characters are exaggerated and ridiculed within the standard romantic comedy plot. And even though one may argue that the humor takes the edge off the clichés, the existence of these stereotypes, which equate youthfulness with attractiveness, success, and social recognition, and which operate on the binaries of young and old and normal and deviant, contributes to reinforcing the ageist tone of the movie.

2.2 Ageism and the Disciplinary Functions of Age Discourses

My Big Fat Greek Wedding, as I have suggested, uses ageist assumptions to amplify the heroine's inappropriateness and otherness. It builds on the characteristics of ageism, which, in a broader sense, "reflects a deep seated uneasiness on the part of the young and middle-aged – a personal revulsion to and distaste for growing old, disease, disability; and fear of powerlessness, 'uselessness,' and death" (Butler 243). In this section, I would like to contextualize the previous age reading of *My Big Fat Greek Wedding* and explain the broader relevance of my interpretation. Ageist attitudes are a central concern for age scholars, who argue that stereotypical and negative associations with old age have profoundly detrimental effects on both the old and the young.[4] Which features and attitudes ascribed to the elderly have been labeled as ageist? And in which forms does ageism appear?

Hodgetts et al. claim that "[e]lderly people have predominantly been represented in a stereotypical manner as ill, incapacitated, senile, lonely, dependent, passive and unproductive individuals" (418). Combe and Schmader show in their study on comedies how "ageism is institutionalized in our comic and satiric tradition" because comedies repeatedly use prejudices against old age, such as "sheer physical decline, dotage and aged

---

4   Also see Nuessel (1982), Kramer (n. d.), or Bearon (n.d.) for the language and social consequences of ageism.

lechery" (84).[5] Moreover, in comedies, the elderly are often represented with the stigma of senility and asexuality (cf. 80, 93). The stock characters of comedies are thus old bachelors, widows, or old curmudgeons – in short, buffoon characters – who, like Toula's father and her grandmother, are either presented as lunatics or as dirty and vulgar people (or both) (cf. 85ff.).

Another form of stereotyping that, at first sight, might appear as positive or harmless is the labeling of elderly women as "little old ladies" (Bearon 1) or "sweet old ladies" (cf. Maierhofer 343), implying a gentle, benevolent, and selfless grandmother figure. These images are generally considered to belittling and patronizing. Another set of more evident stereotypes are expressions such as grumpy old men, geezers, bats, witches, codger, old goat, or crotchety, which are openly derogatory and which can influence how the elderly think about themselves in terms of incompetence, fragility, or helplessness (cf. Bearon 1-2). Other common misconceptions about old age are based on the assumption that the majority of elderly people are often bored or miserable, irritated and angry, live in poverty and alone, and are prone to become victims of criminals (cf. Palmore 89). In the work field, younger coworkers tend to perceive their elderly colleagues as "greedy and demanding, clamoring for material help, always complaining of unfair treatment or deprivation" (Irvine qtd. in Powell, *Social Theory and Aging* 99).[6] Economically speaking, the elderly are imagined as a drain on resources who limit productivity (cf. 100). This assumption increases popular stereotypes of the elderly as "redundant, bothersome and disturbing" (Hazan 26). Such a bias marginalizes and silences the elderly and perpetuates the youth cult in Western societies.[7]

---

5   Combe and Schmader analyze examples from seventeenth- and eighteenth-century comedies (e.g. *The Man of Mode* by Sir George Etheridge) and from contemporary popular movie culture (e.g. *Grumpy Old Men*).
6   Powell quotes from E. Irvine's article "Research into Problem Families" (1954).
7   Idioms such as "sixty is the new forty" or "fifty is the new thirty" stand for a similar emphasis and adoration of youthfulness (cf. e.g. Gullette, *Agewise* 23; or Walden n.pag.). While Gullette views these phrases positively because they represent progress narratives and enable optimistic visualizations of aging, one might also consider such expressions to be ageist because they indicate an orientation towards youthfulness as the only accepted way of aging well (see Chapter 4.1).

Ageist notions also have a significant effect on how younger people imagine their own aging processes. Cassie Phoenix and Andrew C. Sparkes have interviewed undergraduate student athletes about their ideas of a future self and have found that the students often describe future "feared selves," which are "associated with the loss of predictability over a body that had previously been controlled and disciplined in performance terms" ("Young Athletic" 115). The students' future bodies were imagined as "dependent on others, inactive, leaky, painful, and weak" (115). Phoenix and Sparkes found that self-aging, i.e. the aging of the self and the ways in which this process is experienced, perceived, or narrated, is shaped in young adults via three resources: family members, older team members, and the curriculum of their degree course. These resources provide behavioral scripts for future development (cf. "Young Athletic" 111). Phoenix and Sparkes use the term "narrative maps of aging" and they define these maps as "a preview" (110) or "pre-presentations" (109). The influence of role models is vital in the formation of such narrative maps: "[I]n re-presenting his or her experience of ageing, the older person provides the younger person with a *pre*-presentation of what is to come as they age" (Phoenix et. al., "Athletic Identity" 344; original emphasis). Phoenix and Sparkes find a general "preponderance of gerontophobic images" ("Young Athletic" 117) and demonstrate that young adults' assumptions about self-aging are heavily influenced by a binary opposition of youth and old age and the entailing stereotypes about old age.

Phoenix and Sparkes summarize the students' fears of aging in the following way: Middle age is associated with features, such as decreases in physical activity, co-ordination, agility, speed, and strength (cf. 116). It is thus imagined as a loss of the performing body. Old age is envisioned as a period in life, in which weakness, diseases, and pain prevail. Old people are considered to be less active or physically restricted, dependent, leaky, and slow (cf. "Young Athletic" 116). The young body is thus equated with strength, stamina, full control, full functioning, efficiency, and performance whereas the old or aged body represents the decline or loss of these criteria.

Some of these associations also surface in *My Big Fat Greek Wedding*, particularly in the representation of Toula's father and grandmother as odd, senile, and frail, which decisively contributes to the ageist, gerontophobic climate of the movie. Above all, it is the grandmother who is presented as Toula's symbolic future self as an old, unattractive, and demented woman who has lost all autonomy and is ridiculed and not taken seriously. In a sense, these features are already ascribed to Toula, at least at the beginning of the film, when we get to know her. Unsurprisingly, for Toula, this future self is a feared self. Like her grandmother, Toula is presented as a burden to the family and as an object of pity and ridicule. Toula's grandmother is given a voice only once when she mistakes her son for an "ugly Turk" and hits him. Throughout the rest of the movie, she is repeatedly shown as a crazy and oddly speechless old woman and, in this sense, she functions like an ominous shadow that overcasts and aggravates Toula's frustration. Hence, the cultural imaginaries reproduced and fortified in *My Big Fat Greek Wedding* are highly problematic, particularly because the movie is a comedy and invites the viewers to laugh at the oddness of old or aged characters.

Aging as a Moral Enterprise

When Toula is said to look old in *My Big Fat Greek Wedding*, a moral judgment about her social role and position is made, which devalues her as a person. Age scholars maintain that the morality applied to the topic of aging not only designates youth or youthfulness as a desirable aim and old age as its dire opposite, it also insinuates a binary between good, positive, or successful forms of aging and negative or unsuccessful ways of growing old. What does positive aging imply?

The idea of positive aging or successful aging (which I will use interchangeably) sounds desirable and promising at first glance. Successful aging became prominent in 1987 with an article by John Rowe and Robert Kahn (cf. Strawbridge et. al. 727), in which an encouraging vision of aging is mapped out that endorses features in the elderly such as activity, mobility, drive, health, independence, and individuality. Basically, positive aging means that a person maintains "a high quality of life in old age" (Kahn 726). Kahn proposes a measurement of what he calls "successful aging," consisting of three defining components: "a) (relatively) low risk of disease and disease-related disability, b) (relatively) high mental and physical function, and c) active engagement in life, including close relationships with others and continued participation in productive activities" (725). Successful aging then does not mean to not age at all, but to age well (cf. 725). What aging 'well' implies, however, is highly subjective; for this reason, Strawbridge et al. found a significant discrepancy between people who qualify as having aged successfully according to Rowe and Kahn's criteria (18,8%) and those participants who rated themselves as having aged successfully according to their own criteria (50,3%; cf. 732). This inconsistency challenges Kahn's measuring units of physical health and social life as evidence for positive aging. The research conducted by Strawbridge et al. suggests that people might *want* to consider themselves as positively aged (regardless of their physical performance) because having aged positively is a desired and socially recognized status.

Attempts to define positive aging raise further issues. The terminology of 'successful' or 'positive' is problematic because it implies a moral distinction between right and wrong, normal and abnormal, socially acceptable and deviant (cf. Hepworth, "Positive Ageing" 176-7). Strawbridge et al. also comment on the semantics of the term 'successful' which they find questionable

because it implies a contest in which there are winners and losers; most gerontologists are not ready to call someone *unsuccessful* merely because he or she is disabled or diagnosed with diabetes. (728; original emphasis)

Alternative suggestions (such as healthy aging, effective aging, productive aging) are not less problematic (cf. Strawbridge et al. 728). Due to these semantic reverberations, Hepworth considers aging "a moral enterprise" ("Positive Ageing" 180), and Susan Sontag speaks of growing older as "a moral disease" (29).

Despite these critical voices, positive aging is often promoted as a beneficial concept and a favorable vision of old age. Moreover, it is used as a panacea against the (presumed) detrimental effects of old age because it helps people envision a more positive future for their aged selves. Hodgetts et al., however, problematize this praise of positive aging as oversimplistic and argue that

images of the active elderly may not always be as progressive or positive as they first appear. Portrayals of the active elderly in the media drawing on lifestyle often promote an individualized view of ageing, which can lead to ageing being presented as overly self-determined. Such portrayals assign primary responsibility for successful ageing to the individual who can be blamed for failing to comply. ("Between Television" 419)

Hence, instead of providing a larger range of multi-faceted images of aging, the agenda of positive aging potentially increases the repugnance against old age, at least when a person does not manage to age positively. Consequently, the message behind the new aging attitude reads: Aging is an acceptable fact of life as long as a person remains physically young and attractive (cf. Hodgetts et al. 419). This attitude towards aging is, of course, fairly simplistic. And, it continues to endorse the binaries between youthfulness and old age because it basically promotes the prolongation of a youthful lifestyle across the entire life course. The hegemony of youth over old age is upheld and, as Hepworth claims, such action is "repressive of the diversity in later life all gerontologists are exhorted to display and venerate" ("Positive Ageing" 189). In fact, positive aging only sets another set of stereotypes against the ones that Gullette identified as the predominant decline narratives. The new compulsive narrative is that of successful or positive aging. Therefore, Hepworth warns that

> [p]ositive and negative styles of ageing into old age are not objectively distinctive physical conditions waiting to be discovered, but are socially constructed moral categories reflecting the prevailing social preference for individualized consumerism, voluntarism and decentralization [...] [T]hese social preferences foster an accelerating age-consciousness where the fear of ageing into old age tends to predominate, and old age is consequently perceived as a 'social problem' which can only be resolved by normalizing styles of ageing prescriptively designated 'positive' (i.e. as the bodily evidence of 'rational' and independent individual lifestyles) and discoursing or even punishing of styles of ageing defined as deviant (i.e. 'irrational', self-indulgent and, above all, conducive to social dependency). (177)

The moral divide between the features associated with youthful aging and old age thus revolves around voluntarism, self-determination, consumerism, and independence. Instead of reducing the fear of old age, the agenda behind positive aging exacerbates the situation by considering the individual responsible if he or she does not manage to age positively.

The powerful impact of the positive aging doctrine also affects the private lives of age scholars. Erdman B. Palmore, a professor emeritus of medical sociology at Duke University, is an intriguing example of the pervasiveness of the positive aging doctrine. Palmore has devoted his academic career to the combat of ageism. In his private life, however, he goes to great lengths to be a "model of 'successful aging:'"

> I am trying to demonstrate that one can improve with age by becoming stronger through weight-lifting (300 pounds dead-lift); by doing a birthday marathon each year, in which I ride my age in miles on my bicycle (75 this year), and do my age in push-ups and sit-ups; and by doing some birthday adventure such as hang-gliding, bungee-jumping, sky-diving, or white-water rafting. (89)

Palmore's description of his activities reveals how much he has internalized the messages of positive aging: He has a strong belief in infinite progress and growth (each year adds capacity and power) and he (uncritically) strives for boundless youthfulness, energy, vitality, adventure, and a willingness to go to the limits of his physical capacities. The controllability of the body through willpower is demonstrated to an extreme and appears as a form of heroism. To critics of the positive aging doctrine, Palmore is less a hero than a victim in a perpetual pursuit of growth and progress. In a different context, Micki McGee uses the term "belabored self" for describing individuals who are driven by an obsessive obligation to activity, consumerism, corporeality, and endless competition (see Chapter 4.1). Palmore indeed seems to adhere to what Harry R. Moody calls a "frenzy of activity" (238).

Alternative views on aging well were described by one of the pioneers of age studies, G. Stanley Hall, about a century ago. Hall asked residents of retirement homes for their secrets to aging well and found that "all praise early retiring and insist that a generous portion of twenty-four hours must be spent in bed, even if they do not sleep" (qtd. in Katz, *Cultural Aging* 126). Hence, in 1922, when Hall published his study *Senescence: The Last Half of Life*, old age was associated with an entirely different set of desirable practices, such as contemplation, rest, moderation, and composure. It seems that a fundamental change has occurred in American culture's approach towards aging well. Some scholars locate the origins for this ideological change in the neoliberal or economic underpinnings that seem to define positive aging (cf. Hazan 1994, Hepworth 1995, Katz 1999, or Featherstone 2003). Hazan argues, for instance, that the elderly are separated from mainstream society in many different dimensions. One of these dimensions is the economic domain: The elderly are conceived as nonproductive, dependent, and "incapable of making any future returns" (19). The elderly are thus perceived as a social problem because their productivity is only measured in pecuniary ways and not in terms of "a capital of a lifetime of human experience" (19). Economically speaking, the elderly thus represent a monetary deficit and an impending problem. This view of the elderly clearly has ageist undertones.

Positive aging also entails an alternative economic assessment of the elderly, which is, however, no less ageist. In her study "Gold in Gray," Meredith Minkler shows that the elderly have been targeted as an attractive consumer market, a $500 billion market to be specific (cf. 18).[8] Because of their great amount of leisure (and sometimes considerable pensions), retirees can be (and are) praised as ideal consumers who engage in cultural activities, have time to travel extensively, and buy presents for their grandchildren. Of course, this view only focuses on retirees from the (upper) middle class. This market-driven empowerment of the elderly appears to be a positive development, but it has its downsides. It constructs and solidifies two sets of images: the "heroes of aging," who are propelled and courted by consumer culture, and those with "severe bodily decline," who turn into "abominations of human nature" and thus become subhuman or parahuman beings (Featherstone, "Post-Bodies" 227). According to Featherstone, this system is "part of the repertoire of the pornography of old age" (227) because it provokes powerful emotional reactions towards the elderly and reinforces their marginalization. The binary of positive and negative aging is reinforced.

The problematization of positive aging by Katz, Hepworth, and others reveals that the agenda and moral underpinnings of positive aging disqualifies it as a panacea against ageism. Rather, positive aging perpetuates and aggravates the divide between young-old people and old-old people,[9] and, consequently, between youthfulness and old age. Moreover, it attributes particular moralities and desired or undesired qualities to age stages that

---

8   Minkler's numbers are from a study by Phillip Longman (*Born to Pay: The New Politics of Aging in America* 1987).

9   This differentiation into young-old and old-old was suggested by Bernice Neugarten (1974). She defined the age group of the young-old as those who are between 55 and 75 years old, active, healthy and affluent. This group stands in contrast to the old-old (age 75 and older), who need care and support.

can be used to classify or categorize people on the basis of their bodies, social conduct, and attitudes. The notion of age as a moral enterprise and classification device raises important questions: How does an individual fall into one of the two categories – successful or failed? What are the techniques of this moral judgment? And how do the moralities associated with old age and aging inform the age awareness of young adults?

Disciplining Old Age[10]

Even though Foucault never addressed gerontological theory (cf. Powell & Wahidin vii), there is a small field of "Foucauldian gerontology" that studies how age and aging are linked with patterns of normalization, the expert or medical gaze, subjectification processes, surveying and monitoring strategies as well as discourses of dependency and categorization (cf. Powell 93).[11] Foucauldian gerontologists are interested in the ways in which people construct and internalize the moralities and patterns of normalization linked with age (cf. Powell and Wahidin viii). According to Foucault, the discourses of power and regulation materialize in subjectification practices or technologies of the self. Through an interplay of resistance and domination, individuals are constructed

simultaneously as subjects and objects. First, people are seen as objects by someone else, through control and restraint. Second, people are deemed to actively subject their own identity to personal direction through processes such as conscience and mediated self-knowledge. (Powell 105)

Hence, the discourses of power are not unilateral. They only function when people actively engage in and reproduce existing paradigms and discours-

---

10 *Disciplining Old Age* is the name of a book by Stephen Katz from 1996, in which he draws on Foucault's *Discipline and Punish* and argues that "disciplines do not just construct dominant representations of the world but also determine the ways in which the people who inhabit it can be known, studied, calculated, helped, punished, and liberated" (2). For a differentiation of Foucault's concept of disciplining see Kunow's article "Chronologically Gifted" (cf. 33).
11 Jason Powell lists such scholars as Stephen Katz, Emmanuelle Tulle-Winton, Simon Biggs, Azrini Wahidin or Haim Hazan (93-8).

es.[12] According to Powell, the task of elderly individuals consists in contributing to the busyness of their own bodies and in monitoring closely how successfully they perform (cf. 106). If they fail, they are blamed for not fulfilling their responsibilities."In such a [neoliberal] regime older people are exhorted, indeed expected, to become entrepreneurs in all spheres and to accept responsibility for the management of risk" (Powell 107).

The ideas of entrepreneurial thinking and neoliberalism will resurface in Chapters 4.1 and 4.3, where I will discuss how consumerism, managerial discourse, and accountability influence the conception of the self in American culture (cf. Powell 108). For now, I want to stress the importance of self-monitoring and self-responsibility, which are key terms in the processes of social control. According to Hepworth, the domains of social control and normalization patterns go far beyond successful or positive aging: Social practices of all sorts, such as "posture, reflexes, orgasm, diet, breathing, dreams, relationships, psychic plumbing, child rearing" are individual and social areas, in which the allocation of moral values or expectations of appropriate social conduct are tested and negotiated (Stanley Cohen qtd. in Hepworth 188).[13]

The characters in *Away We Go*, Burt and Verona, exemplify the ways in which the practices of self-responsibility and the patterns of normalization function as mechanisms of (self-)control. Burt and Verona negotiate their own normativity through the topics of child rearing (what kind of parents they want to be), dreams (what kind of childhood they want their daughter to have), relationships (what kind of couple they want to be), and bodily functions (what kind of heart beat they want their daughter to have). This negotiation is organized by way of references to age and temporality, which stand for either success or failure.

---

12 The workings of this interplay can be observed in *My Big Fat Greek Wedding*. Toula is the object of her father's control and restraint; she also, however, readily succumbs to his judgments – at least in the first part of the movie – when she describes her situation in a desperate and hopeless tone, which suggests how much of her father's judgments she has internalized.

13 Hepworth quotes Stanley Cohen's *Visions of Social Control: Crime, Punishment, and Classification* (1985).

2.3 SAM MENDES' *AWAY WE GO*

Away We Go (2009) is a movie about Verona de Tessant and Burt Farlander, a young couple in their early thirties who are expecting their first child. When they learn that Burt's parents are leaving the soon-to-be parents by moving to Europe, they realize that they must abandon their current lifestyle – they live in a less than desirable home with cardboard windows and insufficient heating – and find a new place in a family-friendly environment. Verona and Burt decide to embark on a road trip through North America to visit their friends and do a "comparison shopping among lifestyles" in order to find where they want to raise their yet unborn daughter (Ebert n. pag.).

Sam Mendes[14] directed *Away We Go*, which has been described as an independent "road comedy" (Scott, "Practicing Virtue" n. pag.). Dave Eggers and his wife Vendela Vida wrote the original script. With an estimated budget of $17 million, the film grossed only $9,5 million in the United States[15] and received reviews that were critical of the "smug" and "condescending" attitude that the film radiates due to its "bullying, self-righteous tone" (Scott, "Practicing Virtue" n. pag.). The protagonists were criticized for being "implausibly ideal" (Ebert, "*Away We Go*" n. pag.) and for feeling like "two lonely souls in a hostile world" (Harvey n. pag.). According to Dennis Harvey, the characters' attitudes are problematic because they mock and devalue the other characters in the movie as inferior, pitiful, or simply ridiculous caricatures who only make the protagonists glow even brighter.

Despite this criticism, the movie is interesting for its representation of aged young adult characters. Some reviewers even discussed the importance of age in the movie – at least in terms of life stages. A.O. Scott, for instance, finds an "idealism of youth," and a

---

14 Sam Mendes also directed *American Beauty* (1999), for which he was awarded the Oscar for Best Director, *Road To Perdition* (2002), *Jarhead* (2005) and *Revolutionary Road* (2008).

15 The box office information is retrieved from <www.imdb.com>, accessed on 20 May 2013.

flight from adulthood, from engagement, from responsibility, even as [the film] cleverly disguises itself as a search for all those things. But the dream of being left alone in a world of your own making, far from anything sad or icky or difficult, is a child's fantasy. (n. pag.)

Similarly, Roger Ebert, though he is less critical, maintains that parenthood represents a watershed moment for Verona and Burt, which requires adult decisions and radical changes in their lifestyles: "It's not that they can't afford a better home, as much that they are stalled in an impoverished student lifestyle. Now that they're about to become parents, they can't keep adult life on hold" (n. pag.). The key concept of coming of age clearly reverberates in Scott's and Ebert's reviews, and, indeed, Burt and Verona are stuck somewhere between life stages, knowing that they need to mature and find their place in the world. In this sense, they seem to represent prototypical coming-of-age heroes. However, they are stuck in-between life stages, like the "delayed adults" and "perpetual adolescents" described by psychologists and sociologists (see Chapter 3.1). Moreover, Burt and Verona do not fully match the paradigm of teleological progress typical of characters from conventional coming-of-age stories: Even though they embark on a journey, they remain oddly static and unchanging. The references to age and time in *Away We Go* underline this impression. Moreover, the age references suggest disciplinary and self-monitoring dimensions in Burt's and Verona's searches for their future selves.

Aged Losers at a Loss

In *Away We Go*, age references take central stage in the protagonists' search for their future selves. First and foremost, the references to age describe the protagonists as different. As unmarried freelancers with a student lifestyle and practically no family ties, Burt and Verona differ from other characters in the movie who are more settled and have houses, teenage kids, as well as steady jobs. In contrast to Toula's situation, being different in *Away We Go* is mostly a desirable condition for Burt and Verona. At the outset, however, a feeling of otherness and failure in terms of life achievements and proper timing is evoked, which functions as a trigger that motivates Verona and Burt's journey.

Age references occur for the first time when Verona, a 34-year-old freelance illustrator, and Burt, a 33-year-old insurance agent, are on their way to Burt's parents, whom Verona expects to "lean on pretty hard" after the baby is born, as she told her sister earlier on the phone. In the car, Burt receives a phone call from a customer and changes the pitch of his voice to sound older. Verona is annoyed by what seems to be a regular habit of Burt's, who justifies his behavior by saying:

Burt: They expect that from me.
Verona: They expect you to sound like Casey Kasem?[16]
Burt: Verona, most of these guys are in their 50s and 60s. We're talking about millions of dollars in insurance futures. They don't want to be dealing with some 33-year-old that didn't finish college.

In this scene, the age reference is coupled – as so often in *Away We Go* – with the fact that Burt and Verona fear to be losers. Burt feels that his age and inadequate education collide with his trustworthiness. Since Burt only seems to contact his customers' by phone, he uses a fake husky voice to sound more mature, skilled, and reliable. Hence, the reference to Burt's chronological age in the dialog above implies that Burt's sense of inadequacy is twofold: He feels incompetent in terms of his education and because of his (young) age. Both factors are interdependent and connote a lack of experience, expertise, and reliability. The humorous tone of the movie and the way in which the scene is embedded in the film's exposition indicates that this twofold self-condemnation of being an unaccomplished fraud of thirty-three years is not meant to be taken too seriously. After all, Burt is presented as an amiable and kind person.

The second reference to age occurs after Verona and Burt return from the dinner to their shabby home. Having learned that Burt's parents have decided to move to Europe soon, Verona is irritated about what she considers to be a selfish decision. She begins to consider moving somewhere else, too. But then, Verona's doubts set in and she asks:

Verona: Burt, are we fuck-ups?
Burt: No – what do you mean?

---

16 An American radio host, born in 1932.

Verona:	I mean, we're 34.
Burt:	33.
Verona:	We don't even have this basic stuff figured out.
Burt:	Basic, like how?
Verona:	Basic like how to live.
Burt:	We're not fuck-ups.
Verona:	We have a cardboard window.
Burt:	We're not fuck-ups.
V., whispering:	I think we might be fuck-ups.
B., whispering:	We're not fuck-ups.

Verona's feeling of having failed is anchored in her material and financial situation and in her impression of not living appropriately for her age. In addition, she feels alone and realizes that she has no parent generation upon which to rely (her own parents died years ago). Verona seems to believe that, in her thirties, she should have figured out how she wants to live her life. She has failed to live up to this expectation and realizes that she and Burt are stuck in a place that she does not consider a proper home for their unborn child. Again, the references to age insinuate failure and otherness. This association sets the tone of the film: Burt and Verona have not achieved what they expected to have achieved when they would become parents. They are different.

These two references to age occur in the first twelve minutes of the film, after which Burt and Verona start their quest. When the young couple embarks on their journey to Phoenix, Tucson, Madison, Montreal, and Miami, age references recur time and again but in variations. In Burt's case, it is the notion of the "child in a man's body" which characterizes his behavior and attitudes as age-inappropriate[17] and which becomes apparent in the actor's performance and the ways in which the relationship between Burt and Verona is described. For instance, when Verona and Burt start their journey, Verona reminds Burt of their itinerary, which he seems to have forgotten. As a matter of prudence, Verona already stapled it into Burt's jacket. The stapled itinerary functions like a memory aid and denotes Burt

---

17 The "puer aeternus" or "Peter Pan" are well-known variations of the "child in a man's body." The same idea can be found in the contemporary "perpetual adolescent" (see Chapter 3.1).

as a helpless, dependent person. Verona's maternal care belittles Burt and presents him, similar to the earlier example with Casey Kasem, as immature, unreliable, and unskilled in the basic requirements of life. The association of Burt as a "child in a man's body" suggests that despite his chronological age, Burt does not behave like an autonomous, earnest, and prudent adult.

This association recurs when Burt's fixation on breasts is highlighted. Burt hopes that Verona's breasts will grow larger during or after the pregnancy and this (adolescent) obsession is used as a running gag in the movie. When the couple sees Grace, Verona's sister, for example, Burt cannot keep his eyes from Grace's bosom (although he tries). He also dutifully but clumsily praises Grace's new boyfriend (because Verona told him to do so) and he is shown with a gawky body language when he talks to one of his customers on the phone and maladroitly falls from a small stone wall after he spotted a woman with large breasts. The characterization of Burt as a "child in a man's body" functions as a comic device in the movie and marks this character as childish and unusual but, at the same time, as amiable and naive.

Being Ahead or Behind Time

In Verona's case, references to temporality are repeatedly used to suggest her otherness. When Verona meets with her sister Grace in a department store, for instance, they talk about Verona's pregnancy and her feelings about this major and life-changing moment in a woman's life. Verona believes that she should feel different now that she is pregnant, but since she does not, she concludes: "Maybe it's just late coming to me. Like everything else." Verona's mother had her when she was 25 and Verona got pregnant at 34, which she interprets as being late or behind schedule. Evidently, Verona has an acute sense of timing. She considers herself to be belated in both her life decisions and in her feelings. She seems to be off the 'normal' track of time. By using references to temporality and timing, *Away We Go* insinuates that there is a normal or ideal development through time to which Verona does not conform.

Verona's non-conformity also becomes evident when she is described to be ahead of time. Verona's pregnancy and its (advanced) progress are commented upon several times in the course of the movie. These episodes are often embedded in a humorous context, but they also make her stand out against the others. A mocking friend calls her "huge," for instance, and one mother in a hotel remarks knowingly "Any day now," suggesting that Verona will give birth soon. In fact, Verona is only six months along. Apparently, there is a discrepancy between the *perceived* and Verona's *actual* stage of her pregnancy. Her position on the timeline of her pregnancy seems to be flexible and available for external assessment. This availability becomes clear in another scene: When Verona and Burt leave Tucson for Madison, they go to the check-in counter at the airport but are denied access to the plane. After an excruciating, collective appraisal by three airport employees, Verona is judged to be in the eighth month although she insists on being "six months." But none of the women from the ground crew believe her, referring to airline policies that require women in their eighth month to present a note from a doctor. As a result, Verona and Burt have to take the train to Madison. Verona is irritated by this treatment, which she experiences as a form of discrimination. Her pregnancy does not conform to the norm, and Verona learns painfully that her appearing to be ahead of time is judged as an infringement that is immediately sanctioned. Verona and her body do not fit the airline's regulations and norms. The references to timing indicate that the measuring of time, like age, is subjective and contingent; moreover, it can take the form of external control and judgment against which Verona is helpless. Her subsequent breakdown on the train emphasizes her frustration and lack of control.

The next morning, on the train, the references to time recur. The issue of correct timing now refers to the fetus and her heartbeats. Verona measures the heartbeat of her child after breakfast and finds that the rate is too slow. When Burt finds no fault in a slower heartbeat, arguing that he likes the idea of having a mellow child, Verona says: "I don't want mellow now. I want lively now, mellow later." Again, Verona shows an acute sense of timing and temporality. Her urge to control her daughter's bodily functions occurs right after she felt discriminated at the airport and her emotional breakdown in the train. This close narrative succession reinforces the impression that Verona has a conflictual relationship to time. On the one hand, she experiences what it means to be different in terms of timing; on the other hand, she applies normative perceptions of time to her own child. One might interpret Verona's need to regulate time as a way of resuming control over her body after the loss of control she experienced earlier. The measuring of her daughter's heart rate suggests Verona's wish to have at least some power over the management of time. In *Away We Go*, references to time, like references to age, thus indicate a conflictual relationship to social norms, cultural imaginaries about pregnancies, and medical standards of fetal development.

The link between the references to time and the heart beat rate of the baby recurs when Verona and Burt fly to Montreal. In this airplane scene, references to time are associated with failure – similar to the references to age earlier in the movie. Before the airplane scene, Burt told Verona that he did not land the job he applied for in Madison. He thus failed to improve their financial situation with a more secure job and fell short of Verona's expectations. In the subsequent scene in the airplane, Burt has a chance to redeem himself. He hides behind Verona's seat and suddenly screams in order to scare her. He then measures the heartbeat and is satisfied: "We did it." The heart rate of the baby is up. Burt has managed to get control over the heart rate of their child and to bring it within the 'normal' scale. For the first time in the movie, Burt is successful in something and does not feel like a loser. Moreover, in the airplane scene, he counterbalances Verona's incapacity to take control over her timing issues. Conversely, in other scenes, Verona counterbalances Burt's age-inappropriate behavior by appearing to be more responsible and more 'adult.'

In the scene after the airplane incident, age references are again associated with failure. This metaphoric connection suggests once more that Burt and Verona are different from their friends in Montreal, as they are behind time and have failed to achieve financial stability. When Verona and Burt admire their friends' townhouse, they realize that Tom and Munch, who are their peers, are much more advanced in terms of social status.

Verona:	Holy shit.
Burt:	Is this their house?
Verona:	We went to college with these guys. How can they be so grown up? While we are so...?
Burt:	Stunted? (Verona scoffs)
Burt:	Confused? Immature? American?

The implications of being the same age but, in comparison, appearing immature and stunted, make Burt and Verona appear delayed in their development. In contrast to Burt and Verona, Tom and Munch are married, can afford a large house, and have adopted four children, for whom they care in what looks like tender chaos. This lifestyle seems to represent the normative horizon against which Burt and Verona define themselves. Enthusiastic about their friends' striking life, Burt and Verona agree that this is the life they want and decide to settle down in Montreal.

Shortly after this decision, however, the couple receives more thorough insight into the problems and hardships that Tom and Munch have to deal with, including miscarriages, unfulfilled dreams and a sense of having waited too long. In a bar, Tom tells Burt that, a few days ago, Munch miscarried for the fifth time and muses about the meanings of their misfortune as parents.

[...] I wonder if we have been selfish. People like us, we wait until our 30s, and then we are surprised when the babies aren't so easy to make any more. And every day another million 14-year-olds get pregnant without trying. It's terrible feeling this helpless, man. You just watch these babies grow, and then ... then fade.

Tom's sense of being punished for his selfish waiting and wasting his youth corresponds with Verona and Burt's sense of failure that is linked with feeling delayed or belated. To a certain degree, the characters' sense of (temporal) inappropriateness is linked with a broader, generational phenomenon of "people like us," as Tom describes himself and his college friends. After Tom's statement, Burt and Verona's initial fascination with their friends' adult lives and their seemingly age-appropriate behavior, subsides.

The next morning, Verona and Burt are called away from Montreal to comfort Burt's brother, whose wife has left him and their daughter. This sequence in Florida functions as yet another scene that warns Burt and Verona about the imperfections and responsibilities of adult life. In Miami, Burt and Verona eventually realize where they want to live. This chosen place is loaded with references to age, which – again – indicate the couple's otherness and marginalization. The choice of their future home, namely the house that Verona grew up in, a house that is located in a remote area, far away from other people, becomes a physical manifestation of the couple's otherness. Interestingly, however, it is a form of difference that is actively chosen and thus positively connoted. The house appears as a refuge and "precious, hermetic paradise" (Scott n. pag.). The function of the age references thus stays the same: They signify otherness, albeit in a positive sense.

An Old House and a Childhood World

Verona and Burt's future home is explicitly presented as an *old* house. It is run-down and has broken windows and creaky doors (see fig. 8). (Age references thus not only apply to character traits or behaviors, they also describe material objects.) In *Away We Go*, the old house is a perfect fit for the couple because it suggests a wide range of age and time-related associations: It is a secluded and isolated place that represents both Verona's (ideal) childhood, the couple's notions of a perfect childhood, and their future. This future is, however, securely grounded in the past and informed by a profound sense of nostalgia.

Fig. 8: Burt and Verona in their future home

This old environment symbolically stands for a new phase of life into which Verona and Burt have transitioned over the course of the movie. They have found their place in the world. Yet, this new phase in life does not entail a clear transition into a new stage of life, as the coming-of-age narrative would suggest. Verona and Burt have not matured, they remain the same – child-like, off the 'normal' time track, different. A.O. Scott argues that this particular choice is a sign of the characters' naivety and immaturity because it enables Verona and Burt to retreat from a world in which their idealism finds no match. This interpretation is certainly true and underlines my suggestion that the characters do not mature. Yet a focus on the metaphoric dimensions of references to age and time allows a more differentiated interpretation. It seems that Verona and Burt's decision is far more than a perpetuation of their immature lifestyle. Rather, it is a manifestation of an idealization of the past and the future that finds no correspondence in the present, that is in the lives that Verona and Burt observe when they visit their friends. Verona's childhood house signifies a metaphoric environment that suggests a two-sided age trajectory: It stands for the past, for old stories and memories, for a perfect childhood; and it is a projection into the future, which is imagined with identical connotations, such as a perfect childhood, emotional security, and love. The peculiar effect of this ending only partly lies in the perpetuation of the characters' immature behavior. In addition, the vision of Burt and Verona's future life is one that blocks out the present. It only knows the past and imagines a nostalgic version of the future and thus a future that perpetuates the idealized past. In this sense, Burt and Verona's tendency to have 'off' timing in terms of being delayed or premature comes full circle in the metaphoric dimension of the old house. In this environment, Burt and Verona can start their 'new' life as a family and place their own future family life within an older version of Verona's family life.

In a sense, nothing changes. The protagonists' lives, attitudes, and personalities remain the same. Of course, Burt and Verona have realized at the end where they want to live, but the movie suggests that this solution was there all along. When Verona meets her sister Grace, Grace mentions the vacant, old house but Verona evades the topic because it reminds her of her parents' tragic death. In a sense, Verona's accepting to live in her childhood home represents a form of maturation because it presupposes her reconciliation with the premature death of her parents. Other than that, Verona and Burt are presented as strangely static and unchanging throughout the plot. It is true that they have their ups and downs, but their issues seem to be minor in comparison with their friends' problems.

This impression of stagnation is also conveyed by cinematographic devices. Burt and Verona are traveling throughout much of the movie, but they are rarely ever shown actively moving. Often, they sit still – in a plane or in the train – while the world around them quickly moves past them. This cinematographic choice makes sense when one considers that Burt and

Verona do not actually want to move but hope to be settled. They are more or less forced to find a new place to live after their previous plans fell through. The cinematographic devices also support the impression that Burt and Verona are different from the rest. The world that surrounds them is shown as a hectic place and somehow, Burt and Verona manage to remain removed from this frenzy and stay who they are.

Since Burt and Verona remain outsiders, they could be classified as the typical heroes of contemporary American coming-of-age stories, who choose to remain marginalized and who cling to their ideals (cf. Curnutt, Rishoi). Instead of rebelling against the parent generation, these young adults are painfully aware of how much they miss their parents. It is the children's generation that experiences an empty-nest-syndrome and not vice versa. Consequently, Burt and Verona's journey to find their place in the world is a nostalgic search directed towards the past and fraught with idealist notions to which they cling, even if it means to be anti-social. Yet, it seems that *Away We Go* adds a twist to the contemporary coming-of-age narrative as its characters seem to be indifferent to maturation, personal development, or social progress. Passing through time, as exemplified by Burt and Verona, is a passive and strangely static endeavor. At the same time, in being delayed or premature, the characters experience transitions as conflictual if not impossible. Thus, even though the references to age and time are used abundantly in the movie, they do not suggest a transition but indicate a momentary status: of being a loser, having "off" timing, being different. In this respect, similar to *My Big Fat Greek Wedding*, the metaphoric practice of age (and time) employed in *Away We Go* suggests a status of failure and otherness, even though these connotations are mitigated by the amiability of the characters and the humorous tone of the movie.

Failure and otherness also surface in the discussions about perpetual adolescents or delayed adults, who are described as a contemporary generation of young adults in their twenties and thirties who are stuck in their transition to adulthood. Instead of conceptualizing age or aging as metaphoric practices, sociologists are interested in the socio-cultural conditions that shape a generation of young adults who refuse to grow up.

3 Living Across the Life Course

3.1 Shifting Meanings of Adulthood: Perpetual Adolescence and Delayed Adulthood

Journalists and scholars have invented a wealth of labels and neologism to describe the type of "child in a man's body" that Burt Farlander represents: Kidults, adultescents, boy-men, or emerging adults stand for a so-called Peter Pandemic and thus for a refusal to grow up (cf. Arnett 2007, Cross 2008, Hunter 2009, Tierney 2004). Blatterer points out the international reverberations of this phenomenon, listing "'twixters in the U.S. and Australia, 'boomerang kids' in Canada, Nesthocker in German-speaking countries, mammone in Italy, and KIPPERS (Kids In Parents' Pockets Eroding Retirement Savings) in the U.K." ("Adulthood" n. pag.). According to John Tierney, "adultescent" – selected to be the word of the year 2004 by *Webster's New World College Dictionary* – describes an adult who is "too busy playing Halo 2 on his Xbox or watching SpongeBob at his parent's house to think about growing up" (n. pag). The abundance of terms reflects how scrupulously this phenomenon has been observed. And it indicates a plethora of explanations and theories from diverse disciplines such as sociology, developmental psychology, or cultural history that try to understand this "issue of modern immaturity" (Cross 2).

From a linguistic point of view, compounds like kidult or adultescent hint at a porosity or merging of formerly separated life stages, such as being a kid, an adolescent or an adult. It seems that these conceptual boundaries have lost their rigidity and the clear dichotomy between adolescence and adulthood has become blurry (cf. Cuzzocrea & Magaraggia 2012). As a consequence, the transition between stages is more difficult to achieve or to recognize. For some scholars, this blurring comes as no surprise because life stages as such are relatively new concepts that do not constitute universal stages of development but culturally contingent and culturally shaped categories (cf. Gullette 2004, Lesko 1996, Raby 2012). The sociologist Harry Blatterer also takes a cultural constructivist stance when he argues that adulthood is a relatively new concept and became a social category as late as in the twentieth century, when it came to be understood as a default position of maturity and stability (cf. *Coming of Age* 11). Other scholars have deconstructed the meanings of childhood. Neil Postman argued for *The Disappearance of Childhood* in 1982, maintaining that television prematurely adultifies children by confronting them with crime and violence and other adult topics. Perpetual adolescents represent a contrary development: They delay their transition into adulthood because they either do not want to grow up (because they consider adulthood dull and cherish their childhood freedom and sense of adventure) or because they cannot fulfill the criteria of adulthood (for socio-economic reasons). What has changed in American culture that makes entering into adulthood difficult or undesirable? What does adulthood signify? And, which meanings, values, or norms does a person transgress who behaves age-inappropriately by being a kidult or adultescent?

For the sociologist Harry Blatterer and the psychologist Jeffrey J. Arnett, socio-historical changes in Western cultures have triggered the blurring of life stages. Before the 1970s, adulthood was clearly defined due to a stable and growing post-war economy in the era between 1945 to the early 1970s, which facilitated highly predictable private and occupational paths (cf. Blatterer 13-4). The ideals of employee loyalty, stable working hours, ownership, and the model of the suburban "heterosexual nuclear family" with a single income entailed a notion of adulthood, which was defined by "classic markers" or signposts such as independent living, committed relationships, stable employment, marriage, parenthood, and home ownership (14, 16-7). Other sociologists have used terms like chronologization, standardization, periodization, or institutionalization to describe the macrostructural circumstances that represent the normative framework for (what Blatterer calls) the 'standard' meaning of adulthood (e.g. Kohli 1986, Scherger 2007).

In the 1960s and 1970s, as Blatterer summarizes, the predictability of the standard life course was challenged: The oil crises in the early 1970s, changes in the labor market, and globalization, for example, disrupted common patterns of social organization (cf. "Adulthood" n. pag.). Since then, the average age of marriage and parenthood has steadily increased and with growing divorce rates, marriage no longer guarantees stability (e.g. Arnett, "Emerging Adulthood" 478). Furthermore, the neo-liberal pressures in the occupational field result in short-time work and employees are required to be flexible, to accept frequent job changes, and to be willing to relocate upon request (cf. Blatterer, "Adulthood" n. pag.). The catchphrases used to describe these developments are individualization and destandardization (cf. Beck & Beck-Gernsheim 2002, Scherger 2007).[1]

These socio-cultural changes are also reflected in a different perspective of temporality. Referring to Hartmut Rosa's concept of a "de-temporalization of life," Blatterer argues that – since many new adults are married more than once, patchwork-families are increasingly widespread and jobs and career plans are changed several times during the life course – people experience "a quite radical transformation of the temporal unfolding of the life course with the implication that, while institutional arrangements persist, biographies are no longer beholden to a linear trajectory" (*Coming of Age* 18, 44). What is lost, then, is "not the future, nor is it time, but a coherent, collective orientation towards the future" ("Adulthood" n. pag.). The de-temporalization is also a result of the de-institutionalization of the life course, since "institutions themselves no longer provide temporal securities and thus make the long-term projection of biographies more difficult" (*Coming of Age* 44). Especially for those individuals who rely on a standard life course for biographical meaning, the temporal structuring of their lives becomes increasingly difficult and may cause insecurities. Hence, cultural imaginaries of living through time, in terms of an ordered sequence of life stages or a linear trajectory of development, no longer function as orientation guides (cf. 44).

Due to the de-temporalization of life, the experience of time has changed. The notion of a linear passage of time has become obsolete and new temporal models such as asynchronicity or fragmentation prevail (cf. 45). Blatterer ascertains a loss of telos and a "proliferation of options in all

---

1 Also see Scherger 93ff., Blatterer 28-50, and Kohli 2007.

spheres of life" (31). As a consequence, adults need to be flexible, self-reflexive, and become "entrepreneurs of the self" (McDonald qtd. in Blatterer 30).[2] Those who do not know how to deal with the new demands display, according to Blatterer, phenomena such as experiences of "accelerated standstill," "frantic change," "frozen time," lack of direction, and inertia (cf. 45).[3]

Thus, the conflicted relation to time and timing, which Burt and particularly Verona demonstrate so conspicuously in *Away We Go*, might be culturally anchored in the de-temporalization and de-standardization of Western life courses. The ways in which these characters continually attempt to resume control over their time, which seems to have slipped their competency and authority, makes sense in a culture, in which a desire for predictability seems to be nothing but a nostalgic souvenir of the past. In this sense, it is not surprising that a couple like Burt and Verona, who try to provide their unborn daughter with emotional security and protection, symbolically retreat to a past version of a life (namely that of Verona's childhood) and decide to block out the present instability and unpredictability they observe in the lives of their friends and families. One might interpret this decision as a "flight from adulthood, from engagement, from responsibility" (Scott, "Practicing Virtue" n. pag.) or, as I suggest in my age reading, one might acknowledge the depiction of their behavior as a reflection of the contemporary zeitgeist, in which adulthood and maturity have assumed a different meaning.

Redefining Adulthood

The consequences of the macrostructural changes observed by Arnett and Blatterer are interpreted quite differently in terms of the theorization of adulthood. While earlier theories described adulthood with such distinct, institutionalized, and external markers as completing one's education or entering marriage (cf. Raby, "Age" 137), Arnett finds that the so-called Mil-

---

2   Blatterer quotes Kevin McDonald's *Struggles for Subjectivity: Identity, Action and Youth Experience* (1999).
3   The phenomena that Blatterer describes here resonate in *Away We Go, Little Children, Indecision,* and *The Future.*

lennials[4] use different criteria that are more "intangible and psychological," such as "accepting responsibility for one's actions, making independent decisions, and becoming financially independent" (*Emerging Adulthood* vi). Apparently, the markers have become subtler and refer to a form of mental or psychological adulthood. Similarly, Blatterer argues that adulthood is no longer defined by external indicators but by internal markers, such as "personal growth" (*Coming of Age* 75), putting the self in the center (cf. 109), "striving towards self-knowledge" (110), "self-discipline" (88), and "self-reliance" (90). It seems that the passage into adulthood has become a process of an internal, subjective transition and that adulthood itself has become a "state of mind" (61, 88).[5]

James E. Côté identifies a similar change in the definition of adulthood and also stresses the psychological aspects of adulthood rather than its material or exterior dimensions. Adulthood thus implies

to be conscious of the necessity to think ahead; to make choices, the results of which they will have to live with; to be solely responsible for their failings and limitations; and to overcome structural obstacles such as social class, race, gender, and age barriers. In other words, fully benefiting from the freedom requires, among other things, an intelligent self-discipline in dealing with one's self and one's society, often in the absence of collective supports. (127)

Changes in the workplace present new challenges to the individual, such as a "loss of predictability, loss of security/enforced self-reliance, the 'commodification' of self, and a loss of connection" (Moses qtd. in Côté 194).[6] These socioeconomic requirements oblige individuals to become "increas-

---

4   Millennials is the name given to the generation born in the 1980s, who came of age around the turn of the millennium. For further information, see, for example, Neil Howe's and William Strauss' *Millennials Rising: The Next Great Generation* (2000).
5   Of course, the values of being responsible or self-reliant existed before the 1970s and also appeared in earlier definitions of adulthood. Arnett's and Blatterer's point is that these values have received a new and increased importance with the socio-economic changes brought about by neo-liberalism.
6   Côté quotes Barbara Moses' study *Career Intelligence: Mastering the New Work and Personality Realities* (1997).

ingly other-directed" and to do "identity management" on a daily basis (cf. 196-7).

Côté introduces the concept of "youthhood," which he defines as a new phase of life and as a form of psychological adulthood that gives a name to "the institutionalized identity moratorium – an imposed delay of adulthood" which society has granted to young adults due to the changed requirements for adulthood (179).[7] Arnett introduces a different term, "emerging adulthood," which he also defines as a new life stage between 18 and 25. "Emerging adulthood" is

> neither adolescence nor young adulthood but is theoretically and empirically distinct from them both. [...] Having left the dependency of childhood and adolescence, and having not yet entered the enduring responsibilities that are normative in adulthood, emerging adults often explore a variety of possible life directions in love, work, and world-views. ("Emerging Adulthood" 469)

Blatterer criticizes these attempts to further compartmentalize the life course with the introduction of new life stages. Instead, he argues for a new definition of adulthood, which considers adulthood a highly flexible marker that can be used strategically, depending on particular situations. Such a notion of flexible or "liminal adulthood" is also supported by the sociologist Rebecca Raby. Adulthood, Raby explains, used to be considered as a "stable subject position," which was defined as "complete, rational, civilized, independent, and fully social," as opposed to childhood which was "framed as incomplete, emotional, irrational, peer-focused, dependent and closer to nature" ("Theorizing" 69-70). Viewed from the angle of neo-liberal individualization and poststructural theory, however, this binary has come under revision and adulthood has become liminal as well (cf. 70, 72). Hence, "lifelong liminality" has become a new challenge in Western cultures, in which individuals are continually reconfiguring themselves and are permanently struggling with "a lifelong, fluid, contextualized and inter-connected selfhood" (70). Naturally, in such an environment, transitions between life

---

7   Côté borrows the notion of youthhood from the Danish psychologist Sven Mørch (1995). For a critical appraisal of Côté's study, see Michael Shanahan's review in *Social Forces* (2003).

stages are no longer simple or linear trajectories. Instead, they turn into "yo-yo transitions" and are reversible and fragmented (cf. Walther 121).

Not all scholars who try to explain perpetual adolescence investigate into life course theory or life stages. The historian Gary Cross, for instance, suggests that the emergence of modern immaturity embodied in boy-men is not about life stages but about lifestyles (cf. 5). According to Cross, the culture of boy-men today is "less [about] a transition from childhood to adulthood than [about] a choice to live like a teen 'forever'" (5). Hence, if we are dealing with an active choice, why would young adults decide to not become adults? Following Cross, cultural imaginaries connected with life stages are part of the answer: Adulthood has a very negative image, signifying dullness or responsibilities to many young adults, whereas childhood is considered (and marketed) to be adventurous, fun, full of leisure, and free of duties (cf. 5 ff). The media collaborate in this idea of endless fun when they make a person like Hugh Hefner into an icon of boy-man-hood instead of providing a more "compelling image of the grown-up" (12). Cross argues that, as a consequence of socio-economic changes in neo-liberal cultures, financial motivations are one of the explanations for the culture of perpetual adolescence: There is money to be made with boy-men (cf. 18). "Makers of modern consumer and media [...] have figured out how to sell back to men this longed-for image of perpetual youth. Over time, this makes youth, once a life stage, into a permanent and highly desirable lifestyle" (18). Childhood nostalgia is thus openly fostered in Western cultures. According to Cross, delayed adulthood is not necessarily (or merely) a response to overwhelming demands on the individual and thus an indicator of incompetence or failure. Rather, boy-men have made an active choice and have decided in favor of a particular lifestyle that is made attractive to them by consumer industries.

Adulthood as a Social Category and Movable Marker

I want to come back to the sociological perspectives on adulthood because the concept of liminal adulthood provides many interesting correlations with the ideas of age as a movable, flexible, and situational marker. Blatterer finds young adults in a paradoxical situation: Despite the apparent ubiquity of delayed adulthood in Western discourses, most young adults actually conform to standard life courses. Blatterer believes that the old definitions of adulthood or imaginaries about development through the life course "remain ideal evaluative benchmarks," even though they no longer provide adequate temporal trajectories (*Coming of Age* 45). Therefore, despite the fact that young adults "realize they are free in ways they will not be during their thirties and beyond" (Arnett, *Emerging Adulthood* 10), they still conform to normative ideals. Therefore, by the time young adults reach age thirty, most of them will have taken on all adult obligations (cf. 6). And, "[a]t that age, 75% of Americans have married and have had at least one child" (12) and only 30% still feel in-between, meaning that they do not feel that they are fully adults (cf. 149). Hence, there seems to be a normative frame to which most young adults eventually conform, even though they initially reject or doubt it. Does this mean that despite the liminality of adulthood and the blurriness of life stages, adulthood remains a form of "default category" (26), as Blatterer argues? Does it function as a reference point against which the meanings of childhood, adolescence, or old age are defined?

Blatterer supports this hypothesis and maintains that, adulthood has assumed a "taken-for-granted centrality in the apportioning of power" (10). Therefore, it functions like an invisible concept or norm (cf. x). According to Blatterer, the standard life course (in terms of a regular development through life stages that are connected to developmental tasks) represents a means of orientation and regulation and is therefore both a frame of reference and a form of constraint (cf. 36-7). Life stages thus fulfill a social function and are used as a "social category" (Blatterer 26). Côté's concept of "youthhood" is based on a similar understanding and Côté even goes so far as to argue that the new life stage of "youthhood" represents an exclusion mechanism and thus a form of segregation (cf. 185), which contributes to the political and economic disenfranchisement of youth (cf. 174). While Côté's view allows for no agency on behalf of the young, Blatterer understands adulthood as a normative yet also negotiable social category.

Following Blatterer, the normativity connected with adulthood entered the cultural imaginary with the rise of psychology: The notion of maturity became a central "metaphor of adult status" and adulthood became "the default position: a life stage situated between adolescence and old age" (11). During World War II, adulthood entered the social imagination of everyday life and had "come to signify something solid to aim for, a life stage that held the promise of fulfilled wishes and achieved aspirations" (12). Standard adulthood is thus imagined to constitute the "'normal' version of adulthood" (Maguire qtd. in Blatterer, *Coming of Age* 25). Blatterer calls this fallacy a "normative lag" (23) and argues that proponents of the delayed adulthood thesis

> confuse a historically contingent model with contemporary social realities and continue to posit the ideal type as the normative telos to individual development. What is more, the outdated model is often held up as something to be striven for at a time when the realization of standard adulthood is for many not only impossible, but also hardly desirable. (24)

The simultaneous normativity and flexibility of the social category adulthood puts young adults in a paradoxical situation. In some areas, such as the work field, they receive recognition for social practices of flexibility and for having adapted to the new demands while in other areas, they are degraded or sanctioned for not conforming to the traditional ideal of adulthood (cf. "Adulthood" n. pag.). According to Blatterer, these experiences constitute a dilemma for young adults: "Practices may be structurally rewarded while simultaneously being discursively misrecognized as long as the normative ideals of another time remain most readily associated with what it means to be an adult, a full person" (*Coming of Age* 65). Young adults solve this predicament through perpetual negotiations of their biographies. Their approach is a very strategic attitude: They know when to behave like adults because it grants them respect, connectedness, and acceptance; they also know, however, that sometimes, for instance in the work field, it is wiser to "act like a child" (cf. 92). Hence, adult competencies signify performative and situational qualities. Shanahan confirms this interpretation when he argues that

> contemporary young people move in and out of adult statuses with some frequency [...] [because] many of the transition markers are 'reversible,' meaning that an adult status marker can be acquired (e.g. spouse, full-time worker, independent householder) and then relinquished as youth return to their prior status (respectively, unmarried, part-time worker or unemployed, and living with parents). ("Subjective Age Identity" 229)

Blatterer finds the same provisionality and flexibility in the accounts of his interviewees, maintaining that "being grown up does not have to be settled once and for all; it is a way of being that can be drawn upon according to situations and circumstances" (*Coming of Age* 95). For this reason, "there are different, albeit coexisting ways of being grown up" (109).

Life stages are thus connected to cultural imaginaries and contexts that define their meaning in highly complex and situational ways. For sociologists or developmental psychologists, the perpetual adolescent is a symptom of socio-economic and socio-historical circumstances. For filmmakers and novelists, the kidult or adultescent assumes a metaphoric dimension. Sam Mendes' successfully uses Burt's age-inappropriate conduct as an element of comedy, while Tom Perrotta, the author of *Little Children*, uses his perpetual adolescent, Todd, as a troublemaker. Todd and his accomplice Sarah behave like little children and, in doing so, they function as symbolic figures who challenge the bigotry of their suburban environment. Placed in a fictional context, in which the meanings of childhood and adulthood are profoundly contested, Todd's and Sarah's age-inappropriate behavior questions normative concepts of relationships (marriage, adultery, child rearing) or sexuality (porn, pedophilia). References to age take center stage in these negotiations of norms and moralities.

3.2 Tom Perrotta's *Little Children*

Tom Perrotta's novel *Little Children* (2004) was well received among critics who lauded the "amused tenderness of Perrotta's satire" (Blythe n. pag.) and considered it his "breakthrough popular hit" (Maslin n. pag.). Todd Field's successful film version of *Little Children* (2006), featuring Kate Winslet in the leading role, increased the popularity of Perrotta's novel, particularly among international audiences.[8] In his six novels so far, Per-

---

8   In this study, I will focus on Tom Perrotta's novel only. While I consider the film to be a successful adaptation, the novel offers a more fertile ground for an age reading. For a close reading of the film version, see my article "Teenage Nostalgia: Perpetual Adolescents in *Little Children* and *Young Adult*," in which I discuss the relations between nostalgia, coming-of-age narratives, and the liminality of adolescence and adulthood.

rotta has demonstrated a particular interest in the concerns and foibles of white, American, middle-class, young or middle-aged adults. In his early novels, Perrotta dedicates himself to the intricacies of adolescence and the transitions to adulthood: In *The Wishbones* (1997), he describes a 31-year-old aging slacker; in *Election* (1998), he describes the entanglements of a high school student election; and with *Joe College* (2000), Perrotta immerses himself in the world of college students. *Little Children*, as the title suggests, is also set in the world of "youngsters" where "infantilized grown-ups" struggle with their "prefab malaise" (Lim n. pag.). In his two subsequent novels, *The Abstinence Teacher* (2007) and *The Leftovers* (2011), Perrotta focuses on the lives of American suburban families and their struggles with religious bigotry and the consequences of apocalyptic fear.[9]

Little Children portrays "generic American suburb" lives somewhere outside of Boston (Blythe n. pag.). 31-year-old Todd is a stay-at-home dad who flunked his bar exam twice and is preparing half-heartedly for his third trial. He meets Sarah, an unfulfilled mother and housewife, who is "pushing thirty" and who struggles with her current lifestyle, which is diametrically opposed to her former aspirations as an ambitious graduate student (Perrotta 89). Todd's and Sarah's lives are described as a "private hell of failure" (161). For Todd, this hell consists in a limbo between procrastination and a guilty conscience. On the one hand, he knows that his life is quite pleasant: He has a beautiful wife who works as a TV filmmaker of documentaries, a 3-year-old son named Aaron, and a daily routine that, despite its simplicity and boring repetitiveness, is appealing to Todd. On the other hand, Todd senses the pressure and expectations (mostly from his wife Kathy) to eventually get on with his life and to be able to take care of his family financially and thus assume the traditional, male position of head of the household. Todd evades this pressure when he repeatedly watches teenage skateboarders perform their stunts on his way to the library. Instead of actually going into the library and studying for his third (and final) attempt to pass the bar exam, Todd lingers and procrastinates. He joins the local football team – a decision labeled by his wife as a sign of a "premature midlife crisis" (141) – and starts an affair with Sarah, who is as discontent-

---

9   Two of Perrotta's novels were adapted to the screen: *Election* in 1999 and *Little Children* in 2006.

ed as Todd and who represents just another escape from his duties and sorrows.

Sarah is described as a formerly devoted feminist who imagined herself in an academic career but dropped out of graduate school and now marvels at her own life:

[I]f any of the other mothers had asked how it was that Sarah, of all people, had ended up married, living in the suburbs, and caring full-time for a small child, she would have blamed it on a moment of weakness. (9)

This moment of weakness refers to an earlier realization during her college days, when she confessed to herself to be "a failure, a twenty-six-year-old woman of still-ambiguous sexuality who had just discovered that she wasn't really as smart as she'd thought she was" (12). Sarah's earlier sense of entitlement yields to a feeling of having failed and of falling short of her own expectations. In this desperate situation, she marries 47-year-old Richard, with whom she has a 3-year-old daughter Lucy, a daughter from whom Sarah feels strangely alienated. Sarah is unable to make friends with the other mothers in her neighborhood, whom she disdainfully characterizes as a clan of "depressing supermoms" (4) who all seem to have "read the same book" on effective parenting (8). When Sarah starts her affair with Todd, she escapes from her life of boredom and failure, like Todd, but she also (finally) enacts a private teenage fantasy of dating a good-looking high school football hero and Prom King (cf. 150, 213). At the end of the novel, when Todd has a skateboard accident and Sarah realizes that they will not run away nor start a new life together, Sarah bethinks herself of her duties as a mother and joins the "circle of adults" with the bitter realization that she has let herself be seduced by a fantasy because she believed in the possibility that "she was something special, one of the lucky ones, a character in a love story with a happy ending" (354-5).

Sarah and Todd's story is intertwined with several other subplots. The most prominent one is the story of Ronald McGorvey, a convicted child molester who is released from prison, moves to Todd and Sarah's neighborhood, and causes considerable uproar. Particularly Larry Moon, a 33-year-old retired police officer who lives on a disability pension and sees his life in shambles as his wife wants to divorce him, feels called upon to initiate a vigilante group to protect the children in the neighborhood from the child molester Ronnie. Larry's initiative eventually escalates because of his anger and self-righteousness.

In the following age reading of *Little Children*, it will become clear that references to age work differently compared to *My Big Fat Greek Wedding* and *Away We Go*. First, Todd and Sarah do not feel old and are not said to look old, but they are described as 'too young' in their decisions, lifestyles, or attitudes. The age ascriptions are thus directed in the opposite direction of the age spectrum. The characters have not aged prematurely, rather their actions and personal development can be considered belated or delayed compared to their chronological ages. Secondly, Tom Perrotta uses life stages when he insinuates age-inappropriate behavior and thus refers to children (or teenagers) when he describes the misdemeanor of his characters. References to childlike or teenager-like behavior thus designate characters as different from other characters. In addition, by transgressing the norms of (age-) appropriate conduct, Todd and Sarah implicitly challenge the moralities of their surroundings and question what is considered normal, appropriate adult conduct.

"Suddenly Being a Teenager Again"

The title of the novel *Little Children* is the first obvious reference to age. Even though one might argue that the title refers to Todd's and Sarah's toddlers or, in general, to all of the children in the neighborhood who are threatened by the child molester Ronnie McGorvey, it soon becomes clear that it is first and foremost the adults who are described as behaving childishly. The adjective 'little' amplifies their age-inappropriateness.

The first scene of the book presents Sarah among the other mothers on the playground. It is a beginning full of references to childlike or teenager-like behavior. While the setting of the playground makes these references expectable, it is remarkable that they are used exclusively to describe the adults on the playground. Sarah and one of the mothers are described as smoking cigarettes "like teenagers," secretly as if they were committing a crime (4). When Todd appears on the playground, these mothers behave like infatuated teenagers: They call Todd "Prom King" (30), one mother is "smirking like a schoolgirl" (34), another admits that she puts on make-up and thinks about what she is wearing whenever she suspects he may make an appearance at the playground (cf. 32). Sarah is alienated by her observations and comments on the mothers' behavior by asking: "What is this, seventh grade?" (32). The boundaries between who is a teenager and who is an adult blur in this playground scene. The mothers, who constitute a moral authority later in the novel, are described with references to teenage behavior and thus appear as age-inappropriate. Thus, from the very beginning, Perrotta challenges the notions of appropriate and inappropriate behavior and leaves it to the reader to decide who is 'normal' and who is acting oddly.

Sarah becomes a true outcast in the eyes of the other mothers when she kisses Todd, the Prom King, on the playground. The kiss figures as Sarah's personal revenge on the women who had humiliated her before by criticizing her parenting skills. The kiss leads to an affair that henceforth turns the norms and rules of the quiet, white, middle-class suburban community upside down. Todd and Sarah's affair is described as a joint escape into a world of high school fantasies and teenage conduct. This teenage world symbolizes a worry-free, adventurous, and unpredictable life for Todd and Sarah. After their first kiss on the playground, for instance, Todd relives their intimate moment in his fantasy, pondering about the feelings Sarah has unleashed in him:

It was like suddenly being a teenager again, returning to a time when sex wasn't a routine or predictable part of your life, but something mysterious and transforming that could pop up out of nowhere [...] Losing that sense of omnipresent possibility was one of the trade-offs of married life that Todd struggled with on a daily basis. (45-6)

Adult, married life is contrasted with being a teenager and, in this comparison, being an adult appears as dreary, predictable, and boring. This contrast represents Todd's central conflict of living in between two worlds. He is a typical perpetual adolescent.

Todd's predicament revolves around his incapacity to fulfill the expectations associated with adult behavior: being an independent decision maker, showing self-discipline and self-reliance, and believing in personal growth and progress (cf. Raby, "Age" 2012). Todd fulfills none of these criteria of traditional adult behavior. Instead of spending his nights studying at the library, he watches a group of young skateboarders and procrastinates by musing about the "stoic patience of early adolescence" (Perrotta 44): "*I don't know why I'm doing this,* each boy seemed to say, *but I'll keep doing it until I'm old enough to do something else*" (44, original emphasis). Adolescence, for Todd, means to live in the moment, a carefree and untroubled time. Moreover, it signifies a merciful attitude towards failure: When a stunt fails, the teenagers bounce "right up from the pavement, laughing like it was all in the service of an excellent time" (339). Todd, who has failed the bar exam twice and feels the pressure to succeed in his last attempt, finds himself intrigued by an alternative world of teenage playfulness and fun, of hopefulness and moderate ambition.

Todd is repeatedly described as someone who is completely immersed in his child's world or in teenage fantasies: He likes his son's favorite music and repeatedly plays "Train Wreck" with Aaron, throwing himself into the "brainless repetition" of reenacting this game (19). While other parents such as Todd's friend Larry distance themselves from the children's world by mocking their kids' music, Todd loses himself in this microcosm (cf. 48). In Larry's presence, Todd feels alienated and uncomfortable because, by degrading children's music, Larry has established himself as an adult and simultaneously insinuates that Todd is odd and has inappropriate musical taste for a man his age. Todd, clearly, appreciates the state of childhood: "That was one of the sweet, but slightly insane things about being three: Nothing ever got old. If it was good, it stayed good, at least until you turned four" (19). This timelessness and focus on the present moment is a feature that Todd finds appealing and that constitutes, as the novel later spells out, his otherness:

Something has happened to him over the last couple of years, something to do with being home with Aaron, sinking into the rhythm of a kid's day. The little tasks, the small pleasures. The repetition that goes beyond boredom and becomes a kind of peace. You do it long enough, and the adult world starts to drift away. You can't catch up with this, not even if you try. (220)

The children's world signifies peacefulness for Todd, a state of inner balance and seclusion from the adult world.

The jester's cap that Aaron only wears when he is with his father is a symbol of the complicity between father and son. Todd, however, is irritated by the fact that Aaron only wears the cap when he is with his father and tosses it as soon as his mother comes home. For Todd, Aaron's behavior suggests that the boy thinks of the entire day – "the Daddy part" – as a "stupid joke" (21). Todd, who is described as being completely immersed in his son's world, takes Aaron's behavior personally and thus demonstrates how dependent he is not only on his son's respect but also on their mutual involvement in the children's world. In sum, Perrotta's descriptions of Todd's everyday life not only imply irresponsibility (Todd's procrastination) and dependence (on his wife's income), they also insinuate brainlessness, stupidity, repetitiveness, and silliness.

Adulthood, although never addressed directly, figures as the normative background. Perrotta mentions repeatedly that Todd is aware of his age-inappropriate behavior as an adult. As a "grown man" who studied developmental psychology, Todd knows that he should not feel slighted by his son's love for his mother (23). Nor is it age-appropriate for a 30-year-old man to purchase a skateboard for himself (cf. 22). Todd is thus very much aware of the boundaries between childish behavior and the behavior that is expected of adults. But, even though Todd knows that trespassing into age-inappropriate behavior only worsens his situation, he cannot help but act like a child or teenager in numerous situations.

Todd's inclination towards the world of children or teenagers is presented as his strategy of escape from his "private hell of failure" (161). He decides, for instance, to rekindle his former glory as a teenage football player and joins the football team, even though he knows that this is a conscious decision against reason, which Perrotta describes in the following way: "Todd waited for his good sense to kick in" and despite the many incentives to decline the offer, Todd only sees a "thrilling new possibility" (51-2). Perrotta presents Todd's decision to join the team as an active decision to be a seventh grader again (cf. 51-2). Todd's affair with Sarah represents a similar escape strategy. When Todd sees Sarah for the first time after their kiss, Todd realizes that she is dressed like a grown woman on a date, which contradicts with his memory of her on the playground where "she'd been girlish and sloppy" (101). Todd concludes: "She was dressed all wrong" (101). Obviously, Todd wants to surround himself with people who radiate an age-inappropriate aura similar to his own.

In his analysis of *Little Children*, Michael O'Connor argues that the characters have "regressed back to teenage mentalities" (n. pag.), which suggests a failure to grow up and thus a deterioration of the characters and a form of degeneration. This interpretation is reminiscent of Scott's analysis of *Away We Go* and his suggestion that Verona and Burt glorify youth and escape from adulthood. Perrotta indeed makes allusions that one might associate with a form of deficiency: When Todd watches the skateboarders, he realizes that there is "something unresolved or defective at the core of his being," a "flaw or lack" that is inexplicable to him given that he always impersonated a "successful, well-adjusted kid" (26). Todd's flaw, as these descriptions indicate, is however not only a matter of idleness or cowardice. The reader learns that Todd's childhood was not carefree or ideal at all given that his mother died in a car crash when Todd was about 11 or 12 years old. Hence, *Little Children* suggests early in the novel that Todd's nostalgia for and fascination with the ideal of a carefree and innocent childhood is a more complex matter than a naive glorification of past days. In other words, Todd's "defective" core insinuates a symbolic meaning that goes deeper than this character's refusal to mature.

As in Todd's case, Sarah's relation to her past is complicated. It implies social exclusion, alienation, and a deep-rooted conflict that originates in her feeling of having failed and fallen short of her own expectations. Sarah is described as living in "Kidworld," (79). She has difficulties "to tell one weekday from the next" and has the impression that "they all just melted together like a bag of crayons left out in the sun" (7). When Sarah compares her daily routine with her husband's days at work, which he is allowed to spend "being an adult," she realizes that her own life entirely revolves around her daughter's needs and tantrums, which leaves her frustrated and exhausted (78). Sarah even begins to imagine a complicity between herself and Steve, the host of *Blue's Clues*, a TV-show for children, maintaining that "[h]e reminded her of herself: a smart, somewhat passive person who'd somehow gotten trapped in Kidworld" (79). Evidently, Sarah feels trapped herself.

References to childishness or being like a child also appear in other contexts. When Sarah is introduced by an older friend Jean to a local book club, where the elderly members are encouraged to bring younger members as "little sisters" because the club "could use some fresh blood" (90), Sarah's youth implies newness and, again, singles Sarah out as different from the other elderly ladies. Elsewhere in the novel, references to childishness imply a lack of comprehension and a physical incompetence. When Todd is described as "a kid who didn't yet realize he needed glasses to see the blackboard" (299), the reference to childlike behavior implies that Todd is too dreamy or innocent to realize his physical condition. With this description, Todd appears like a person who does not face reality. Todd's cognitive incompetence is also referred to in terms of a childlike state: When he gets into Larry's car, without wondering about the purpose of this ride, Todd feels "like an idiot" and concludes that "the average five-year-old would have known better" (48). Similarly, when he allows himself to be persuaded by Larry to join the football team, Todd has to admit that "[a]t this point in his life, he was no more a quarterback than he was a seventh grader" (51). Hence, Todd's incompetence to play football is linked with his status as an adult. When Todd then decides to join the team in the position of the quarterback, he tacitly allows himself to be a seventh grader again.

Ambiguous Meanings:
References to Children and Teenagers

References to age stages are not only used describe Todd's evasive maneuvers. May McGorvey, Ronnie's mother, uses references to younger age stages when speaking about her adult son in order to sugarcoat the fact that he is a convicted child molester. When Ronnie breaks his arm, for instance, she believes: "It was like he was a child again, needing her for everything" (291). Ronnie is imagined as dependent and helpless. Seen from May's perspective, references to childishness insinuate innocence and purity and thus demonstrate her refusal to accept her son's criminal behavior. When Ronnie smokes a cigarette, his smoking is compared to "sucking on it [the cigarette] like a kid drinking out of a straw" (65). Again, in linking Ronnie's behavior to that of a child, May's difficulty to make sense of her son's behavior becomes clear. Still, she is aware of the fact that "[i]t wasn't natural for a grown man to be living with his mother, no hobbies and diversions, just reading the paper and watching TV all day" (66-7). Applied by May, references to being a child provide a possibility to symbolically reduce her son's social exclusion and deviancy, which, ironically, is caused by his inappropriate behavior towards children. The ambiguity in the meaning of childlike behavior insinuates that Ronnie is both unnatural and deviant but also a "boy" and thus in need of sympathy and help. The evocation of childlike behavior can marginalize characters like Todd and Sarah, but it can also enable a character like May to endure (or defy) the abnormality of her son.

This semantic variety is a typical effect of references to childlike behavior. There are, for instance, two implications of being or behaving like a seventh grader that exist side-by-side in Perrotta's novel: While it signifies physical incompetence in Todd's ascription (when he ponders upon whether or not to join the football team), it refers to silliness and ridicule in Sarah's case when she labels the other mothers' attitudes towards Todd as typical teenage (or seventh-grade) conduct (cf. 32). The variety of implications also becomes clear in a scene where Kathy and Sarah describe Todd as a child or teenager. On the morning of Todd's bar exam, his wife Kathy smiles at him "as though he were a child returning to school after a brief illness" (212), implying that he is an anxious, fragile, and insecure child who needs support and affirmation. When Todd meets with Sarah (instead of going to the bar exam as his wife suspects), Sarah praises his trickery with the words "Quite the Boy Scout" (213), insinuating with this reference that – instead of being needy and frightened – Todd is actually cunning, bold, and adventurous. In *Little Children*, such references can combine two almost contradictory perceptions of a single person, which demonstrates not only the situation-specific versatility of references to age but also challenges the very existence of categories such as childhood or adulthood and the normative or moral implications they involve. Morality, after all, is a central topic in this novel about child molesting and adultery. The references to childhood, as I am suggesting, function as resourceful metaphors that insinuate meanings beyond those directly associated with age and aging. This metaphoric dimension becomes clear when Todd is compared to the pervert Ronnie (see page 138).

Like the references to childishness, references to teenage behavior indicate a range of different meanings. Ronnie is described as a "restless teenager" (239), for instance. His body is "in constant motion," which is a warning sign in Ronnie's case because he had been "antsy just like this the morning he exposed himself to that poor little Girl Scout" (240). It is implied here that Ronnie's teenage behavior puts him beyond anyone's control, a stereotypical (and problematic) notion associated with adolescence as a phase of storm and stress and unpredictable hormone rushes (cf. Lesko 1996, Payne 2010).

A strong sexual drive is also insinuated in the description of Richard, Sarah's husband, who feels like a "horny teenager" (113) when it comes to pornography.[10] Richard has an ambivalent attitude towards porn: When he behaves like a "responsible adult," Richard condemns pornography because of its violence and exploitation of young women; but when he is in his horny teenager state, he thinks that it is "incredibly cool" (113). Like Todd and Sarah, Richard gives way to his teenage fantasies and meets with Slutty Kay, an internet porn star, realizing that this is not the way an adult behaves ("Grown men didn't belong to fan clubs" 299). And yet, Richard cannot help but escape into the teenage world because the adult world has become unbearable to him, representing a "suburban cage and forcing him onto the hamster wheel of corporate drudgery" (117). Adulthood thus implies "claustrophobia and resentment," being caught in a situation that forces Richard to throw away "the best years of his youth" (120). His teenage fantasies then function like a symbolic escape from the intolerable, restrictive coercions of adult life. In Richard's case, references to teenage and adult behavior reflect his mental condition and his contradictory and unstable attitude towards responsible adult behavior on the one hand and irresponsible teenage behavior on the other hand. References to the age stage of adolescence, made in connection with chronologically adult characters, thus point to conflictual situations and indicate a possibility for symbolic escape and resistance.

A "Grown-Up Art" of Power Play

Age references in *Little Children* also involve disciplinary implications. When Todd's football teammates call their opponents crybabies, for example, they degrade these adult men by marking them as weak, pathetic losers.[11] The disciplinary function of references to age stages also recurs in

---

10 Richard also attributes insecurity and anxiety as features of being a (horny) teenager when he maintains that "[i]t was as if he were back in high school, pining after some girl in chemistry class, knowing he'd never find the nerve to talk to her" (114).

11 The loser reference also appears in *Little Children* but is less prominent. Sarah, for example, seems to have much sympathy for losers like Todd and Ronnie. Her husband Richard attacks her for defending Ronnie and for seeing him as a

more complex negotiations of authority and power. During a dinner at Todd and Kathy's house, to which Sarah and Richard are invited, references to age stages function as an affective amplifier in the silent war between Kathy and Sarah, as Kathy suspects that Sarah is having an affair with her husband. The reader follows Kathy's emotional roller coaster ride during the dinner which is framed by repeated age references. Kathy's first impression of Sarah, for instance, is described as an act of disparagement of her rival: "[Sarah's] lipstick was the wrong shade of red, clashing both with her skin tone and her shirt, as though she were a teenager who still hadn't quite mastered the grown-up art of color coordination. Kathy almost felt sorry for her" (258). Kathy's description of Sarah as a teenager belittles her rival. For Kathy, this devaluation implies that Sarah is harmless because she is neither attractive nor seductive. Hence, Sarah does not need to be taken seriously because she represents no danger.

In a next step, references to age are used by Kathy as a means of denigrating Richard whom she criticizes for his physical appearance. Given that Richard is about fifteen years older than the others, he is indeed chronologically older but he is not as old as Kathy describes him. Kathy first compares Richard to the old veterans whom she interviewed for a documentary. This comparison was used before when Kathy tried to emphasize Todd's delusional behavior, comparing him to a particular old veteran who thinks that he is still a young man and thus lives in a permanent state of denial (cf. 144). In Richard's case, this reference to the old, feeble veterans of the documentary, who are probably about twenty years older than Richard, highlights Richard's lack of attractiveness in Kathy's eyes. Kathy compares Richard to "old geezers," noting their unpleasant habits (sly winking, snoring), unappealing physical looks (saggy pecs, expanding waistline, ear wax, nose hair), and their neediness (cholesterol and blood pressure medicine, in need of compassionate understanding; 260-1). Kathy concludes her comparison of Richard to an old veteran with the statement: "Just the thought of it was enough to make you start sleeping with teenagers again" (261). Ironically, Kathy's husband behaves like a teenager.

The fact that Kathy exaggerates her age ascription in this case suggests an affective function of age references because they amplify Richard's re-

---

"pathetic loser" and not a scary pervert (270). Richard contradicts her and argues that "[t]hose are the ones we have to worry about" (270).

pulsiveness. Richard is not simply chronologically older than the other characters at the table (which is a fact); he is imagined as a senile, disabled, and repugnant old man. Richard's physical shortcomings, however, soon wear off in Kathy's perception and she begins to use Richard's behavioral qualities as an older man to denigrate her own husband. Hence, the reference to age which first indicated negative features is now used to stress the positive aspects that advanced age can entail. Kathy therefore notes sympathetically: "Despite [Richard's] yucky clothes and weak chin and annoying tendency to wink, there was a kind of expansive ease about him, a wealth of experience and opinions" (261). Richard now appears as a man of gravitas, dignity, experience, achievement, and wisdom – features that (childish or teenage) Todd lacks entirely: "[Todd] was a thirty-one-year-old man who'd accomplished nothing with his life except to father a child and avoid paying work for longer than she'd imagined possible" (261). The versatility and contingency of age references mirror Kathy's emotional instability and undermine her authority in this situation. While the narrative makes it clear that her strategic use of age references is an attempt to restore her own sense of security and confidence, she still emerges as a highly apprehensive and insecure character.

Kathy's insecurity and doubts reappear when she senses the sexual tension between Todd and Sarah. The power relations change again and Kathy realizes that "Sarah seemed to have been transformed into an entirely different woman. Not beautiful, but powerful nonetheless" (271). In Kathy's perception, Sarah is thus no longer an awkward teenager but a potent woman. In an attempt to reverse this power relation for her own benefit, Kathy falls back on her strategy of disciplining Sarah through references to age: She notices the color of Sarah's nail polish, which is

> a hideous metallic blue, the kind of color a trashy twelve-year-old would have loved, nothing you'd ever expect to find on the feet of a grown woman, the mother of a young child. You would have to be crazy to wear nail polish like that, or so deeply in love that you were beyond caring. (271-2)

In this example, Kathy's references to age have lost their disciplining power. They still mark Sarah as crazy and different (because of her age-inappropriate looks). Nevertheless, the effectiveness of Kathy's denigration strategy has decreased: Kathy falls apart and realizes that Sarah is having an affair with Todd and that Sarah has "stolen her husband" (272). The creative potential of age references in fictional contexts becomes clear in this scene. Age references assume metaphoric meaning and support attempts to control and devalue another character or to stigmatize a rival as a lawbreaker. At the same time, Kathy's practice of using age metaphors is an attempt to restore order within emotional chaos.

Sarah experiences a similar emotional roller coaster ride during her book club meeting. When Sarah is introduced into the club, which the members call the "Bellington Ladies Belletristic Society," she meets a group of vibrant, free-spirited, and curious elderly women who surprise Sarah in their candidness regarding the constraints of married life and the freedom they have rediscovered after their husbands passed away. These women represent an alternative to Sarah's experiences with old age, which are mainly informed by her mother's secluded, constrained, and altogether deplorable condition (cf. 178). Sarah feels connected to this "community of smart, independent, supportive women" and feels inspired by their strength and carpe diem attitude (191). "It was like being back at the Women's Center" (which Sarah had frequented as an undergraduate), and she recognizes "what she'd been missing, the oasis she'd been unable to find in graduate school, at work, or even at the playground [...] it was a huge relief to be back inside the circle again" (191). This image of a circle is significant because it implies that the elderly women help Sarah to not feel singled out or alienated by her surroundings. In this scene, age references insinuate an intergenerational connection. Sarah is far from reproducing Kathy's ageist stereotypes of old age (in terms of old geezers) and instead feels that she is in good hands among the elderly women, where competition, achievement, and exterior appearance are secondary to more indulgent and tolerant values of mutual support, patience, and endurance. The book club women remind Sarah of what it means to feel accepted and valued.

Sarah's re-found sense of belonging and approval is disturbed when her archenemy from the playground, Mary Ann, also joins the book club. Mary Ann has previously condemned Sarah's poor qualities as a mother and wife. As an immediate response, Sarah feels a hostile atmosphere rising and feels suddenly excluded from the community of the elderly women. This sense of exclusion is emphasized by references to age: Both Sarah and Mary Ann are called little sisters now (cf. 192). As a response, Sarah feels like someone who has "been given a beautiful present, only to have it ripped away a moment later and handed to someone else" (192). Her new position is thus characterized by powerlessness, lack of understanding, and subjection. The same effect applies to Mary Ann: When she is asked to open the discussion, the ladies of the Belletristic Society smile at her "like kindergarten teachers" (192) and thus belittle her in – what seems to be – a condescending attitude. Figuratively speaking, Mary Ann and Sarah are on the playground again, fighting immaturely over whose interpretation of *Madame Bovary*, the book that is being discussed, is correct.

But then, the situation changes: Sarah manages to free herself from the age-graded position (maybe because Mary Ann is degraded by the same metaphoric practice). Sarah reclaims her earlier invigorated position, feeling

calm and well prepared, an adult among her peers. Maybe she'd grown up in the past five or six years without realizing it. Or maybe she was just happier now than she'd been back then. She looked at Mary Ann with what she hoped was a kind of empathy. (194)

Sarah symbolically matures from a child's position to that of an adult. In doing so, she is able to control the situation. After all, it is Sarah who provides an interpretation of *Madame Bovary*, which finds approval by the elderly women of the book club. Sarah interprets the character Madame Bovary, who appears like her soul mate, as a strong woman who dares to fight for her dreams but fails because of a too narrow-minded social environment.[12] Thus, Sarah wins out over Mary Ann and feels strengthened in her intellectual competencies and moral righteousness. Again, the refer-

---

12 Sarah provides a very empathetic interpretation of Emma Bovary's behavior: "It's not cheating. It is the hunger for an alternative. The refusal to accept unhappiness" (195). With this interpretation, Sarah reframes her own adulterous behavior and concludes that her conduct is not perverse, as Mary Ann wants her to believe, but an act of resistance and thus a refusal to accept the dullness and desperation of her life. According to Sarah, Emma Bovary's fault lies somewhere else: "Madame Bovary's problem wasn't that she committed adultery [...] It was that she committed adultery with losers. She never found a partner worthy of her heroic passion" (196).

ences to age amplify the scene's emotional atmosphere of tension, acceptance, and denigration.

The book club scene reveals further complexities in the metaphoric practice of age. Sarah's ascribed or subjectively felt age status is accompanied by a constant change in her position of authority. The age references indicate that Sarah vacillates between the status of an outsider (as a little sister) and that of an insider (as part of a community of older women). The communal spirit among the elderly women invigorates her by making her feel like an esteemed adult among peers, which implies authority, competence, and a sense of calm. At the same time, this position becomes fragile as soon as Mary Ann enters the group of women. Therefore, in the book club scene, references to age are flexible and contingent markers which can either rejuvenate or mature Sarah, depending on the corresponding situation.

A similar versatility of the age references can be observed in the descriptions of Todd's attitude towards sex. References to age either suggest Todd's closeness to his wife or to his lover, depending on whether or not sex is described as grown-up or teenage sex. On one occasion, for instance, Todd maintains that the sex with Sarah has made him mature because he has learned that beauty is not a vital element of sexual attraction. At another occasion, Todd describes the sex with Sarah as "uninhibited grown-up sex" (221), only to maintain by the end of the novel that Sarah radiates "adolescent clumsiness" whereas the sex with his wife Kathy is the result of "hard-won adult experience" (333). References to age thus express Todd's situational emotions and point to his unstable position between two women.

The "Definitional Instability" of Life Stages

In *Little Children*, references to age challenge power positions and norms. Perrotta plays with the meanings of life stages, at times questioning them and sometimes even inverting them. As a consequence, references to age not only reflect a field of power, as Krekula argues (cf. 25), they also become a mode of resistance against age grading, age discrimination, and normative conceptions of life stages and development.

When Sarah is introduced in the first chapter of the novel, Perrotta draws attention to a peculiar contradiction regarding age-related behavior: Adult mothers on a playground behave like teenagers upon seeing a good-looking man, while at the same time they consider themselves as moral authorities regarding parenting or the safety of their community. The inconsistency in these observations challenges the meaning of adulthood: Can one take seriously the authority and self-righteousness of an adult woman like Mary Ann, who is extremely silly and immature one moment and dominant and condescending the next? Or, in the words of Sarah,

[w]hat was adult life but one moment of weakness piled on top of another? Most people just fell in line like obedient little children, doing exactly what society expected of them at any given moment, all the while pretending that they'd actually made some sort of choice. (9)

Perrotta questions the values of traditional adulthood, such as active decision-making or independence. He suggests that the boundaries between childlike and adult behavior are porous or liminal (see page 116-7). Being an independent decision maker does not define a person as an adult. It is rather the obedient fulfillment of social expectations, weakness, and pretense that seem to characterize the adults in the novel. Perrotta presents these adult yet immature women at the playground as the moral authorities of their community, who punish the adulterers Todd and Sarah with the same strategies of social exclusion and moral superiority they use for the child molester Ronnie. From the very beginning, this supposedly superior morality is called into question. Perrotta invites his readers to assume a similarly distanced attitude as Sarah, who, in the first paragraph of the novel, is presented as an anthropologist who watches the evolving spectacle that unfolds before her eyes. With this critical position in mind, the spectacle of suburban bigotry is refracted through the lens of age stages.

As the novel unfolds, almost all characters claim at one point to be 'normal' and express this status by affirming their adulthood. Larry Moon, for instance, the 33-year-old retired ex-cop is very persistent in assuming and maintaining a position of adult rationality and moral astuteness, particularly since he is constantly degraded by others into the role of a dependent child or that of an unproductive slacker (cf. 252). The vigilante group that Larry initiates as an attempt to protect the children of the neighborhood appears like an act of redemption in light of his previous history. Larry Moon accidentally shot and killed an adolescent in a mall and was then diagnosed with post-traumatic stress disorder. Larry's position within the community is thus very unstable. Like Ronnie, he has committed a crime against a child. Larry's harassment of the child molester Ronnie figures as his attempt to regain a more stable and respected position in the community – a position that is denied to Ronnie for good.

Hence, even though Larry and Ronnie appear as antagonists, they have much in common: Both Larry and Ronnie have violently broken the rules and have injured the sanctuary that childhood represents in Western cultures. While Larry accidentally shot a teenage boy, Ronnie molested (and presumably killed) a girl. Larry and Ronnie also share a similar history: They both lost their parents, and Larry can sympathize with Ronnie's desolation (cf. 255). Moreover, Larry and Ronnie know what it means to suffer from social isolation and the authoritative ways of others who control and dominate their lives. When, for instance, at a church meeting, Larry and Ronnie run into each other and get into a fight, Larry exerts the same kind of humiliation he experienced just minutes before by his wife, who was "employing the overly rational tone favored by people talking to lunatics or very small children" (252). He angrily yanks Ronnie out of the church, drags "the cringing pervert" by the ear "like a misbehaving child" (254), and humiliates Ronnie by transferring the same age-degradation that Larry's wife exerted on him. When Ronnie then shouts "You're the pervert! [...] You're trying to rape me or something?" (253), Ronnie and Larry have reversed roles and the boundaries between good and evil, normal and perverse have been nullified. Perrotta uses the references to age with an interesting twist: He conflates the presumed innocence and powerlessness of children with lunacy and even perversity, demonstrating once again how seemingly natural the linkage between adulthood and normativity has become and how flawed this connection actually is.

Ronnie's position within the novel is ambiguous. Obviously, as a pedophile and assumed murderer, he represents a transgressor and threatens the civic righteousness of his white, suburban environment. Without wanting to euphemize pedophilia, I would like to suggest that Ronnie has a much more complex function in the novel than representing evil incarnate because he has much in common with the other characters, such as Larry and Todd. It is this connection that makes Ronnie's perversity more complicated and, at the same time, reflects his perversity and lunacy back to those characters in the novel who judge him. From the perspective of an age reading, Ronnie is a character who acts inappropriately for his age because he is a grown man who shows sexual interest in children instead of people of his own age. A similar age-inappropriate infatuation is presented in Todd's unusual interest in young skateboarders. Todd watches them for hours and feels attracted to them (although not on a sexual level). This analogy between Todd and Ronnie is substantiated when Todd watches the skateboarders one night, musing about Sarah and their kiss on the playground. Among other aspects that Todd likes about Sarah, it is the fact that she is "short and boyish" that intrigues him (46). In the following paragraph, Larry shows up and shouts to Todd: "Hey, pervert! [...] Like the little boys, do you?" (46). Even though Larry is teasing Todd, Todd is startled and cringes at the word pervert. The perversity here refers to a second dimension of Todd's inappropriate behavior: He is not only watching teenage skateboarders for hours, he is also dreaming about a woman other than his wife and is about to commit adultery. The accusation of perversity recurs in the novel and constitutes an important theme associated with age and age stages.

For an age critic like Gullette, the connection between pedophilia and age or age-inappropriate behavior is no surprise. As Gullette maintains in *Agewise*, "[i]n a consumerist hypersexualized environment where bare-midriffed fifteen-year-olds are the pedophilic standard of desirability, becoming older is coded as a set of deficiencies" (125). Therefore, "[p]edophilia is almost too perfect an allegory of decline's relationship to growing older" (205). Gullette makes clear that ageist notions of aging are not only comparable with deficiency but also with a sense of perversity, and it is exactly this association that is insinuated in *Little Children* when Todd's and Sarah's age-inappropriate behavior is used as an indicator of their felt deficiency in life. The juxtaposition of their childish behavior with Ronnie's pedophilic misconduct indicates the irony and subversive quality that metaphoric practices of age can unfold.

With the introduction of the child molester Ronnie, the boundaries between perverse and normal become brittle and are revealed as artificial. Adult behavior is no longer a guarantor or gauge of normalcy and this fact becomes evident in Mary Ann's realization of personal failure. Mary Ann, Sarah's archenemy, is a character who stands for the moral authority of the neighborhood and functions (like Larry) as an alleged guardian of childhood and good motherhood. She is established as the epitome of reasonable, organized, and dutiful adult behavior. Mary Ann has rigid moral beliefs, such as the necessity to castrate pedophiles or the depravity of adultery (cf. 27, 194). At the end of the novel, however, when the neighborhood is turned upside down and the boundaries between right and wrong are blurred, Mary Ann's presumed flawlessness crumbles and her position of supposed exemplary adult behavior is swiftly but relentlessly dismantled. In short, interspersed vignettes, Perrotta describes how Mary Ann's children rebel against their mother's rigid rules. Then, her husband Lewis criticizes the sex schedule Mary Ann has set up and his wife's parenting ("Our son is four years old [...]. You have to stop talking to him about Harvard" 327). At the end of the novel, it becomes clear that Mary Ann's purportedly reasonable adult choices have resulted in misery: She realizes that her marriage is floundering, that she never loved her husband, and that she only married him to avoid becoming an old spinster.

As it turns out, Mary Ann and Sarah have much in common; they merely took different roads. Todd has triggered similar feelings in Mary Ann as in Sarah, conjuring up in each of them images of a different version of adult life that echo their earlier, teenage fantasies. Like Sarah, Mary Ann realizes that she did not live up to her dreams and that her present situation is marked by a feeling of inferiority and poor decision-making. The results of her decisions are bitter: Her initial authority and power are dismantled and the moral grounds of her adult or age-appropriate behavior turn out to be highly unstable and artificial.

In *Little Children*, the "boundaries of 'normal behavior'" (42) emerge as unstable and negotiable. When Perrotta describes how Todd and Kathy met in college, he has their sociology professor argue that we live in "an era of definitional instability" (171), referring to definitions of marriage and domestic relationships. As the story progresses, norms and age stages continue to be challenged and it becomes clear that not only gender roles or institutional bonds like marriage are at stake. In Perrotta's novel, definitional instability applies to all kinds of social interaction and social practices, in which concepts of normativity and deviance define age roles, social conduct, human relationships, and moral values.

At the end of the novel, Sarah is on the playground with Larry, Ronnie, and Mary Ann. She has realized that Todd will not show up to elope with her and she envisions a future as a struggling single mother, destined for a complicated relationship with her daughter Lucy (cf. 352). She then decides to rejoin "the circle of adults," which is, however, a circle of losers and failed adults, who have fallen short of living up to the expectations of proper adult behavior and who have violated the code of conduct in terms of age-appropriate sexual relationships (Ronnie), age-appropriate gainful employment (Larry), or age-appropriate candidness about one's own faults and indulgence with other people's faults (Mary Ann). As the novel ends, adulthood no longer implies moral authority but symbolizes bleakness and failure. Sarah imagines a disillusioned vision of her future with her daughter, which she describes as "a sudden vivid awareness of the life they'd lead together from here on out, the hothouse intimacy of a single mother and her only child" and the "probably unhealthy bond that for better and worse would become the center of both of their identities, fodder for years of therapy" (353-4). Interestingly, this new version of her life feels good to Sarah because it is real and palpable in contrast to the alternative of a fantasy life with Todd (cf. 354).

In Todd's case, adult behavior also resumes center stage at the end of the novel. When he is offered a skateboard to ride for the first time and accepts, even though he is supposed to meet with Sarah in order to elope with her, he realizes that his affair with Sarah was only an adventure to spice up his daily boredom: "What he loved most about Sarah was how beautifully she fit into his old one [life], distracting him from his imperfect marriage and the tedious obligations of child care, supercharging the dull summer days with a sweet illicit thrill" (350). By not meeting Sarah as planned, Todd (more or less) 'decides' to persevere and to meet the challenges of married life. The fact that this decision coincides with his fall during a skateboard stunt and thus his failure to act out his escape into the teenage world of skateboarders is ironical.

One might interpret Todd's decision to stay with his family as a new sense of maturity in Todd's life. And this maturity comes as a hard-won lesson, entailing physical harm (he is unconscious for five minutes and seems to have sustained a brain concussion), which appears like the price he has to pay for finally joining the adult world. Todd's acceptance of his adult status is ambiguous, however. When he wakes from his unconsciousness after the fall, he wonders if he should become a policeman. On the one hand, this idea indicates his willingness to become the provider of his family. On the other hand, Larry, to whom Todd speaks about his plans, used to be a policeman and failed to provide for his family. Todd's plans of assuming an adult position thus appear questionable, particularly in view of the fact that the job of a policeman is, according to a study from the *Children's Mutual*, in the top 10 of the most popular professions among five- and six-year-olds (cf. Booth n. pag.). Earlier in the novel, Todd also wonders why he chose to become a lawyer instead of a cop or fireman,[13] which are far more "exciting" and "cool" careers because both involve action and adrenaline rushes (Perrotta 100). Instead, he had decided to become a lawyer. "Why had it ever seemed like a good idea to put on a suit every morning and spend his day researching copyrights or figuring out ways to exploit loopholes in the tax code? What kind of life was that for a grown man?" (100). The adult world that Todd describes here is marked by boredom and futility. From this perspective, Todd's plan to become a policeman at the end of the novel is as much an adult decision as the fulfillment of a child's dream.

In *Little Children*, references to age assume several functions: (1) They elucidate the relationships between the characters and indicate the major conflicts, (2) they are used as metaphors that suggest a variety of emotional states and social positions of the characters in the novel, and (3) they dismantle boundaries between normal and deviant behavior and challenge the cultural imaginaries associated with life stages and age-appropriate behavior. The focus on the metaphoric practices of age adds an alternative perspective on perpetual adolescents, who are not only a contemporary phenomenon of particular socio-economic circumstances, but can also become a symbolic figure in fictional contexts, embodying the porosity of norms, authorities, and moral judgments. The figure of the age-inappropriate perpetual adolescent personifies conflict and a lifestyle that, on the one hand, glorifies youthfulness and, on the other hand, refuses maturity and responsibility. Juxtaposed with other characters (Ronnie) or problematic actions (adultery, pedophilia), the figure of the delayed adult in *Little Children* exposes the bigotry and hypocrisy of middle-class suburban life. Perrotta discusses these themes by assuming the point of view of the marginalized – the perverts, adulterers, and sex addicts – who threaten established norms, rules, and expectations through their age-inappropriate behavior.

---

13 The profession of fireman also appears in the top 10 of the most popular jobs (cf. Booth n. pag.).

Coming of age, or even a late or secondary coming of age is not an issue in the novel. On the contrary, Todd and Sarah have already come of age in terms of marriage and parenthood (though they are unhappy with their respective social situations). They refuse to accept the mature lifestyles in which they find themselves and, instead of envisioning (or believing in) a progression towards a more satisfactory version of their lives, they regress into teenage fantasies and, in some sense, experience a similar (though rather mental) rejuvenation as Toula in *My Big Fat Greek Wedding*. Since the teenage fantasies cannot be upheld, as Sarah realizes at the end, she can only imagine a bleak future of therapy and an unhealthy relationship with her daughter.

Let us take a step back and recapitulate. The three fictional narratives discussed so far start out with descriptions of characters who are in a crisis: They are unhappy with their lives of missed chances and unfulfilled expectations; they share a sense of personal failure; they are unhappy because they are unmarried (Toula) or, if they are married, the marriage is partly responsible for their unhappiness (Sarah and Todd). The characters realize painfully that they fall short of social (or their own) expectations in terms of careers, self-fulfillment, or financial status. Being in their early thirties, they have a life crisis.

3.3 Normativity and the Life Course

According to some life course scholars,[14] a crisis at age thirty is not surprising. On the contrary, it is even considered to be normal. Age thirty figures as a watershed in the studies of Robert J. Havighurst (*Developmental Tasks*

---

14 Life course scholarship was officially introduced as a scientific discipline by sociologist Leonard D. Cain, Jr. in 1964. The disciplinary boundaries of life course theory are diffuse and the research field is diverse (see Elder et al. "Emergence" 4). Karl Ulrich Mayer (2003) and Shanahan & Porfelli (2002) subdivide the field into sociological life course theory and life span psychology. While sociological research on the life course is interested in the social, cultural, or historical structures, psychologists try to understand the ways in which individuals develop in a social environment due to their genetic, emotional, and cognitive abilities.

and Education, 1974) and Daniel J. Levinson (*The Seasons of a Man's Life*, 1978). Levinson argues that the so-called 'Age Thirty Transition' "frequently begins with a vague uneasiness, a feeling that something is missing or wrong in one's life and that some change is needed if the future is to be worthwhile" (71). The following feelings might occur in a young adult facing the 'Age 30 Transition:' instability, feeling of fragmentation, no clear occupational direction, insecurity, rootlessness, having no center in life, feelings of doubt, and experiencing a moment of crisis (cf. 83). The young adult is "plagued by choices and contradiction" (83) and by the knowledge that he has to give up the "little boy within himself" (60). Levinson claims these feelings to be normal: 57% of his sample[15] experienced these feelings (cf. 83), and 62% of the men went through a moderate or severe crisis (cf. 87). Likewise, for the women in Levinson's subsequent study, it was "bewildering to discover, at around 30," that life "has major imperfections [...] and that [they] still have some 'growing up' to do" (*Woman* 117). Hence, as Levinson claims, a crisis at age thirty occurs in many people's lives, suggesting that it is a normal aspect of the human life course.

Similarly, in her book *Passages: Predictable Crises of Adult Life* (1976), journalist Gail Sheehy considers the transitional phase between ages 28 and 32 a normal crisis, calling it the 'Catch-30 Passage.' This passage is a "[t]ime of crisis, of disruption or constructive change" which is "not only predictable but desirable" because it means growth (21). Moments of crisis at particular ages are thus naturalized as ontogenetic aspects of the life course and intrinsic components of human development. In choosing the name 'Catch-30 Passage,' Sheehy makes an allusion to paradoxical and absurd predicaments known as 'Catch-22,' which is a quite dramatic label compared with her rather optimistic description of this time of change:

A restless vitality wells up as we approach 30. Almost everyone wants to make some alteration. [...] The restrictions we feel on nearing 30 are the outgrowth of the choices of the twenties, choices that may have been perfectly appropriate to that stage.

---

15 Between 1968 and 1970, Levinson interviewed a sample of 40 men who were 35 to 45 years old, lived somewhere between Boston and New York, and came from four different occupational subgroups. In his follow-up study *The Seasons of a Woman's Life*, published in 1996, Levinson interviewed a group of 45 women in the early 1980s.

Now the fit feels different. We become aware of some inner aspect that has been left out. It may make itself felt suddenly, emphatically. More often it begins as a slow drum roll, a vague but persistent sense of *wanting to be something more*. (138)

In Levinson's concept of the 'Age 30 Transition,' men and women around age 30 undergo a similar re-evaluation of the current life structure. They feel a necessity to consider the future by asking questions such as: "What have I done with my life? What do I want to make of it? What new directions shall I chose?" (84). As a result, they feel an "increasing internal need and external pressure to [...] get more order, purpose and attachment into their lives" (*Man* 80).

Externally, there are pressures to 'grow up,' get married, enter an occupation, define his goals and lead a more organized life. In the self there are desires for stability and order, for roots, membership in the tribe, lasting ties, fulfillment of core values. (*Man* 79-80)[16]

From the perspective of Levinson and Sheehy, the crises of Toula, Verona, or Todd are thus normal and predictable symptoms of a desirable development. Crises are considered intrinsic aspects of the life course, which is conceptualized as a universal structure of human life. Hence, is the cultural and historical situatedness within which the fictional narratives of this study unfold irrelevant to an understanding of the characters' life crises?

Levinson, like his colleagues Havighurst and Erikson, would agree because they understand the life course as a universal structure of human life that exists quite independently from social and cultural influences. Contemporary life course scholars such as Blatterer contradict this essentialist view of human development (see Chapter 3.1).[17] And yet, Blatterer con-

---

16 Levinson remains vague when he speaks of the external and internal pressures. In his later study on female life courses, this elusiveness is persistent (cf. *Woman* 326).

17 In the 1960s, two approaches dominated the field of life course research: Some scholars considered individual development to be a matter of a universally patterned life course, emphasizing the structural forces that influence the life course. Others contested this view and argued for the individual malleability of the life course (cf. Clausen 1993).

cedes that the concept of universal life stages or life courses still exists in people's cultural imaginaries. They remain "evaluative benchmarks" even though the reality is quite different (*Coming of Age* 45).[18] Indeed, as Arnett proves statistically, most people's life courses turn out to be similar (cf. *Emerging Adulthood* 12). And Blatterer finds that most of his interviewees eventually led lives that incorporated the milestones of standard adulthood (cf. *Coming of Age* 120). Apparently, the notions of universal life courses and standard life stages play a significant role in the cultural imaginaries associated with life stages and aging. The remarkable incidence that all of the young adult characters in this study have a similar life crisis at or around age 30 with similar fears and concerns thus seems to support the universalist theories of life course scholars. But how relevant are these essentialist imaginaries of the life course today? And which functions do life course imaginaries have in highly individualized cultures that promote agency, flexibility, and self-responsibility?

Life Course Imaginaries

Imaginaries of the life course have a long cultural history. As early as 600 BC, Aesop maintains in his fable "The Man, the Horse, the Ox and the Dog" that a man's life is divided into three stages (youth, adulthood, old age) and that each stage is attributed a characteristic feature (impatience, industriousness, peevishness), which is symbolized by animals.[19] In Shakespeare's comedy *As You Like It* (1623), the notion of the "Seven Ages of Man" presents a life course imaginary that subdivides human life into seven stages: infant, school-boy, lover, soldier, the justice, the pantaloon, second childishness (cf. Act II, Scene 7). Each stage is linked with a characteristic behavior, and there seems to be a circular concept behind the overall sequence of the seven stages. Pictorial representations of Shakespeare's life course imaginary therefore often align the seven stages in a circle so that

---

18 Blatterer does not directly address "universal" life stages. He refers, however, to the imaginaries of postwar life courses and the standard model of adulthood, which, as he argues, remain a romanticized ideal in many people's minds.

19 Aesop's story has survived over the centuries. The Brothers Grimm, for example, picked up the idea of life stages in "The Duration of Life" ("Die Lebenszeit" 1840).

the infant stage and the second stage of childishness are placed side by side.[20]

The American artist Thomas Cole painted the series *The Voyage of Life* in 1842, in which he depicts four stages of life: childhood, youth, manhood, and old age. The paintings depict a voyager who travels in a boat on the River of Life. Each painting shows a landscape, which reflects a season of the year and reproduces the stereotypical equation of spring with childhood and winter with old age. The four stages of life are associated with particular moods or challenges, which are reflected in the colors of the sky (the bright colors in "Youth"), the condition of the river (troubled water in "Manhood"), the voyager's orientation towards a castle in "Youth," or the atmosphere insinuated by the landscape (soft meadows in "Childhood" and rocks in "Manhood").

The notion of the life course as a linear, ascending and descending staircase or "Lebenstreppe" emerged in the sixteenth century (cf. Lucke et al. 2009). The following painting is from 1900 (see fig. 9).

Fig. 9: Die Lebenstreppe

The staircase of life is very symmetrical in its partitioning of the life course into equal life stages. Each step of the "Lebenstreppe" comprises ten years and is associated with a task. The third decade, for example, shows a couple

---

20 The "Wheel of Life" or "Wheel of Becoming" is also a circular representation of the life course.

with two children and defines the thirties as a decade for marrying and starting a family. This representation of the life course is problematic, however, because it presents a lifetime of 100 years, which does not correspond with the average life expectancy at that time.[21] Interestingly though, the division of the life course into stages and the meanings (and tasks) associated with particular stages in the staircase of life continue to appear in the studies of Erik H. Erikson, Daniel J. Levinson, and Robert J. Havighurst.

Erikson, for instance, uses eight stages of development, Havighurst six, and Levinson creates four larger eras, which he subdivides into several periods. Each stage is related to particular tasks that need to be fulfilled before a person can enter a new phase of life. In Erikson's model, each stage is associated with a crisis or conflict of opposites, which must be solved in order to gain a virtue and to move onto the next stage (cf. 150-1). Similarly, Havighurst assigns developmental tasks to each stage. Levinson's model, which is the most detailed and compartmentalized of the models, is more process-oriented in comparison to Erikson's rather static division of stages because Levinson suggests that the decisions made in a life stage are only provisional; they can be revised in later stages. Each transition between two stages functions like "a bridge, or a boundary zone, between two states of greater stability" (*Man* 49-50). Stages and transitions thus alternate regularly throughout the life course with the possibility that some eras may overlap at times (cf. *Woman* 413). Evidently, these concepts of stages are based on a linear and sequential understanding of how people move through their life course. Despite the rigid stage structure of their models, Levinson, Erikson, and Havighurst emphasize individual agency and put less emphasis on the influence of society.[22] The studies by Erikson, Levinson, and Havighurst have been reproached for being ethnocentric, androcentric, and universalist and for committing an "ontogenetic fallacy" by assuming that "change in adulthood [is] a natural property of the individual which tends to be uni-

---

21 According to the German Federal Institute for Population Research (Statistisches Bundesamt), the life expectancy was 51,58 years for men and 58,30 years for women born in the year 1909. Cf. <https://www.destatis.de/DE/ZahlenFakten/GesellschaftStaat/Bevoelkerung/Sterbefaelle/Tabellen/ModellrechnungLebenserwartung.html>, accessed on 9 September 2013.
22 Also see C. Wright Mills (1959) or Glen H. Elder (1974), who emphasize the influence of social factors on the life course.

form across individuals and relatively unaffected by context" (Dannefer, "Adult Development" 109).

Imaginaries of the life course can also refer to spatial images, such as mental maps, cartographies, or navigational charts (cf. Levinson 1978, Settersten 2003, Burnett 2010). According to Burnett, the social ideas and images about the life course "are a rich form of data, revealing the life course paradigm as a calendar and map, a sort of clock by which our identities are kept or challenged, and our social locations defined or changed" (2). Similarly, temporal imaginaries function as mental representations of the life course. Timetables, social clocks, deadlines, and notions of being on-time or off-time are recurring metaphors (cf. Settersten, "Age Structuring" 85ff, Burnett 2, 24-38). The concepts of the social clock[23] or biological clock are also very popular temporal life course imaginaries in contemporary Western cultures.[24]

The U-bend shape of the life course (see fig. 10) is an alternative visualization, which suggests a reversed structure of the staircase of life. In the 1990s, the economics researcher Andrew Oswald suggested this U-bend shape when he studied psychological well-being over the life course (cf. "U-bend of Life" n. pag.). He found that middle age does not represent a peak in life, as the "Lebenstreppe" suggests. On the contrary, people in midlife are typically less happy compared to their younger or older selves. Despite Oswald's empirical evidence, however, the cultural imaginary of the rise-and-fall shape of the life course seems to prevail in people's minds.[25] Cultural imaginaries are thus quite powerful in shaping people's

---

23 Rook et al. have critically reviewed the social clock theory and find that the idea of a social clock, which dictates normative timing of life events, still exists in cultural imaginaries of the life course. They note that, despite empirical counter-examples, the "intuitive appeal of the 'social clock hypothesis'" continues to support the assumption that "being out of step with one's peers" can cause "feelings of personal inadequacy and incompetence" (234).

24 See my article "Let the Countdown Begin: Aging Experiences of Young Adults in Countdown Blogs" (2012), for a discussion of a blog called "Watch me turn 30" that uses a logo with a bomb to symbolize the deadline that age thirty represents.

25 *The Economist* quotes a study by Peter Ubel et al., which found that people believe that 30-year-olds are happier than 70-year-olds, even though when both

concepts of self-development and seem to form shared cultural knowledge despite individual experiences or empirical proof of the contrary.[26] But why is the rise-and-decline shape so prominent?

Fig. 10: Visualization of the U-bend from The Economist

Control Functions of the Life Course

According to Richard A. Settersten Jr., life course imaginaries are naturalized and "internalized [...] frames of reference," which

a) prescribe and proscribe social action,
b) are based on a consensus about rules of differentiation between normative and non-normative social action and
c) represent mechanisms of control which ensure the implementation of these rules. (cf. "Age Structuring" 86)

---

age groups are asked to rate their own well-being, the 70-years-olds emerge as the happier group ("U-bend of Life" n. pag.).

26 Also see the website of *Transgenerational Design Matters* (an "educational, research, and advocacy organization"). It shows "Four Views of Aging," which are presented graphically and show a rise-and-decline shape in four variations (cf. <http://www.transgenerational.org/aging/perceptions.htm>, accessed on 22 November 2011).

Similarly, Steven Katz argues that

> on a macro-scale, life courses are aggregations of knowledges, structures, ethics, and hierarchies through which the complexities of aging are refracted and socially organized. On a micro-scale, they are lived-out embodiments of time from which people distill a rich and versatile archive of meaning, memory, passion, and identity. ("Growing Older" 190)

In this sense, age imaginaries and life course imaginaries have similar cultural functions as mechanisms of control or as categories of differentiation. In addition, both types of imaginaries are associated with values that become visible when a person develops unsuccessfully. In Sheehy's assessment of life crises, cultural values of development, growth, and success are considered universal outcomes of (successfully managed) crises (cf. 21). Transitions in the life course thus carry a potential for growth, while failed transitions signify decline or stagnation. Erikson maintains that, if a person does not manage to develop successfully through the life course, he or she lacks a sense of unity, inner strength or the knowledge "to do well" (cf. 56). If, for instance, young adults have not successfully established a sense of who they are, they will become isolated and will not be able to enjoy intimate and satisfying relationships (cf. 114-5). Levinson argues that if people feel unable to make decisions that advance them in their personal development through the life course, this evasiveness might be caused by "resignation, inertia, passive acquiescence or controlled despair" (*Man* 52). The resulting situation is "surface stability," which leads to decline in the long run (52). Correspondingly, Havighurst has a clear yet uncritical notion of the gratification system that underlies development, arguing that "failure [to complete a task] leads to unhappiness in the individual, disapproval by society, and difficulty with later tasks" (2). Developmental tasks are thus duties in the life course which "constitute healthy and satisfactory growth in our society" and which a person must learn "if he is to be judged and to judge himself to be a reasonably happy and successful person" (2).[27]

---

27 According to Havighurst, the developmental tasks a thirty-year-old should have fulfilled are: 1) selecting a mate, 2) learning to live with a marriage partner, 3) starting a family, 4) rearing children, 5) managing a home, 6) getting started in

If we apply these judgments to Sarah or Todd from *Little Children*, we see how their life crises and feelings of failure are echoed in the descriptions by Havighurst and Erikson. According to these life course psychologists, Todd's refusal to grow up is thus not a response to or a symptom of a particular cultural or social setting. It is rather a sign of his very individual, psychological incapacity to achieve a new stage in his life because he fails to complete developmental tasks in previous stages. From this perspective, Todd appears as a stock character in the story of universal human development.

Indeed, life stages and life crises seem to be closely related to the structure of a (social) drama. When Levinson describes the 'Age 30 Transition' in *The Seasons of a Man's Life*, his depiction is quite literary (*Man* 51):

[A] man alone on a body of water trying to get from Island Past to Island Future. He fears that he will not reach Future. He feels that he can move neither forward nor backward, that he is on the verge of drowning. A man may experience himself as swimming alone, as rowing in a leaky boat, or as captain of a luxurious but defective ship caught in a storm. There are wide variations in the nature of the vehicle, the sources of threat and the nature of Past and Future. The critical thing is that the integrity of the enterprise is in serious doubt: he experiences the imminent danger of chaos, dissolution, the loss of the future. (*Man* 86)

The allegory that Levinson uses to describe this moment of transition in many ways echoes Victor Turner's symbolic anthropology and his studies on liminality. In *The Ritual Process: Structure and Anti-Structure* (1969), Turner describes people in transition as being "neither here nor there; they are betwixt and between" (95). Liminal people are outside of society, which involves a disengagement from duties and tasks and presupposes a preparation for the next status or stage. Turner defines four stages in what he calls the "social drama" of crisis resolution: 1) breach, 2) crisis, 3) redressive action (or, if the crisis cannot be solved, regression to the crisis phase), and 4) reintegration (*Dramas, Fields and Metaphors* 38-9). With this connection to the field of drama, Turner links the empirical approach of life course

---

an occupation, 7) taking on civic responsibility, 8) finding a congenial social group (cf. 96-106).

theory with literature and fine arts by revealing the structural kinship and the narrative connections between life courses and life stories.

Such a dual approach to life course imaginaries in terms of social structures of organization and control, on the one hand, and individually constructed biographies, on the other hand, opens up the notion of life course imaginaries to more complex and bi-directional negotiations of development through time. Victor W. Marshall and Philippa J. Clarke, for instance, use a "'duality of structure' approach that combines agency with a view of structures as including resources" (301). According to Marshall and Clarke, this approach holds "the most promise for capturing the complexities of aging" (301). Anthony Giddens' "theory of structuration" also represents such a "duality of structure" approach, as it tries to bridge the divide between structure and agency and defines its relationship as a complex, dialectical, and dynamic interaction: While structure (understood as rules and resources) influences human behavior, human beings also influence social structure through their behavior, which then reproduces the structure (cf. *The Constitution of Society* 2, 17). Through repeated action therefore, the structure is not only reproduced but also reinforced. Hence, agency and structure are mutually dependent and closely related; they are two sides of the same coin (cf. 25).

Life course imaginaries are thus – at least partly – actively constructed by individuals, and life course psychologists and sociologists have developed several interesting concepts which combine structural, individual, and narrative influences on life courses. Walter R. Heinz, for instance, speaks of "doing biography," which implies that individuals conceive of their lives as "biographical projects" (55), in which the self becomes the "architect of the life course" ("Self-Socialization" 55, 59).[28] Life scripts, for example,

---

28 Anthony Giddens speaks of reflexive biographies (cf. *Modernity and Self-Identity* 53ff.) and Ulrich Beck argues that individuals need to understand themselves as centers of action ("Handlungszentrum") or as planning offices ("Planungsbüro"), in which people's biographies are negotiated and forged according to their abilities, orientations, relationships, and aims (cf. *Risk Society* 135). "Choice biographies," Beck maintains, reflect the imperative to make an "active effort" and to choose wisely among the many options one has. And yet, a choice biography (or "do-it-yourself biography") is a risky endeavor because it can

constitute such narrative frames that demonstrate the complex interaction between individual agency and the control function of life course imaginaries.[29] "Legitimated résumés" represent a similar concept. According to John W. Meyer, "legitimated résumés" consist of elements that "are fixed in advance" and that individuals carry over time (cf. "Self and the Life Course" 242, 251). In order to receive social recognition, individuals must provide legitimate reasons, motives, and aspirations for their life choices. For Meyer, the act of choosing is not a sign of freedom or sovereignty but a coercion: "[I]ndividuals *must* choose" and *must* give reasons for their choices from an "available list of reasons, motives, and aspirations" which can be used and which are marked by values such as progress, fairness, productivity, social efficiency, self-esteem, activity, and initiative (cf. 245, 248, 253; original emphasis).[30] According to Meyer, violations against the coercion to provide a "legitimated résumé" result in alienation. A deviant self is thus an alienated self.

Trajectories, according to the definition by German sociologists Fritz Schütze and Gerhard Riemann, provide a particularly interesting conceptualization of the relation between life scripts and life narratives because they focus on unsuccessful development.[31] Trajectories are "biographical processes of long-term suffering and cumulative disorder, of being overwhelmed by outside forces which lead to a successive loss of control over

---

quickly turn into a "breakdown biography" (*Individualization* 3) suggesting that an unsuccessful life course is the result of individual failure and wrong choices.

29 The concept of scripts was developed by R.C. Schank and R.P. Abelson (1977). Also see the work of Dorthe Berntsen and David C. Rubin (2002, 2003, 2004).

30 Likewise, Giddens maintains that "in conditions of high modernity, we all not only follow lifestyles, but in an important sense are forced to do so – we have no choice but to choose" (*Modernity* 81).

31 The concept of trajectory is "theoretically vague," as Sackmann and Wingens admit (95). Elder simply defines trajectory as a "pathway defined by the aging process or by movement across the age structure" ("Perspectives" 31). Likewise, Meyer's use of the term "trajectory status" (255) refers to the sequential and thus temporary aspect of the life course. In a similarly neutral way, Shanahan and Macmillan define the life course trajectory as "a term that does not prejudge the direction, degree, or rate of change in its course" (*Biography* 79).

one's life circumstances" (Riemann, "Doing Biographical Research" 22).[32] Schütze and Riemann understand trajectories as any form of "disorderly social processes in general that bring about suffering" ("'Trajectory'" 335). "Deviant careers," for instance, can be part of a trajectory, as can illness, general failure, an occupational career (unemployment), an exam (failing), or a love affair (lovesickness) (cf. 338). Practically any number of events in a person's life that take the form of a sequence and that can be narrated can turn into a trajectory. From this perspective, it comes as no surprise that a character like Sarah in *Little Children*, experiences her own life story in terms of a trajectory: She failed as an academic, she married a man she does not love, and she feels alienated from her daughter and from the community of mothers on the playground.

Trajectories, the cultural imaginaries of the "Lebenstreppe," and also Gullette's age narratives of progress and decline share an interesting visual aspect: a curve with an upward and a downward vector with both vectors being connected by a climax or turning point. While the "Lebenstreppe" and decline narratives associate the downward movement with old age, the trajectory offers more interpretative freedom: illness, deviance, failure, unemployment, or lovesickness can become reasons for a perceived downward movement. This connection offers an explanation for the various meanings attached to cultural imaginaries associated with age. When Verona in *Away We Go*, for instance, speaks of feeling old when she anticipates a loss (namely a loss of control and support after learning about her parents-in-law's plans to move abroad), this feared loss can be associated with Gullette's decline narrative of aging. The semantic openness of the trajectory model allows for further associations, such as failure. Moreover, like the decline narrative, the trajectory counters the narrative formula of the coming-of-age story, which – at least in its traditional form – suggests progress and growth instead of decline and loss.

In *The Corrections*, Jonathan Franzen also seems to allude to the concept of a trajectory when he describes the deeply dysfunctional Lambert family.

---

32 Anselm Strauss and Barney Glaser introduced this particular concept of trajectories in their study *Time for Dying* (1968), in which they explore the medical work and organization that surrounds courses of (perceived and not necessarily actual) dying.

Moreover, the youngest daughter, Denise Lambert, experiences particular pressure from her surroundings to conform to or provide a legitimated résumé. Her brother Gary and her mother Enid have clear expectations of an ideal life course for Denise and force her repeatedly to justify, reconsider, or undo her life decisions. Denise is 'doing biography' (cf. Heinz, "Self-Socialization" 59), but she does not conform to her family's expected life script in terms of career choices, relationships, or sexuality. As a consequence, she has to deal with the implications that her age-inappropriate behavior triggers, namely alienation and a sense of failure. At the same time, the dual or bi-directional concept of life course imaginaries and their functions allows Franzen to have his characters make active and creative use of their deviance from standard life course imaginaries. References to age assume a central metaphoric function in this novel, which is predominantly concerned with the consequences of old age for the Lambert family. Applied to Denise, who is far from being old, the metaphoric practice of age appears as a creative practice to negotiate discipline and revenge, control and resistance. The metaphor of age casts Denise as different, yet, at the same time, Denise is shown to actively participate in her marginalization through her age-inappropriate behavior.

3.4 Jonathan Franzen's *The Corrections*

The Lambert family, which Jonathan Franzen describes in *The Corrections*, consists of Alfred Lambert, the 79-year-old father of the family who suffers from Parkinson's disease and dementia; Enid Lambert, the 73-year-old mother of three children who feels misunderstood by her husband and disappointed by her children; Gary Lambert, the 45-year-old husband to Caroline, father to three children, and a vice president at CenTrust Bank, who fights but eventually surrenders to his wife's suspicion that he is depressed; Chip Lambert, an almost 40-year-old professor of literature who has an affair with a student, loses his job, and embarks on a shady business enterprise to Lithuania; and Denise, a 32-year-old bisexual chef at a successful high-end restaurant whose self-destructive relationships with men and women continually undermine her professional success and personal happiness.[33]

In *The Corrections,* which was awarded the National Book Award in 2001, Franzen weaves a web of intertwining vignettes, in which each member of the Lambert family is portrayed. On more than 600 pages, he demonstrates the intricate dynamics of guilt, revenge, search for approval and atonement from which the family members suffer. As Gary, the oldest son, remarks on his mother's incomprehensible stubbornness, the issues of the characters appear to be symptoms "of a larger malaise" (169).[34] And it is this larger malaise of American culture in the late 1990s that Franzen sets out to describe in his Great American Novel (cf. Davis 162, Strecker 123).

In a review of the novel, the *Village Voice* describes *The Corrections* as a novel about "family [...] money, the market, big pharma, unbridled Russian death capitalism, the goofiness of academic American postmodernism, gourmet cooking, therapy, and, maybe above all else, passive aggression" (Baron n. pag.). Michiko Kakutani from *The New York Times* describes *The Corrections* as "a sort of American 'Buddenbrooks'" and as

> a harrowing portrait of America in the late 1990's – an America deep in the grip of that decade's money madness and sick with envy, resentment, greed, acquisitiveness and self-delusion, an America committed to the quick-fix solution and determined to try to medicate its problems away. (n. pag.)

The Corrections is, above all else, "a novel of family dysfunction," Emily Eakin from *The New York Times* maintains (n. pag.). Franzen explicitly describes the Lambert family as a gerontocratic family, in which old age and aging play a central role, and Kunkel's interpretation of *The Corrections* as a "novel of generational conflict" further emphasizes the significance of age in the novel (Kunkel n. pag.).

In his essay "Perchance to Dream in the Age of Images: A Reason to Write Novels," which Franzen wrote five years before *The Corrections* was published, he discusses the topic of age or aging. Franzen demonstrates a

---

33 Kunkel provides a list of the characters' ages in his review "Treatment for Therapy" (n. pag.).
34 The notion of a "larger malaise" appears when Enid experiences a painful emptiness in her life, which becomes apparent in her obsession with Christmas.

heightened sense of temporality and shows himself as a keen observer and concurrent victim of the "ephemerality of every story or trend of fashion or issue" (42). Franzen relates the fast pace of consumer culture, which he calls "a form of planned obsolescence," to the difficulties that fiction writers encounter when non-fictional texts, television, and Hollywood are much more popular and catch the readers' and critics' attention (cf. 39, 42). He feels compelled to "Address the Culture and Bring News to the Mainstream" (54) and thus sees himself in the predicament of needing to find a way out of "the hegemony of overnight obsolescence" without "confirming and furthering it" (42). Franzen's own response is his belief in the value of the novel to *not* offer fast, binary solutions to problems. He continues to believe in a form of fiction "that raises more questions than it answers" (53). Franzen's concept of planned obsolescence in consumer culture evokes a sensibility to the cultural meanings of age that is similar to Margaret Morganroth Gullette's observations on the fashion cycle in consumer culture (see Chapter 4.4). In his article, Franzen addresses a feared obsolescence of the value of novels in consumer culture and, in his novel *The Corrections*, this notion of obsolescence seems to be transferred to the topic of age and aging and its consequences on a Midwestern family.

References to age appear frequently in *The Corrections* and often they describe the biological or chronological effects of aging for Enid and Alfred Lambert and the consequences that old age entails for their three children Gary, Chip, and Denise. Denise's role is unique in this context because she is far from old age and, yet, she is repeatedly described as looking old or behaving inappropriately for her age. References to old age amplify the fact that Denise is a deeply torn, self-destructive, and complicated character with severe problems when it comes to relationships and love.

"Too Young to Be So Old"

The fictional Midwestern town of St. Jude is the Lambert family's hometown and, named after the "[p]atron saint of hopeless causes" (467), it sets the tone of the novel, in which all of the characters desperately strive for personal happiness and sanity. It is in this town, which is described as a town of "gerontocratic suburbs" (3), a place of "stillness" and "deadness" (201), in which Denise, the youngest child of the Lambert family, grew up. Over the course of the novel, the reader learns that for Denise, her family was a dark place of old people. When she visits an industrial site in Philadelphia with her boss Brian Callahan, the mood of decay and rotting reminds her of her family.

> [S]he recognized the mood from having been born into a family of older people who kept mothballed wool and iron things in ancient boxes in the basement. She'd gone to school in a bright modernity and come home every day to an older, darker world. (445)

Old age is a pervasive and influential factor in Denise's life. Not only does she come from a gerontocratic world, her life choices also bind her to older men. Denise has two affairs with men twice her age, Don Armour and Ed Sterling, before she marries a chef, Emile Berger, whom her mother Enid describes as *"too OLD for her"* because he "is going to be an old man in not too many years" (60, 141; original emphasis). Denise is twenty-three when she marries middle-aged Emile Berger, who is an "asylum" for her and who makes her feel "infinitely adult" (438). These feelings, however, do not last. Their teacher-disciple relationship (with him being the experienced chef and her being the trainee) soon reverses when Denise tries to "teach *him* a thing or two" (438; original emphasis). Emile, however, does not take Denise seriously. This lack of recognition by her husband-mentor causes a change of heart in Denise:

> She felt more skilled and ambitious and *hungry* than her white-haired husband. She felt as if, while working and sleeping and working and sleeping, she'd aged so rapidly that she'd passed Emile and caught up with her parents. Her circumscribed world of round-the-clock domestic and workplace togetherness seemed to her identical to her parents' universe of two. She had old-person aches in her young hips and knees and feet. She had scarred old-person hands, she had a dry old-person vagina, she had old-person hands prejudices and old-person politics, she had an old-person dislike of young people and their consumer electronics and their diction. She said to herself: 'I'm too young to be so old.' (438-9)

The repeated references to Denise's premature aging evoke stereotypical cultural imaginaries associated with old age, such as loss of vitality and libido, stubbornness, stagnation, and conservatism as well as dissociation from other generations (see Chapter 2.2). The incongruity between Denise's subjective old age and her chronological youthful age indicates the looming crisis in Denise's marriage. But there is more to this incongruity.

Denise is only properly introduced in the fifth of seven chapters, entitled "The Generator," in which Franzen focuses entirely on Denise and her relationships and conflicts. In the earlier chapters, Denise is described through the reactions she triggers in the other characters. She has a particularly strong effect on her mother and her brother Gary, who repeatedly use age references when they criticize Denise's behavior. According to Enid, for instance, Denise's marriage with Emile Berger, in whose restaurant she works full-time, is detrimental to her daughter's youth. Not only is Emile too old for Denise, she is also "ruining her hands and wasting her youth" (138) by being immature, overly romantic, and impractical in her devotion to this man and her job (cf. 139). Enid cannot get over the fact that her daughter "had just turned twenty-three and had a beautiful face and figure and her whole life ahead of her" and is now dating a person like Emile who is so much older (139). Interestingly, Enid is unsure about the alternatives: "As to what exactly a young woman was supposed to do with her physical charms while she waited for the maturing years to pass, now that girls no longer got married quite so young, Enid was, to be sure, somewhat vague" (139). And yet, Enid's judgment is clear: Her daughter is off-track in terms of age-appropriate behavior and, therefore, Denise does not match Enid's personal imaginaries of a normal life course.

Enid's normative understanding of life courses surfaces in her wish to have a daughter who behaves like the other young people in St. Jude, who – like the gerontocratic environment of the town – seem to fulfill traditional standards of marriage. Enid's ideals are evoked when she describes the weddings of Denise's peers. These "good St. Jude Kids" are described with adjectives such as nice, charitable, good, super young, polite to older people, upbeat, loving, stable, and traditional (cf. 135). These features constitute the values and virtues that inform Enid's normative understanding of how young adults should behave. Enid perceives a "miracle of niceness" when she looks at the children from other families (135).

[Y]oung men of this caliber [i.e. those who are nice and traditional] continued, even as the twentieth century drew to a close, to be *the norm* in suburban St. Jude. All the young fellows she'd known [...] all these clean-cut and *handsome* young men (whom Denise, as a teenager, to Enid's quiet rage, had dismissed with her look of "amusement"), had marched and would be marching down heartland Protestant aisles and exchanging vows with nice, normal girls. (136; original emphasis)

Besides the idea of youthfulness – the adjective 'young' is mentioned three times – "matching" is one of Enid's main concerns. Enid believes that couples should have "similar backgrounds and ages and educations" (136). When a couple does not match in this respect, when for example "the bride would be heavier or significantly older than the groom," Enid feels sorry for them and "just *knew* the marriage was going to be a struggle from day one" (137; original emphasis). Her daughter's match, Enid imagined, would be a "tall, broad-shouldered, possibly Scandinavian young man" whom she would marry in an elegant wedding (137). Enid's deliberations serve as a dramatic built-up to Denise's disclosure of having married a 'non-matching' man, namely Emile Berger, who is twice her age. When Enid learns about her daughter's marriage, she gets sick. The condition of Enid's health and Denise's (age-)inappropriate behavior thus appear to be causally connected in the narrative succession of events. And this linking between age-inappropriate behavior and sickness is only the first of many instances in which age references appear as a metaphoric practice.

Enid's understanding of norms surfaces prominently in a cautionary tale that she repeatedly tells to Denise, namely the story of Norma Greene, a former friend of Enid's (cf. 142, 475, 491). Again, Franzen links Enid's notions of "*the norm*" – and it is probably no coincidence that the woman's name is Norm-a – with references to age. Norma had been involved with a much older, married man, who had promised her repeatedly and for years that he would leave his wife. Norma had hoped and waited for a happy ending – her surname Greene alludes to this hopeful attitude – but after years, Norma realizes that her lover will never leave his wife and feels that she has become too old to find a new, younger partner or to have children herself. While Enid understands the appeal of an older partner who can afford luxuries and has already achieved some status in life, she clearly objects to Norma's choice: Norma had "gone on dates with other men, but they were younger and they didn't seem matoor to her – Floyd was fifteen years older and very matoor, and I do understand how an older man has a matoority that can make him attractive to a younger woman" (143). This overuse of "matoor" makes Enid's monologue sound ridiculous. Nevertheless, Enid makes her point: Timing is crucial in a woman's life, and older men can be distracting in that respect. With her cautionary tale, Enid condemns her daughter's decision and predicts a tragic ending for Denise's marriage.

The cautionary tale also implies another judgment: Not only does Enid sanction Denise's choice to marry an older man, she also insinuates that Denise might currently be in an extramarital relationship with a married man (which is true at that point in the novel). Denise understands this implication immediately and suspects that Gary has given away her secret. Even though Denise rejects her mother's accusation, Enid is convinced that Denise has imposed a second assault on her mother's sense of morality. In short, one can say that Enid's understanding of the norm is informed by youthfulness and proper timing. Immoral or deviant behavior, on the contrary, is associated with old age or age-inappropriateness.

Gary shares his mother's attitude regarding life decisions and life courses and also believes that Denise is behaving age-inappropriately. He condemns her behavior by labeling her as prematurely old. According to Gary, Denise is wasting her life.

Denise at thirty-two was still beautiful, but long hours at the stove had begun to cook her youthful skin into a kind of terra-cotta mask that made Gary a little more anxious each time he saw her. She was his baby sister, after all. Her years of fertility and marriageability were passing with a swiftness to which he was attuned and she, he suspected, was not. Her career seemed to him an evil spell under the influence of which she worked sixteen-hour days and had no social life. Gary was afraid – he claimed, as her oldest brother, the *right* to be afraid – that by the time Denise awakened from this spell she would be too old to start a family. (237-8; original emphasis)

This passage clearly indicates Gary's normative and judgmental ideas on life courses and the problems he has with people who violate his expectations. The disciplinary objective behind Gary's rigid views is expressed in an urgency that he tries to impart to Denise: "Well, just remember," he says to her, "there's more to life than cooking. You're at a stage now where you need to start thinking about what you really want and how you're going to get it" (251). The task that Gary believes Denise should address soon resembles the developmental tasks formulated by Erikson or Havighurst, namely bearing a child and starting a family.

Clearly, Gary imposes his own sense of a 'good' and 'normal' life on his sister's life course decisions. At the same time, Franzen makes clear that Denise's non-conformity also affects her brother on a personal level.

It frustrated him that people could so happily drop out of the world of conventional expectations; it undercut the pleasure he took in his home and job and family; it felt like a unilateral rewriting, to his disadvantage, of the rules of life. (566)

Realizing that Denise's deviance is rewarded with professional success and public recognition and noticing how Denise shows off her 'otherness' instead of being ashamed by it, Gary feels that his own rule-abiding life has been undermined. The sacrifices he made to establish his normal life lose value and his disciplinary authority is challenged or resisted by Denise.

References to age emphasize the dual effect of Denise's age-inappropriate behavior. Her deviance rewrites Gary's (and her mother's) rules of life. And, similar to the references to age in *Little Children*, the disciplinary function of marginalizing a character through age references is complicated by the fact that the authority behind Gary's and Enid's disciplinary endeavors is questioned over the course of the novel. Being diagnosed as depressed by his wife Caroline and eventually surrendering to her judgment on his failing mental health, Gary has actually lost the grounds on which he bases his moral superiority (cf. 209). He can only passively observe that right and wrong, healthy and insane, young and old fall together, which undermine his binary convictions of righteousness. Like Perrotta, Franzen thus points to the brittle ground on which moral judgments are based and, simultaneously, he creates an important link that recurs in Denise's relationship with her father, namely the connection between references to age and the topic of (mental) health.

A similar porosity of moral authority can be detected in Enid. Even though Enid has strict definitions of normal behavior and good decision-making, she herself has made a poor decision in the choice of her husband. As a young woman, Enid was looking for financial security and emotional happiness and when she met Alfred, she perceived him as "a full-lipped thick-haired well-muscled boy in a man's shape and a man's suits" (308). References to age stages indicate a crucial ambivalence in Alfred, who is attributed a boyish as well as a mature and manly side. This ambivalence recurs when Enid assesses her decision years later:

What to believe about Al Lambert? There were the old-man things he said about himself and the young-man way he looked. Enid had chosen to believe the promise of his looks. Life then became a matter of waiting for his personality to change. (308-9)

Alfred did not change over the years. While his looks still keep reminding Enid of the young boy she sees in him, his old-man speeches are now predominant. Apparently, Enid made the wrong choice by getting confused with the simultaneous boyish and manly appearance of Alfred. When Denise seems to make a similar mistake by choosing a man who is not age-appropriate, Enid sees her own poor judgment repeated.

In the Lambert family, corrections are an all-pervasive endeavor. Not only are the children "[c]orrecting their parents' lives by their own, they also have been subjected to corrections," as Kunkel observes ("Treatment for Therapy" n. pag.). In Denise's case, the corrections are rooted in a conflict that Franzen describes as prenatal. On the one hand, this conflict is created by Enid choosing the wrong husband. On the other hand, Alfred is also responsible for Denise's issues. When Enid was pregnant with Denise, Alfred raped his wife. As a result of this domestic violence, as the narrative suggests, Denise learned even before her birth that her parent's relationship is doomed. "[T]he unborn child could see as clearly as anyone. She had ears and eyes, fingers and a forebrain and a cerebellum, and she floated in a central place. She already knew the main hungers" (318). Due to Alfred's violence towards his wife, the unborn Denise is "already drenched in sticky knowledge" (322). Alfred's guilt towards his daughter spurs his wish to "make corrections" but he soon has to understand that "he'd squirted such filth on her when she was helpless. She'd witnessed such scenes of marriage, and so of course, when she was older, she betrayed him. What made correction possible also doomed it" (323). Later in the novel, when Denise reflects upon the Callahan marriage, "that other married couple in her life, that other incompatible pair," it becomes clear how damaged Denise actually is: Her parents had "let the proxy war unfold inside their daughter's head" (496). A profound doubt in loving relationships and her parent's internalized conflict are so deeply rooted in Denise's psyche that she considers the break-up of the Callahan couple as a comparatively easy task: "*Easy for you guys*, she thought. *You can split in two*" (496; original emphasis).

For Denise, however, her parents' conflict has become part of her personality and her wish to free herself from this burden turns out to be a profoundly self-destructive endeavor. As a result, most of Denise's relationships are somehow connected to her parents – either because the partners remind Denise of her parents or because the men are little younger than her father.

Looming Crises and Age-Inappropriate Relationships

Whenever Denise's relationships with men are described, age plays a major role because Denise only seems to be drawn to much older men whereas men her own age are entirely unattractive to her (cf. 420, 428, 435-6). Denise had her first affair at eighteen with Don Armour, a colleague of her father's who was twice her age, married, and had children – like her own father Alfred. When Denise and Don start flirting, references to both childhood and old age recur. These references describe the complex dynamic between the unlikely couple. Armour's physical appearance, for instance, is described both as young and old, similar to Enid's impression of Alfred. On the one hand, "[h]e wasn't good-looking. His head seemed too large, his hair was thinning" (421). At the same time, Denise is aware of the "boyish whorl of his pencil-gray hair" (425). The fact that he drives "a big American sedan similar to Denise's mother's, only older" (426) establishes yet another link between Don Armour and Denise's parents.

When Denise and Don have sex in her bedroom, Denise

> felt returned to a childhood world of Grimm and C.S. Lewis where a touch could be transformative. His hands made her hips into a woman's hips, his mouth made her thighs into a woman's thighs, her whatever into a cunt. These were the advantages of being wanted by someone older – to feel less like an ungendered marionette, to be given a guided tour of the state of her morphology, to have its usefulness elucidated by a person for whom it was just the ticket.
> Boys her own age wanted *something*, but they didn't seem to know exactly what. (428; original emphasis)

Through her alliance with an older man, Denise matures into a woman. Her sexual coming of age, however, does not fully match a typical coming-of-age story because Denise's first sexual experiences with an older man are a matter of maturing only on the outside. What is actually happening, as I want to suggest, is an act of revenge disguised in a maturation plot of sexual awakening.

Moreover, the references to age complicate the situation. Denise is not described as a teenager, which she is at that point, but as a child who believes in magical worlds and fairytales. Her childlike state is further emphasized when Don Armour forces Denise to have oral sex.

> Kneeling by the bed, he drew the sheet up over her shoulder and stroked her head as she had to assume he often stroked his daughters' heads [...] Then the theater of his stroking expanded into regions that she had to assume were off-limits with his daughters. (430)

When Denise whimpers, Don Armour pushes "her southward" (430). The references to childhood clearly evoke incest and pedophilia. The connection between Don's abuse of a childlike Denise and Alfred's rape of his wife, when she was pregnant with Denise, suggests that Denise's infatuation with older men is somehow related to her father's trespass.

Denise's affair with Don Armour is clearly conflictual. On the one hand, her affair with an older man helps her mature – at least in terms of the rite of passage that her loss of virginity signifies. On the other hand, it is this man who forces her into the position of a helpless child. This situation not only repeats her mother's powerlessness but also questions her newfound maturity. Denise's relation with this older man turns out to be a deeply self-destructive endeavor. And, it is also destructive for her father: A decade later, Denise learns that Don Armour used the affair to blackmail Alfred out of his job and retirement funds. The consequences of Denise's age-inappropriate affair thus have powerful repercussions.

In the fifth chapter, Franzen continues to describe Denise's personal development as a young woman via her age-inappropriate relationships. Again, Denise has an affair with a man twice her age. Again, this man, Ed Sterling, the father of a college friend, is married. Denise once describes to her brother Gary what makes married, older men so attractive to her: "You see a person with kids [...] and you see how happy they are to be a parent, and you're attracted to their happiness. Impossibility is attractive. You know, the safety of dead-ended things" (251). Clearly, Denise's faith in relationships is deeply disrupted. Not only does she foreclose that she might ever have a happy relationship herself, she also implicitly undermines those relationships around her that seem to be happy. The third, much older man who Denise dates is the man she marries, Emile Berger, much to the chagrin of her mother Enid. When this marriage fails, Denise has her first lesbian relationship with Becky Hemerling, which is also deeply dysfunctional and which ends when Denise realizes that "she wasn't a lesbian after all" (441).

Being professionally very successful, Denise is still searching for private happiness when she meets the Callahan family. Brian Callahan offers Denise the position of executive chef in his new restaurant, The Generator, and introduces her to his family. Brian is married to Robin Passaforo and has two daughters. The Callahan family becomes a surrogate family to Denise, and Denise seamlessly integrates into this union (cf. 450; 469-70). The harmony, however, does not last long, and Denise's inner conflict surfaces again and radiates its destructive force.

Brian's age is not specified, but we can assume that he is the same age as his wife Robin, who is three years older than Denise. In the description of Brian, telling references to age are used: He is a man with "winning blue eyes and sandy hair and little-boy freckles" (442). It is, however, not the "boy" in Brian that Denise falls in love with. When Brian surprises Denise with a trip to an industrial site in Philadelphia, the place where he wants to open his new restaurant, Denise is reminded of her gerontocratic hometown. The industrial site triggers associations of oldness, decay, and waste. It is in this scene that Franzen describes Denise's home as a "family of older people," "an older, darker world" (445). Denise is impressed by the place, as she is by Brian. When Brian and Denise then embark on a food journey through Europe, Denise learns about Brian's marital problems and is convinced that their marriage will not last. And indeed, soon after, Brian tries to seduce Denise. When he kisses her, Denise is reminded of Don Armour (cf. 457), her first age-inappropriate affair. When Brian continues kissing her, Denise feels a "Robin-faced balloon of *wrongness*" swell inside her and she stops Brian. Eventually, Brian and Denise end their affair and Denise becomes sexually involved with Robin.

Denise's attraction to Robin evolves slowly and is also accompanied by scattered references to age. Robin is described, for example, as wearing the clothes of a graduate student (cf. 403, 493). When Denise is on her way to visit Robin's Garden Project, she notices several signs of both freshness and decay in the streets and houses that she passes.

Early autumn in Philadelphia brought smells of fresh seawater and tidewater, gradual abatements in temperature [...] Denise passed an old woman in a housecoat standing watch while two dusty men unloaded Acme groceries from a corroded Pinto's hatchback [...] Friable houses with bedsheet curtains. Expanses of fresh asphalt that seemed to seal the neighborhood's fate more than promise renewal. (461)

When she arrives at Robin's garden, it is a garden "full of childhood memory" (462). In the following months, Denise and Robin get closer and Denise realizes her predicament: "She had a thing for a straight woman who was married to a man whom she herself might have liked to marry. It was a reasonably hopeless case. And St. Jude gave and St. Jude took away" (471). In the following spring, Robin and Denise get closer. When they have sex for the first time, Denise enters a "new territory" because it is the first time that she experiences sex in a new way, with ease and pleasure, and realizes that "only now, at the age of thirty-two, did she *get* what all the fuss was about" (480-1; original emphasis). When Denise is on her way to see Robin another time, references to adolescence suggest Denise's youthful exhilaration as she notices "the skins of adolescent eggplants, young peppers and cukes and sweet corn, pubescent cantaloupes" (481). These references are ambivalent, however, because the light reflected in the skins of the plants is the "compromised" light of a city with drugs, filth, diseases, and pollution. The idyll of the new couple is interrupted when Brian surprises Denise and Robin in their love nest. Even though he is oblivious of what is happening, Denise feels "the bad child's impulse to cry when caught red-handed" (482). At the same time, she realizes that Brian reminds her of her father: A chair broke during Robin's und Denise's lovemaking and when Brian picks up the remains of the chair, Denise is "pierced now by the resemblance to Alfred in his intelligent sympathy for the broken object" (482).

From now onwards, the references to Denise's parents increase and it becomes ever more apparent that Denise's corrective impulse to free herself from her parents' legacy only leads her deeper into the familiar spiral of guilt, dependency, and self-destruction. When Denise secretly goes into the marital bedroom of Brian and Robin, she is reminded of her parents' bedroom.

As she lay down on the unmade parental bed, she remembered the smell and the quiet of the St. Judean summer afternoons when she would be left alone in the house and could be, for a couple of hours, as weird as she wanted. (484)

When Denise discovers a condom wrapper and realizes that Robin and Brian still have sex, she feels betrayed and jealous and, soon after, Robin and Denise break up.

Shortly after the break-up, Denise is fired and loses the woman she loves, the surrogate family with which she felt at home, and the prestigious job that made her famous in the culinary scene. Denise starts dating and continues to have age-inappropriate relationships with other women. This time, however, she is not dating older partners but much younger women, namely a high school graduate and a college student (cf. 580). Hence, references to age indicate highly conflictual relationships suggesting that Denise's attempt to emancipate herself from her dysfunctional family heritage only draws her deeper into self-destruction.

Triggers of Diseases

In *The Corrections*, the references to age are also linked with physical and mental diseases. This association structures the narrative in such a way that each time Alfred and Enid learn about another of their daughter's age-inappropriate relationships, their health decreases and one of them becomes (permanently) sick. When Denise informs her parents on the phone about her marriage with Emile Berger, for example, Enid feels sick. When she comes out of the bathroom, she realizes that Alfred has changed and that his hands have started to shake violently (cf. 140). A week later, Alfred is diagnosed with Parkinson's and Enid cannot help but see a causal relation:

[A]n underground branch of [Enid's] intelligence persisted in connecting his disease with Denise's announcement and so in blaming her daughter for the subsequent plummeting of her own quality of life, even though Dr. Hedgepeth had stressed that Parkinson's was somatic in origin and gradual in its onset. [...] Enid was pretty well convinced that Denise and Emile had ruined her life. (140-1)

Franzen's description of Enid's irrational connection between Denise's marriage with Emile and her husband's deteriorating health stresses Enid's self-conception as the designated victim of an ungrateful family. Franzen continues to link Denise's deviance with the onset of spreading diseases in her family. When Alfred and Enid learn, for example, that Denise's age-inappropriate marriage has failed, Alfred's health deteriorates once more. In addition to Parkinson's, he is now also afflicted with dementia, mistaking sunflowers for children and being clearly confused.

In the sixth chapter, during the Christmas holiday in St. Jude, Denise learns that her father knew about her affair with his colleague Don Armour, who blackmailed Alfred for a better job position. Alfred was forced to accept early retirement, fearing that Denise's affair would otherwise become public and thus ruin the family's reputation. Out of shame, as it is suggested, Alfred even accepted a considerably smaller pension. From then on, Enid feels a sense of refusal in Alfred: He is no longer interested in other things and he becomes passive (despite his doctor's advice to remain active) and sits in his chair all day long (cf. 74). In unison, the Lambert family diagnose Alfred as depressed and Franzen implies two reasons that might have triggered Alfred's depressive state: On the one hand, as a workaholic, retirement left Alfred with nothing much to live for. On the other hand, the realization that his daughter betrayed him with a man twice her age nullifies his attempts to correct his own misdemeanor towards Denise. Denise's age-inappropriate relationships thus seem to inflict a succession of mental and physical illnesses on her family.

Franzen's interest in mental illnesses also appears in his essay "Perchance to Dream in the Age of Images: A Reason to Write Novels" from 1996. Franzen defines contemporary American culture by describing it as a

> reductively binary culture: you're either healthy or you are sick, you either function or you don't. And if that flattening of the field of possibility is precisely what's depressing you, you're inclined to resist participating in the flattening by calling yourself depressed. (44)

In this binary culture, Franzen argues, depression has lost its "social stigma" and "has become fashionable to the point of banality" (44).

In *The Corrections*, depression is one of the major themes and almost all of the characters are somehow affected by it. As I have tried to show, the onset of Alfred's depression is associated with references to age, specifically references to age-inappropriate behavior. And there are more examples, in which Franzen seems to bring together depression and age or aging. Gary, for instance, is highly aware of his own aging when he diagnoses himself with depression. His slowly surfacing acceptance of his mental state is concomitant with his realization "that he survived from day to day by distracting himself from underground truths that day by day grew more compelling and decisive. The truth that he was going to die" (182). Instead of linking Gary's awareness of aging and decline with a mid-life crisis, Franzen explains Gary's condition as depression and "Anhedonia," which is defined in the novel as a "physical condition characterized by inability to experience pleasure in normally pleasurable acts" (188).[35] When Enid, who constantly complains about the aches and pains of getting older (cf. 168), goes to see a doctor on a cruise ship for her anxiety attacks, she is prescribed Aslan, an antidepressant and "personality optimizer," which "exerts a remarkable blocking effect on 'deep' or 'morbid' shame" (366). Aslan is supposed to help Enid "feel emotionally more resilient [...] [m]ore flexible, more confident, happier" with herself and assist her in dealing with her husband's and her own rapid decline in the face of old age (371).[36]

Franzen pushes the topic of depression to absurdity when he describes a sales event that Gary and Denise attend in search of a solution for their father's Alzheimer's. They are presented the heal-it-all drug "Corecktall," which promises to be a panacea for all kinds of diseases, from Parkinson's to Alzheimer's to depression (217). The drug is even marketed as a cure for social misdemeanor with the potential to change "the brain of the criminal" for the better (238). Depression emerges here as a cash cow for the pharmaceutical industry. And, in extending the scope of the issue to a national and even global dimension, Franzen has one of the minor characters, a passenger on the cruise ship, wonder "if we're depressed because there's no frontier anymore. Because we can't pretend anymore there's a place no one's been. I wonder if aggregate depression is on the rise, world-wide" (379). In

---

35 Much of Gary's knowledge about his condition comes from fictitious self-help books (which his wife Caroline seems to devour) with such titles as *Feeling Great, Hands-Off Parenting: Skills for the Next Millennium* or *Middle Ground: How to Spare Your Child the Adolescence YOU Had.*

36 For a more detailed discussion of this connection, see my article "Depression and Aging in Jonathan Franzen's *The Corrections*" (forthcoming in 2014).

addition, Chip argues elsewhere that "the structure of the entire culture is flawed" because it can "define certain states of mind as 'diseased'" (35-6). This binary rationale of a socially contingent status of either health or disease is reminiscent of the binary opposite of youth and old age (see Chapter 2.2). Furthermore, as will become clear in the next chapter, Franzen's association between age and depression is not only an artistic decision.

4 Mental Health and Age

4.1 Positive Thinking and Entrepreneurial Selves

Quoting a French study,[1] the sociologist Alain Ehrenberg gives evidence for a causal relationship between age and depression.

Depressed people between twenty and twenty-nine years old have as many health problems as do non-depressed individuals between forty-five and fifty-nine years old; depressed women aged forty-five to fifty-nine have the health profile of a person over eighty. "Depressed people," the authors [of the CREDES study] write, "are old before their time." (181)

The CREDES study measures aging in terms of an increased liability to health problems and focuses on the physical dimension of aging. Being prematurely aged when one suffers from a mental illness like depression is thus directly connected to the materiality of the body. According to Ehrenberg, depression has become part of the public discourse and "people admit more readily to being depressed today than they did in the past" (181). The social stigma connected to depression seems to have softened. And yet, de-

---

[1] The study was conducted by a French research center, CREDES (Centre d'études et de documentation sur la santé). It found that between the early 1980s and the early 1990s, "the rate of depression increased 50 percent in France" (Ehrenberg 181).

spite the public acceptance of depression as a physical pathology, it is also a social fact (xxviii):

> [I]t is the situation of every individual in Western society [...] contemporary depression is the marriage between the traditional melancholia of the exceptional person and the modern egalitarian idea that anyone can be exceptional [...] I do not approach depression as a weakening of social bonds but, rather, as an attitude, a mindset heavy with multiple social practices and representations of ourselves in a society in which values associated with autonomy (e.g. personal choice, self-ownership, individual initiative) have been generalized. Depression, then, is a pathology of grandeur [...] Thus, depression brings together all the tensions of the modern individual. (xxx)[2]

Following Ehrenberg, depression is thus linked with particular sociocultural values and virtues, which also appear in discussions of old age and life courses, such as positive aging and doing biography (see Chapters 2.2 and 3.3). Jonathan Franzen suggests a similar association of depression to a social and cultural setting when he has his character Chip argue that consumer economy is a crucial factor in producing the tensions of the modern individual.

> "I'm saying the structure of the entire culture is flawed," Chip said. "I'm saying the bureaucracy has arrogated the right to define certain states of the mind as 'diseased.' A lack of desire to spend money becomes a symptom of disease that requires expensive medication. Which medication then destroys the libido, in other words destroys the appetite for the one pleasure in life that's free, which means the person has to spend even *more* money on compensatory pleasures. The very definition of mental 'health' is the ability to participate in the consumer economy. When you buy into therapy, you're buying into buying. (*The Corrections*, 35-6)

---

2   According to Ehrenberg, melancholia once stood for the troubled self during the Age of Enlightenment and became the illness of the artist during the Romantic period (cf. xxx). At the turn of the last century, neurosis marked the anxiety of the bourgeoisie. And today, depression has become a democratic, egalitarian phenomenon, affecting everyone and therefore representing "the manifestation of the *democratization of the exceptional*" (218; original emphasis).

In Chip's reasoning, depression is primarily defined by a lack, namely a lack of desire to participate in consumer culture. Insinuating that a particular lack or deficiency activates a spiral of social practices that aim at reintegrating a person into the circle of consumer economy, Chip evokes a rationale that we have already encountered with the cultural imaginaries associated with old age, which is also often defined as a lack – a lack of physical health, physical strength, vitality, attractiveness, productivity or efficiency. What are the "lacks" or losses that define depression?

In his study *The Weariness of the Self: Diagnosing the History of Depression in the Contemporary Age* (1998), Ehrenberg examines how depression has turned into a social and cultural pathology that is characteristic of the late twentieth century. In a social history of depression, Ehrenberg traces how the invention of antidepressants in 1957, followed by the launch of Prozac in 1988, led to the medical diagnosis of a widespread unease and weariness. According to Ehrenberg, the symptoms of depression are "illness, unhappiness, misfortune, and failure" (xxix). Depression constitutes a "mood disorder that turns all feelings grey" and it is characterized by [p]sychomotor slowing, sleep disorder, apathy, indifference, and a lack of initiative (cf. 167). The depressed individual suffers from a "pathology of motivation" and a "pathology of time" (233) because the depressed self cannot project himself or herself into the future and therefore has no future. Therefore, "[f]rozen action [e.g. apathy] sculpts the depressive universe. It is a kind of 'stoppage of time'" (188). Moreover,

[t]he depressed person has trouble forming projects; he or she lacks energy and the minimum motivation to carry them out. Inhibited, impulsive, or compulsive, she has trouble communicating with herself and others. With no project, motivation, or communication, the depressed person stands in exact opposition to our social norms. (233)

Ehrenberg's definition of the depressed person is reminiscent of the stereotypes towards the elderly. While the old person violates the imperative of youthfulness, the depressed person breaches the requirements of being the center of action and the planning office of his or her identity and life (cf. Beck, *Risk Society* 135). After all, as Ehrenberg argues, "[a]ction these days has become an individual enterprise. [...] Individual initiative has moved to the top position among criteria that measure a person's value" (Ehrenberg

183). Tellingly, the antidepressant Prozac has been labeled the "action pill" (xvii). A central criterion of depression thus consists in a lack of energy or activity.

Ehrenberg situates the individual in a social environment in which the self is perceived as an entrepreneur who follows the culture's norms of "project, motivation and communication" (233).[3] The aim of every personal endeavor consists in conquering your personal identity, and, evidently, this idea of a conquest evokes the image of a powerful and heroic warrior who seizes his identity like an estate or property (cf. 183). Possession and ownership clearly resonate in this imagery and, therefore, Ehrenberg argues that "ownership of the self has become our lifestyle" (221). Strategies for conquering and owning (oneself) not only represent activities that echo belligerent (and maybe stereotypically masculine) features, they also become markers in the process of identity construction. These features are highly dependent on "personal resourcefulness" and the question is no longer "'Do I have the right?' but, rather, 'Am I able to?'" (222-3). Following Ehrenberg, identity formation is thus a question of capacity, competence, and power. Hence, rules or laws, whether religious or secular, no longer constitute the sole background for decision-making. Instead, the normative framework consists of abilities and skills, of personal initiative and motivation – and of choice. The individual is thrown back onto himself or herself. Self-responsibility, which dominates the discourses of age and aging so profoundly, thus also plays into depression.

The flipside of this entrepreneurial form of self-construction, as Ehrenberg argues, lies in the fact that this new freedom of identity construction is paid with a high price.

The individual, free from morality, creating herself by herself and aspiring to the superhuman (acting upon her own nature, surpassing herself, being more than herself), is now our reality. But, instead of possessing the strength of the masters, she turns out to be fragile, lacking in being, weary of her sovereignty and full of complaints.

---

3   Ehrenberg's academic work demonstrates his fascination with entrepreneurial concepts and his notion of the self is intricately connected to Foucault's idea of the self as an entrepreneur, a concept which, as he maintains, has become "a reference point for socio-political action" since the 1980s (*Weariness of the Self* 183). Also see Ehrenberg's study *Le culte de la performance* (1991).

[...] Depression, then, is melancholia plus equality, the perfect disorder of the democratic human being. It is *the inexorable counterpart of the human being who is her/his own sovereign*. We are not speaking of the human being who has acted badly but, rather, of the human being who cannot act. Depression is not conceived in terms of law, what is allowed and what is forbidden, but in terms of *capacity*. (218-9; original emphasis)

Those who fail to perform adequately face feelings of inadequacy and deficiency, which are amplified by a seemingly clear attribution of responsibility: Since motivation comes from the inside, a lack of motivation must be the fault of the individual. From this perspective, it is not surprising that Denise's mother links her daughter's failure (or unwillingness) to find a suitable husband with a moral deficiency in Denise (cf. Franzen, *The Corrections* 135).

The similarities with the agenda of positive aging are intriguing. As discussed in Chapter 2.2, the notion of successful aging relies on a similar morality that celebrates the active and busy body and that puts the blame of an old, unhealthy, and passive body on individuals because they have let themselves go and have neglected their duties to take care of their bodies through exercise, diet, and the like. David Ekerdt identifies the agenda of compulsive activity promoted by those who support positive aging as a "busy ethic" (239). Similar to the "work ethic," the busy ethic allows retirees to justify their leisure time and pensions by compelling them to activate a "busy ethic" which legitimates leisure as "earnest, occupied, and filled with activity" (239). (This pressure is also exerted on Alfred Lambert in Franzen's *The Corrections*.) The "busy ethic" that defines retirement today thus establishes retiree's leisure as a morally desirable lifestyle because it "defends retired people against judgments of obsolescence, it gives definition to retirement role, and it 'domesticates' retirement by adapting retired life to prevailing societal norms" (240). Staying busy is thus not only a strategy for fending off aging. It is a psychological device that is specific to a culture that ascribes moral values to work. Therefore, "busy bodies," as Katz maintains, constitute an ideal in later life, at least in neoliberal societies (cf. *Cultural Aging* 121ff). Powell argues that "older people are exhorted, indeed expected, to become entrepreneurs in all spheres and to accept responsibility for the management of risk" (Powell 107). Those who do not follow the "busy body" agenda face practices of discipline, control, and exclusion and are labeled as "problem persons" (Katz, *Cultural Aging* 138).

Positive Thinking

Mental health discourses are influenced by similar disciplinary regimes that define proper social behavior. The cultural critic Barbara Ehrenberg demonstrates in her study *Smile or Die: How Positive Thinking Fooled America and the World* (2009) that positive thinking – note the terminological similarities with positive aging – represents a cultural agenda that is based on a binary logic of classifying social conduct: Either you are depressed or you learn to (and work on) thinking positively. Ehrenreich argues along the lines of Ehrenberg by referring to the widespread accessibility of antidepressants in the 1980s and the simultaneous surge of motivational literature and coaches. According to her observations, the self is the result of a constant effort of self-monitoring, hard work, self-modification, and resourcefulness (cf. 223). In this context, positive thinking emerges as a "mental discipline" and as a form of "social control" (202-3). The "thought control" is accomplished by the individuals themselves who believe that they 'only' need to change internally and work on their attitudes in order to bring about a change in their social reality (203). An individual's attitude is also affected by an imposed vocabulary, which encourages 'positive' expressions, such as victor, fighting, fierce, and brave, over words with negative connotations, such as patient or victim (cf. 26). According to Ehrenreich, the belligerent vocabulary is a symptom of megalomania, narcissism, and solipsism (cf. 190).[4]

Ehrenreich's analysis echoes some of the notions I have discussed in relation to positive aging, such as self-responsibility and failure. For example, the consequences that Ehrenreich draws from her observations are very similar to Jonathan Franzen's comment on the binary morality in American culture: "In this moral system, either you look on the bright side [...] – or

---

4   Ehrenreich's symptoms resemble the characteristics of entitlement and navel-gazing that journalists have located in contemporary young adults (cf. Alsop 2008, Lim 2007, or Twenge 2006). The title of Jean Twenge's study, for example, speaks for itself: *Generation Me: Why Today's Young Americans Are More Confident, Assertive, Entitled – and More Miserable Than Ever Before* (2006).

you go over to the dark side" (Ehrenreich 195). According to Ehrenreich, the normativity of "this ideological force in American culture" relies on the following classification of normal and deviant behavior: "[C]heerfulness is required, dissent a kind of treason" (31). Attitude thus becomes a marker of differentiation: Cheerfulness categorizes a person as normative, while skepticism, sadness, or inactivity are signs for deviance. Ehrenreich criticizes this culture of oppressive and enforced positivity arguing that it is delusional, unrealistic, and dangerous (cf. 10-13).[5]

In tracing the consequences of the positive thinking ideology, Ehrenreich establishes a set of binaries within which individuals negotiate their position in contemporary Western cultures. These binaries are mutually exclusive and entail serious consequences: One option is to be excessively naive and positive, active, self-motivating, and unrealistically optimistic; the other option is to be depressed, discouraged, apathetic, weak, and weary, which is accompanied by a diagnosis of being 'ill' or deviant (cf. 5, 8f., 22f., 54-57). If people feel failed and depressed, nobody else is to blame but the individuals themselves because, as the moral system in Ehrenreich's study purports, they actively chose to be losers (cf. 43).

These rigid binaries of success and failure, normal and perverse, inside and outside, also surface in the novels and films that I have discussed so far. Dichotomies of moralities and norms form the backdrop against which (or within which) characters like Toula, Todd, or Sarah try to position themselves by negotiating their lifestyles, life decisions, and career choices. These dichotomies seem to be closely connected with the cultural imaginaries linked with age and aging, depression, and other forms of social 'inappropriateness.' The characters, as I have demonstrated in the previous chapters, call themselves (or are called) old or age-inappropriate and, repeatedly, they consider themselves losers who have failed on a personal level. What does it mean to be a loser in a culture that stresses self-responsibility and self-monitoring? And why is the notion of being a loser so prominent in people who have age experiences?

---

5   One of the examples for the destructive force of positive thinking that Ehrenreich mentions is the financial crisis of 2007, when a cheerful optimism silenced voices of doubt and reason and led to a massive national and international economic crisis.

Crises of the Weary Self: Losers vs. Entrepreneurs

In his study *Born Losers: A History of Failure in America* (2005), the American historian Scott A. Sandage examines the cultural meaning of failure in American society and undertakes a cultural reading of failure in the United States of the nineteenth and twentieth century.[6] In Sandage's argument, the role of economy takes center stage. Discerning a particular rhetoric of failure, Sandage notices that the vocabulary of the nineteenth century increasingly associates economic terms with morality. Originally, the word failure used to signify a breakdown of business, or "a breaking, becoming insolvent" as Noah Webster's dictionary affirms in 1828 (qtd. in Sandage 11-2). Failure was thus exclusively related to the business sphere. Only three decades later, the meaning of failure had extended to the self, signifying a "deficient self, an identity in the red" (2), or in Webster's terms, "some weakness in a man's character, disposition, or habit" (from the 1857 revision, qtd. in Sandage 12).[7] Failure thus evolved from a business term to a personal trait. 'Success' and 'failure' became classifications that appraised and categorized lives.

Likewise, depression is both an expression for an economic and a psychological condition. The *Oxford English Dictionary* defines depression, among other meanings, as a

> lowering in quality, vigour, or amount; the state of being lowered or reduced in force, activity, intensity, etc. In mod. use *esp.* of trade; spec. *the Depression*, the fi-

---

[6] Sandage claims that the American Dream not only reflects a scenario for success but also for failure because it gives everyone "the chance to be a born loser" (278). Sandage acknowledges that the "from-rags-to-riches" formula is increasingly treated with skepticism. However, he argues that the reason for failure is still ascribed to the person and represents a "deficiency of the self" (259). Failure is an individual responsibility that excludes social circumstances. It is perceived as a character trait and thus as one's destiny. Failure stories are thus deeply rooted in American culture and identity.

[7] The *OED* reports a similar etymology, noting 1642 as the first occurrence of the word in terms of a "failing to occur, be performed, or be produced." In 1702, "failure" is first mentioned in relation to business, implying the "fact of failing in business; bankruptcy, insolvency."

nancial and industrial 'slump' of 1929 and subsequent years. (n. pag.; original emphasis)

and as

[t]he condition of being depressed in spirits; dejection [...] Psychol. Freq. a sign of psychiatric disorder or a component of various psychoses, with symptoms of misery, anguish, or guilt accompanied by headache, insomnia, etc. (n. pag.)

Hence, in the English lexicon, economy and personal identity seem closely interwoven. Similarly, life narratives are often marked by a business vocabulary of measurement and balancing:

we 'take stock' of how we 'spend' our lives, take 'credit' for our gains, or try not to end up 'third rate' or 'good for nothing' [...] Someday, we hope, 'the bottom line' will show that we 'amount to something' [...] we 'balance' our whole lives, not just our accounts. (Sandage 265)

In a similar way, Peter Miller and Nikolas Rose argue that there is a discursive field connected to economy that uses "particular technical devices of writing, listing, numbering and computing that render a realm into discourse as a knowable, calculable and administrable object" (5). Business thus becomes "the dominant model for our outer and inner lives. Ours is an ideology of achieved identity; obligatory striving is its method, and failure and success are its outcomes" (Sandage 265).[8] Following Sandage, identity, failure, depression, and economy are thus closely connected and failure can lead to a "deficient self, an identity in the red" (2). When we remember how swiftly Verona in *Away We Go* associates her dire financial situation with her age and with her self-description as a loser, we can see how the metaphoric practice of age is linked with current discourses in contemporary American culture.

---

8   In an article on 'Countdown-Blogs' by thirty-year-olds, I have traced how this economic rhetoric influences the ways in which young adults negotiate their age awareness during a life transition by applying strategies of calculation, schemes, lists, and reviews. See "Let the Countdown Begin – Aging Experiences of Young Adults in Countdown Blogs" (2012).

The counter-image of the loser is the entrepreneur of the self,[9] a concept developed by the French philosopher, sociologist, and historian Michel Foucault in his lectures on governmentality and biopolitics at the Collège de France in 1979. Foucault interpreted the entrepreneur as a central metaphor of American neoliberalism and redefined human capital, enterprise, and the role of the individual within the economic system by applying an economic grid to the private sphere of family, marriage, household, parenting, or education (cf. *Naissance* 249-50). He found that American neoliberalism influences the worker in such a way that it expects him to develop from a passive object within an alienating system of exchange and consumption into an active economic subject who is no longer the dependent partner of exchange and satisfier of needs but an active producer of his own satisfaction (cf. 232).[10] Thus, in Foucault's theory, man no longer represents human capital within a large business machine but becomes an entrepreneur himself and of himself:

Homo oeconomicus is an entrepreneur, an entrepreneur of himself [...] being for himself his own capital, being for himself his own producer, being for himself the source of [his] earnings. (*Birth* 226)

According to Foucault, this redefined position of man within the workforce and within society also affects his social relations, which become susceptible to careful and constant scrutiny, cost-benefit analyses, and optimization (cf. 236, 247). Similarly to Sandage's observations, economization in Foucault's view not solely refers to money or the pecuniary outcome of an enterprise. Instead, economical reasoning permeates all aspects of individual

---

9   In the early nineteenth century, political economists such as David Ricardo, John Stuart Mill, or John Kells Ingram used the concept of the 'economic man' as a theoretical construct to understand and predict, in a laboratory-like situation, how man will react to a moral dilemma (cf. Rolle 122). Foucault differentiates between a classic concept of the 'homo oeconomicus,' in which man is "one of the two partners in the process of exchange," and the neoliberal understanding of the 'economic man,' which he develops in his lecture (*Birth* 226).

10 Foucault speaks of male workers and entrepreneurs only. For the sake of simplicity regarding the integration of quotes from Foucault's lectures, I will do so as well while implying the female worker and entrepreneur.

(or private) life and influences how people design their life courses and relations in life.

Living in a culture, in which one is expected to function as an entrepreneur, does not automatically produce entrepreneurs of the self. The character in Benjamin Kunkel's novel *Indecision*, Dwight Wilmerding, whom I will discuss in the next chapter, is the perfect example of a character who fails to be such an entrepreneur. In her study *Self-Help, Inc.: Makeover Culture in American Life* (2005), McGee describes the drastic repercussions of entrepreneurial thinking and suggests a counter-image to the entrepreneur of the self: the "belabored self," who is exhausted by his or her efforts to remain "marriageable and employable" (12), to create a sense of stability in a world that requires constant flexibility and mobility. The belabored self is constantly confronted with the frightening image of "endless insufficiency" and inadequacy (17 f.). He or she thus oscillates between "exhilaration and exhaustion" (169), always trying to be authentic, displaying effortlessness and boundless energy (cf. 171). Beyond constantly working on the self, the entrepreneur of the self is isolated, considering everybody else a competitor or rival. This "fantasy of a disengaged, masterful, rational, and controlling self" (173) has a serious downside: Not only is this fantasy based on the domination and exploitation of others, as McGee claims, it also bans the "failed and defective forms of selfhood – childhood, illness, disability, or aged infirmity" (174).

Benjamin Kunkel's (anti-)hero Dwight Wilmerding is a particularly interesting case of a failed and defective self. Dwight is not only a perpetual adolescent, he also suffers from a mental problem, abulia, which implies that he is incapable of making decisions. Dwight wavers between exhilaration and aimlessness. With his self-induced unemployment, being evicted from his apartment, and unable to commit to a girlfriend, he appears and sees himself as a loser. His acute age awareness is used in a playful and ironic way, particularly as Kunkel's novel is patterned on the coming-of-age plot. Dwight's sense of feeling old, however, is used in a much more complex way than as a simple sign of his delayed maturation.

4.2 BENJAMIN KUNKEL'S *INDECISION*

28-year-old Dwight Wilmerding is a former prep school student who went on to study philosophy in college and now lives in New York City. He works as "an assistant communications technician subcontracted to Pfizer" before he is "pfired" early in the novel (133; original emphasis). Dwight has no aim, no ambition, and he is diagnosed by his roommate with "abulia," a disease of the mind defined as "the impairment or even [...] the *loss* of your ability to make decisions" (31; original emphasis). Dwight is a typical perpetual adolescent, who sees no point in growing up or finding his place in life. He has compiled a long list of his own problems, which range from "ambivalence" and "laziness" to "lack of funds" and a "lack of Der Unternehmungsgrund der Individuums [sic]" and thus a lack for the "*ground for the individual's action*" (18, 32-3; original emphasis). Dwight is clearly not an entrepreneur of himself.

According to A.O. Scott, Dwight's situation represents a generational problem, which is caused by

> an alienation from his [Dwight's] own experience brought about by too much knowledge, too many easy, inconsequential choices, too much self-consciousness. Bred in a culture consecrated to the entitled primacy of the individual, he discovers that he lacks a self, a coherent identity, maybe a soul. He feels that he could be anyone. (Scott, "Among the Believers" n. pag.)

The many 'lacks' that Scott identifies are part of Dwight's sense of inappropriateness and failure, which increases when he remembers an upcoming High School reunion, when he loses his job, and when his lease expires and he has to leave his apartment and roommates. Borrowing money from his father, Dwight travels to Ecuador on vacation, where he meets Brigid – his travel mate, mentor, love interest, and future fiancée.

Indecision was published in 2005 and quickly became one of the top selling debut novels with 32-year-old debut author Benjamin Kunkel being lauded as the new "wunderkind" of the American literary scene (McInerney n. pag.).[11] The novel, told from the perspective of the first-person narrator

---

11 Kunkel is also the founding editor of the magazine *n+1* and a freelance writer for various prestigious American newspapers.

Dwight, is described a "memoir on the growth of my [Dwight's] mind" (237) and has frequently been associated with the genre of the *Bildungsroman* (see Kakutani 2005, McInerney 2005, Rosenberg 2011, Schäfer 2011). In his review of *Indecision*, Jay McInerney, for example, finds that the novel shares many features of the *Bildungsroman*, but, in the end, the generic *Bildungsroman* hero accepts the values of society whereas Kunkel's hero rejects the American consumer society, becomes a democratic socialist, and works for an organization that fights for Bolivian economic rights. Even though he enjoys the "fresh and funny" feel of the novel, McInerney wonders if *Indecision* is, after all, "nothing so much as a self-conscious, postmodern homage/parody of the genre" (n. pag.). Similarly, Schäfer problematizes the label of the *Bildungsroman* in her analysis of *Indecision*. According to Schäfer, who examines the aspect of self-narration in Kunkel's *Indecision*, the genre of the *Bildungsroman* is alluded to by the rite of passage Dwight experiences in Ecuador and by the "succession of various stages of self-recognition" that Dwight goes through (112). Schäfer finds that the concept of the *Bildungsroman* can only be applied to a certain extent because Dwight actually remains an "unchanged self" (120). At the end of the novel, Dwight is as materialist and competitive as before his conversion into a democratic socialist (cf. 130). Therefore, Schäfer argues, Dwight's transformation "is based on narrative self-fashioning rather than actual character change" (127).

Dwight Wilmerding has also been compared to Holden Caulfield, the hero from J.D. Salinger's *The Catcher in the Rye* (1951). And indeed, the similarities Kakutani finds between these two characters, who are over fifty years apart (in terms of publication), are surprising (cf. "Who's Afraid"). At the same time, many critics like A.O. Scott consider *Indecision* a very contemporary generational portrait, which sets Dwight apart from Holden Caulfield and which insinuates yet another interpretation of Dwight as a perpetual adolescent of the new millennium. From this perspective, Dwight appears as a "post-Grunge-era slacker" who "suffers an early midlife crisis" (McNally n. pag.). For John McNally, Dwight "had more advantages than most, yet he continues to live like an 18-year-old," whose "childlike innocence" makes him very likeable (n. pag.). Similarly, Kakutani argues that 28-year-old Dwight "acts like he's still 17" (n. pag.). According to Schäfer, Dwight lives an "adolescent life-style" which is "unfit for a 28-year-old" and which marks him as a "late bloomer," a "flat-out loser" who suffers from a "feeling of inadequacy" (110, 132). These interpretations of *Indecision* suggest that the central conflict in the novel is Dwight's chronological age and his actual behavior in relation to the cultural expectations of a man his age.

Dwight repeatedly reflects upon contemporary life by referring to sociological and cultural theories. He is described as a person who has a "sociological sense of [his] life" (32) and who feels like a "scrap of sociology blown into its designated corner of the world" (26). The novel evokes all kinds of cultural theories, such as the coercion to choose,[12] entrepreneurial selfhood, or the effects of consumer culture. Dwight reflects profusely upon his own situation, but, as the novel demonstrates, all his knowledge of philosophy or his sister's insight into cultural anthropology and psychoanalysis do not help Dwight. Instead, despite his intellectual resources, his sociological and philosophical insight only amplifies his navel-gazing, self-conscious, and undecided attitude. Dwight is unable (or unwilling) to conform to the expectations of his surroundings and therefore feels (and is treated) as an outsider.

The ironic tone of the novel further complicates a categorization of Dwight and his fictional memoir. McInerney stresses the "post-ironic" tone of the novel and its "hazy new frontier between sincerity and irony" (n. pag). Similarly, Schäfer finds that Dwight's journey to self-knowledge is a "comic quest" (105), which "playfully parodies the *bildungsroman*" (107; original emphasis) with its "self-reflective and self-ironic tone" (112). According to Schäfer, Dwight's "adventurous quest for an adult identity parodies the nostalgic search of twenty-something Americans for meaning in the post-ideological age of the early 2000s" (18). Kunkel comments upon the ambiguous use of irony in an interview on *NPR*:

The term is always misused, irony. I think when you sense a difference between what you mean to be and what you are, you're being ironic and you're essentially just being human. That's no particular aspect of any generation. But what irony referred to was a kind of an inability to take seriously anyone's thoughts or feelings

---

12 In the *NPR* interview, Kunkel explains that Dwight's predicament of indecision lies in the fact that he cannot deal with the "explosion of freedom without any sort of similar capacity to handle the opportunities that spread themselves before [him]" (n. pag.).

and ultimately an inability to take seriously one's self. And I think Dwight manages slightly by the end of the novel to begin to take himself a bit seriously. (Simon n. pag.)

McInerney agrees that the ironic tone changes over the course of the novel, presenting an ending that is "a hazy new frontier of hip sincerity, of irony subordinated to a higher calling" (n. pag.).

Irony also plays a central role in relation to the topic of age because the ironic tone in the novel is amplified by references to age. Dwight's age awareness, together with his mental condition, point to his non-conformity and deviance in a consumer-oriented, materialist, post-Fordist culture. At the same time, Kunkel presents Dwight as a character who does not suffer too severely under these circumstances and actually enjoys his ambiguous situation. From this perspective, Dwight – the belabored, pessimistic, and lethargic self who does not (or cannot) conceive of his life as an entrepreneurial project – shows a new facet of the perpetual adolescent and Kunkel seems to use this figure to underline the silliness of his protagonist's behavior and condition. Dwight's apathy is presented as a cliché, or, as Vaneetha, a woman Dwight dates sporadically, argues: He lives a cliché that is "not even a fresh cliché" (26).

"Age Sure Takes It's Toll:" Metaphors of Age and Time

Age is a recurring issue for Dwight and it is mentioned regularly when he comments upon his conduct or feelings. The most obvious examples occur when Dwight mentions the physical changes he observes in his body, which are quite exaggerated, as an older reader might claim. Dwight is proud, for instance, that he has not gone bald, but he notices that his hairline has receded (cf. 8-9). In Ecuador, he decides to "become the satisfied denizen of my somewhat flabby and already declining body" (174). He also realizes that a hangover at twenty-eight is more difficult for him to endure than ten years ago. "Age sure takes its toll," he concedes when he mentions that, after a night of heavy drinking, he feels like waking up with "a tag on my toe" (39). In these moments, he feels closer to death than to life (cf. 39). When Dwight visits his father, he recognizes his own graduation picture and is reminded of the passing of time: "College seems like a long time ago," Dwight muses (93). His father, however, relativizes his son's age awareness and emphasizes Dwight's lack of maturation: "Don't make a career out of your childhood or you'll never adapt yourself to any other" (93). Hence, while the father sees his son clinging to childhood, Dwight's comment suggests that, for him, childhood or adolescence are long gone. Apparently, references to age and experiences of temporality stand for contradictory emotions or states of mind – depending on who utters them and to which end.

In Dwight's case, references to age indicate the profound confusion that characterizes Dwight and, despite some references to old age, they predominantly refer to child-like or adolescent behavior. In Ecuador, for instance, Dwight has the impression that his backpack is handled "like an abducted child" (99) and this "kidnapping feeling" suggests how ambivalently he experiences the situation himself. When Dwight and Brigid travel through Ecuador, they "are sitting pressed together on a torn vinyl seat, knees up high like overgrown kids" (113). In the tram in Quito, references to childhood indicate that Dwight is an outsider in the tram (and, generally, in Ecuador): When the train stops for a longer amount of time, the passengers (and Brigid) begin to sing a mournful song until the tram resumes. "Such a musical people, the Ecuadoris," Dwight thinks, only to remark in the next sentence that he "felt left out along with the crying infants and sullen old men and wished to learn right away this apparently national song" (111). The references to childhood describe Dwight's sense of isolation and marginalization. He is different from the people around him and even though he would like to belong, he feels excluded.

Dwight also experiences a series of trigger moments that are accompanied by references to age. When Dwight loses his job right before the tenth reunion with his high school classmates and when he has to leave his room in the apartment he shared with friends, he first prides himself (and his roommates) on being immature:

Out of everybody we knew our immaturity was best-preserved, we dressed worst and succeeded least professionally – and at times I could get into feeling that for the old crowd to set foot on the scarred linoleum of our kitchen must be like entering this circling, slow eddy in the otherwise one-way flow of time. Outside was the streaming traffic, the money bazaar, the trash-distributing winds with their careerist velocities. And here inside Chamber St. was this cozy set of underachievers." (17-8)

Dwight establishes a clear line of demarcation between himself and "the old crowd," given their opposite lifestyles (success-driven vs. underachieving), life concepts (linear vs. circular), and velocity (fast vs. slow). But then the dichotomies begin to blur. When he describes his housing situation, Dwight links it with the topic of death. He speaks about a rock band he likes, called the Grateful Dead, and their singer Jerry, who passed away in 1995.

> But Jerry *had* died. And soon our lease would be up! And so would I end and die too! I tried not to be reminded of the eternal endingness of everything by Ground Zero down the street. (18)

The sense of panic caused by the death of a rock band member fuels Dwight's contemplations on his own mortality. Again, however, Dwight's awareness of aging seems exaggerated and bizarre in the face of the actual deaths at Ground Zero and the political seriousness of the terrorist attacks on September 11. The ridiculousness of Dwight's epiphany is emphasized when the reader learns that Dwight was on Ecstasy when the planes crashed into the World Trade Center. Contrary to the devastating events, Dwight felt entirely optimistic at that moment in time. Obviously, this "very ironical act" and Dwight's sense of finitude and mortality is not meant to be taken too seriously (Kakutani n. pag.).

Similarly, hereafter, Dwight's relation to age is presented as ambiguous and somewhat insubstantial. When Dwight describes Brigid, the woman he falls in love with during their journey through Ecuador, she is portrayed as "this Brigid person, woman, girl, certainly by now a friend" (201). This age-ambiguous description recurs in an email to his parents:

> I have met a girl and amazingly, but too complicated to explain, this girl or at 30 really a full-fledged woman [...] is a friend of Alice's [...] So it will surprise you less if I say that Brigid, the girl/woman, has convinced me to become a socialist. (222)

Dwight perceives Brigid as a girl because she resembles himself in his own childishness and interest in adventure or drugs. But she is also a "full-fledged woman" because, in contrast to Dwight, she has a clearer vision of who she is and what she believes in. Brigid is thus more mature and able to help the boy-man Dwight grow up. This ambiguity of age references also extends to Dwight's own perception of himself. Towards Brigid, he says: "Right now I'm twenty-eight. If a young twenty-eight" (173). Dwight suggests here that he considers twenty-eight to be old and he uses the modifier 'young' to relativize his chronological age. In Dwight's case, the modifier 'young' reveals the playfulness and exaggeration involved in the metaphoric practice of age used in *Indecision*.

When Dwight travels through Ecuador, the references to age and time recur. After an almost lethal bus accident, Dwight realizes that "[*l*]*ife* is short" (117; original emphasis). Together with his travel companion Brigid, he eventually reaches the "Valley of Longevity" where they stay for several days (189). The Valley appears like a paradise to Dwight and he overwhelmingly praises it as a place where "mestizo Methuselahs cradled over the course of their absurdly long lives in the permanent equatorial summer of this gentle, fertile valley where on most days the high averaged out at seventy-eight" (189). A sense of timelessness is evoked when Brigid, after taking some drugs, imagines a fruit that would help people experience "a paradise in which there is no lack of time. I would like for everyone to have so plentifully much time" (207). Again, it is difficult to take these ideas seriously because both Brigid and Dwight are on drugs. It is ironic, once more, that the Valley of Longevity – as a place for very old people – is praised by a perpetual adolescent like Dwight and thus by a character who is reluctant to grow old and presents himself as someone who is troubled by the ravages of time.

Kunkel does not directly refer to perpetual adolescence to explain Dwight's condition, but he alludes to several other concepts, drawing on a wide range of ideas from philosophy, sociology, psychology, and anthropology, particularly when Dwight's sister, Alice, who appears like the embodiment of a cultural elite, tries to contextualize and theorize outsiders like Dwight. Alice is an anthropologist who went to Yale and obtained her PhD from Columbia (cf. 7). She has special interests in consumer culture, psychoanalysis, and developmental psychology. In fact, Alice makes a scientific comment on almost every topic that she discusses with her brother. She profusely analyzes Dwight's situation from various sociological and cultural angles and even starts psychoanalytic sessions with him.

During one of these sessions, Alice explains her brother's situation of stagnation and aimlessness by arguing that her and her brother's generation has learned to believe that "the future could always be cancelled at any time" (141).

> [T]here was a serious question of whether we'd live to see twenty-five. Remember adults would ask us about what we wanted to be when we grew up? And didn't you always feel like you were humoring them, no matter what you said? And then,' Alice went on, 'how it came as a shock to discover midway through prep school, with the Wall coming down, that there really *was* something to prepare for after all. Yet you had no plans for adult life – none. We could never imagine growing up because the future could always be cancelled at any time. So beyond a certain narrow time frame our desires ran into a kind of horizon and had to stop. There was *no such thing as the long term*. (141-2; original emphasis)

To Alice, it is not surprising that Dwight leads "a preliminary life" (55) or that he feels that he is too slow for the "efficient digestion of modern – or postmodern life" (18). From her perspective, Dwight is a symptom of the culture and times in which he grew up.

With her claim that, for Dwight's generation, the "long term" never existed, Alice offers an interesting explanation of her brother's situation and conduct. The narrow time frames, within which her generation's plans and personalities are framed, not only seem to influence the narrative style of Dwight's fictional memoir, in which he jumps from one topic to the next, dwelling upon a subject no longer than a few moments. These short time frames also challenge the linear, long-term development of identity formation that the coming-of-age story suggests. Instead of a continuous progression towards social acceptance or towards a future life, Dwight and his sister seem to belong to a generation which no longer believes in the future or in teleological development. Thus, instead of a sense of time that is processual and consecutive, Dwight seems to act upon temporary ideas and spontaneous mental leaps. Moreover, this concept of time suggests that when young characters experience age awareness, it is rather 'age' as a momentary status than 'aging' as a processual development they have in mind (also see page 70.)

Dwight's generation seems to suffer from an additional problem, which challenges any traditional notion of coming of age. According to Alice,

[p]art of it is that we belong to a social class and a generation where our parents live too long and remain too economically powerful. [...] Neither mom nor dad shows any sign of declining, much less *dying*. Any fairy tale [sic], the hero or heroine's parents are dead or as good as dead. Otherwise the fantasies can't come true. (134-5; original emphasis)

Ironically then, Alice experiences an older generation as one that stubbornly subsists instead of making room for the younger generation. The demographic changes, however, do not reduce generational conflict. According to Alice, Dwight's generation suffers under parents who refuse to leave their place, that is who refuse to age and die, but who are nevertheless strangely "fucked up" and thus do not represent a moral authority (135). The changes in generational relationships, in her opinion, are difficult to cope with because the imaginaries that a culture feeds upon, namely the fairy tales, have remained unchanged and still influence how young adults evaluate their situation. The 'fantasy' of maturation becomes increasingly difficult to fulfill.[13] Yet, Alice's analysis of her generations' situation cannot be taken too seriously. First, Alice's ideas are quickly superseded by other theories, concepts, and explanations and are thus not really followed through. Second, Dwight's and Alice's awareness of the many theories does not change their situation nor does it help Dwight. Instead, Kunkel's characters seem to brag with their academic and cultural knowledgeability, which is, however, more of an intellectual game than an actual attempt at solving the problems. Contemporary generational theories, embodied by the concept of the perpetual adolescent, for example, as well as traditional narrative frames, such as the coming-of-age story, are thus evoked, challenged, and ultimately superseded by other theories, such as theories on consumer culture and mental illnesses.

Age, Abulia, and Consumer Culture

During his reunion speech at the end of the novel, the ridiculousness of Dwight's age awareness increases and is linked with socio-economic prob-

---

13 In this sense, Alice seems to echo Blatterer's observations on the simultaneous existence of standard life course imaginaries and more contemporary lifestyles (see Chapter 3.3).

lems. "Brevity," he begins his speech, "brevity is the spice of life. And, I guess, when these last ten years have passed in the blink of an eye, it's only appropriate that I should speak briefly, and not detain you any more than I already will" (231-2). Dwight continues his erratic speech:

Life is brief. And youth briefer than life. Except for some people. Lots of people actually, especially in the third world, where lots of people die very young. For us, however, youth has been appallingly expanded, in our remarkable time, when there are more people alive on the planet today than have ever even existed before, and when therefore the things we do have a special new importance, and also, by the same token, each individual possesses a special new irrelevance, because of the same numbers – anyway, for us, during this time, youth has expanded to dimensions apparently without historical precedent [...] So all I mean to say is that youth, brief youth, long-lasting youth, is for contemplating choices with your ever-changing mind. And yet the time has surely come for choices to be made [...] Because it seems to me that we, in this room, for reasons of cruel and unusual socioeconomic conditions, have an especially big range of decisions we could make, and so there is a particular burden. (232-4)

Dwight randomly touches upon seemingly unrelated topics, some of which are often discussed in sociological studies, such as the effects of superaging and demographic changes, choice as a coercion, and perpetual adolescence (c.f. e.g. Meyer 1987, Giddens 1991, Peterson 1999, or Blatterer 2007). There are no new insights or surprising solutions that Dwight can offer. In fact, he is as cryptic and confused as ever when he speaks about the simultaneous importance and irrelevance of people and their deeds.

Dwight is aware of the socio-economic injustice in the third world, particularly with Bolivian men, who are his peers. When Dwight describes his new job in Bolivia at the end of the novel, he reflects upon the social problems caused by the cultivation of coca in Bolivia. He illustrates the socio-economic situation of young men in Bolivia and then quickly comes to the point: Bolivian young men his age often die before they turn twenty-nine, which is Dwight's age at this point in the novel, either from the unhealthy working conditions in the tin mines or from their use of coca which gives them some relief from the hardship of their lives. Dwight remarks: "This is my age now, and I can testify that it does creep up" (236). Dwight relates to the fate of his Bolivian counterparts through age, but his comment that age creeps up indicates his particular (Western) cultural background. For Dwight, as he maintained earlier, the creeping up of age implies that he has become aware of the passage of time and feels his body starting to decline, which – when he drinks too much – makes him feel close to death (cf. 8, 39, 93). In comparison to the Bolivian men, Dwight's apprehension of aging is trivial and ridiculous and, to some extent, Dwight realizes that his age awareness is preposterous compared to the socio-economic conditions and their lethal effects on young Bolivian men.

Alice, who has written a fictitious book called *Consumer Survivalism*, in which she critically examines the "American garage-filling culture" (116),[14] sees a connection between consumer culture and aging. In a conversation with Brigid, Dwight summarizes his sister's study with the following words: "I think the idea is how people buy more things than they could ever actually *use* in order to like secretly convince themselves that they'll live some absurdly long time. Like long enough to actually use all the stuff they buy" (116; original emphasis). In summarizing Alice's ideas, Dwight links people's urge to consume with their desire for longevity. Dwight then changes the subject with the following transition: When asked by Brigid if he shares his sister's politics, he responds in a way that trivializes the severity of the issue: "I don't know. Haven't finished the book yet. My opinion is that good books, just like bad ones – don't you think they're better if they're short?" (117). The next paragraph then starts with "*Life* was short" (original emphasis) and Dwight speaks about the bus accident in Ecuador that triggers another realization of his mortality. Once more, these incoherent shifts between topics characterize the inconsequentiality with which Dwight pursues his thoughts.

Dwight's assumed mental illness, abulia, is also conditioned by Western consumer culture and, like Dwight's age awareness, abulia is presented both as symptomatic of a particular cultural malaise and as a bizarre and ridiculous status of the hero. Abulia is indeed an existing neurological disease, but in the novel, it is used for satirical purposes. An amateurish diagnosis by his roommate Dan convinces Dwight to take part in a clinical trial

---

14 The publisher that Kunkel mentions for Alice's fictitious book is "n+1 books," which is an allusion to the print journal *n+1* of which Kunkel is one of the editors.

of the drug Abulinix, which is supposed to cure abulia. Chronic indecision thus becomes the label for Dwight's problems, but it is a questionable label. Within only two pages, Dan diagnoses Dwight's problem and potentially cures him because he knows about a drug for treating abulia. Dwight concedes that "only now that I held the panacea in my hand did I recognize abulia as my major basic overriding problem" (32). Thus, from early on, the constructedness of the disease itself is exposed and ridiculed.

Henceforth, Dwight clings to the idea that abulia might be the cause for all of his problems. Conveniently, to improve his situation, he only has to wait for the effects of the drug Abulinix to set in. Over the course of the novel, Dwight meticulously counts how many days he has been taking Abulinix and increasingly asks himself whether the drug will change who he is and to which kind of life-altering decisions it will lead him (cf. 40, 85).[15] The comical climax occurs when, towards the end of the novel, Dwight finally realizes how he wants to live his life. He attributes this decision to Abulinix and considers himself cured only to find out little later that he was actually given a placebo and not the drug itself (cf. 223). Obviously then, Dwight did not suffer from an actual neurological disease but from what his sister Alice compares to a symptom of a cultural malaise: "Just like social phobia suddenly exists, even though it was created by the pharmaceuticals about four years ago. Like neurasthenia used to exist but now somehow it's died out" (59).

Abulia serves as yet another silly component that Kunkel uses to characterize Dwight and ridicule contemporary American culture, particularly pharmaceutical companies, their shady methods, and the naivety of people like Dwight's father who believe in (and profit from) mental illness. Not only does Kunkel present pharmaceutical companies as negligent drug developers that employ careless people like Dan and let him steal a box of an untested and unapproved drug. Kunkel also comments upon the ways in which the media advertises drugs such as Abulinix and brings them to the attention of the general public (cf. 29). The ultimate deconstruction of abulia (and other diseases of the mind) occurs in a conversation between Dwight and his father, when it becomes clear how mental illnesses represent cash cows for pharmaceutical companies and private investors.

---

15 Like Franzen's character Gary Lambert, Dwight is very much concerned with the ways in which drugs alter a person's identity and personality (cf. 79).

During this conversation, the senior Mr. Wilmerding highlights "the role of pharmaceuticals in our American society," which he considers to be "the new frontier" because drug companies represent "the place to be" (78).[16] Dwight senses that his father is intrigued by new investment opportunities in the pharmaceutical industry and invents a new disease, "mild, low-level autism" (MLLA), which he defines as an "epidemic in this country" that "affects especially white suburban males" (81). It is a "mild inability to recognize the basic mental reality of others" and represents a "[t]otal potential cash cow [...] it's definitely an issue out there" (81). Dwight's father buys into Dwight's sham and becomes intrigued.

The dialog between Dwight and his father is accompanied by references to age, which are used to suggest changing positions of power throughout the conversation. This function of the references to age resembles the metaphoric practice of age used in the dinner scene in *Little Children*. When Dwight feels inferior, for instance, he is called a "child of divorce" and the conversation evokes in him "infantilizing" conversations with his father (76, 77). Conversely, when Dwight has the upper hand, Mr. Wilmerding is described as a credulous, naive child with a red nose, which is interpreted as a "nose tipped with red like that of a kid come in from the cold" (81). In fact, the red nose is more likely due to Mr. Wilmerding's alcohol consumption, as both father and son are quite drunk at that moment. The references to childhood contribute to the dynamic of the conversation and emphasize the interlocutors' shifting roles and positions of power.

Kunkel mocks advisors like Dwight's father, who – in a classical coming-of-age story – would represent either the benevolent mentor and the wisdom of (old) age or the dominating, overbearing parent generation. In Kunkel's novel, the father figure is presented as a divorced and bankrupt drunkard who likes to quote from Hippocrates or Shakespeare. Amusingly, however, he misquotes Hippocrates and claims that "Vita longa, ars brevis" instead of "Ars longa, vita brevis" (91). His role as a parental advisor is

---

16 Mr. Wilmerding's comments are almost identical with the words Franzen uses to describe the role of depression in American society. And like Franzen, Kunkel also immerses his characters in a philosophical discussion about the effects of drugs on the meanings of identity or the soul (cf. 78-80).

thus ridiculed and the fact that Dwight's father is dead drunk when they have their father-son conversation only emphasizes his incompetence.[17]

Kunkel ridicules a plethora of academic discourses from developmental psychology, psychotherapy, sociology, and philosophy, which follow each other in quick succession and render themselves somehow pointless and ineffective. After all, even though Dwight can draw on a rich arsenal of theories, interpretations, and explanations of his predicament, he does not find a solution among these theories. All theoretical knowledge seems to be pointless as long as it is not preceded by actual experience or, as Dwight maintains in the beginning of the novel, "knowing the clichés are clichés doesn't help you to escape them. You still have to go on experiencing your experience as if no one else has ever done it" (26). The novel, however, ends with an idealistic solution to Dwight's problems that represents, as McInerney argues, "a hazy new frontier of hip sincerity, of irony subordinated to a higher calling" (n. pag.). As a democratic socialist, Dwight moves to Bolivia to work for the Bolivian Action Node that fights for Bolivian economic rights (cf. 235-6). Dwight somehow manages to break out of his mental imprisonment of indecision and leaves the consumer culture that he despises behind – at least on some level.[18]

I would like to come back to Dwight's sense of age and time in the novel. Similar to Verona and Burt, who experience how quickly time pass-

---

17 In the conversation between Dwight and his father, references to age appear repeatedly. Mr. Wilmerding quotes Shakespeare with a phrase from the fool in *King Lear*, which reads: "Thou shouldst not have been old till thou hadst been wise" (94). Dwight's father suggests that his son is acting inappropriately for his age because he plays dead instead of living his life and making experiences and thus ultimately becoming wise (cf. 94). He thus labels Dwight as prematurely old. When Dwight decides to "start a new life," his father comments his son's plans in the following way: "Ah you'll grow old doing that" (95).

18 Kunkel relativizes this idealistic solution by showing that Dwight has not undergone a complete personality change. On the day of the reunion, he still tries to outrank his former classmates and borrows his father's Audi, accouters his girlfriend Brigid, and presents himself as a matured, successful young man. He is thus still materialist and competitive (cf. Schäfer 130) because, as Dwight admits, he wants "the whole reunion fantasy" (*Indecision* 227).

es and thus realize how little time they have to make important decisions, Dwight experiences both: When he looks at his graduation picture, he shares Verona and Burt's experience of acceleration. Yet Dwight also feels a stoppage or deceleration of time and explains this impression in a variety of ways. Quoting the fictional philosopher Knittel, he argues that "[p]rocrastination is our substitute for immortality" and that "we behave as if we have no shortage of time" (18). Knittel provides convenient explanations for a privileged and intelligent upper-class character like Dwight who never tires of commenting on the ways in which his generation suffers from the many choices it has to make and for the lack of individual action that characterizes Dwight's procrastination and stagnation (cf. 19). But in the end, Knittel only serves to provide quotations that Dwight throws into his account in a know-it-all manner only to get distracted soon after and focus on a new topic in the next sentence. In a conversation with Alice, the topic of consumer culture surfaces again and Dwight, inspired by Knittel, links the purchase of commodities with the consumers' desire for longevity or immortality (cf. 116). Exaggerated consumption, the novel suggests, thus functions as a substitute for immortality and, given the repeated association of age, mental illness, and consumer culture in *Indecision*, one wonders: Does consumer culture actually influence the perception of living in time or the availability of time in general? And does a consumer economy have the power to shape people's imaginaries of aging, as *Indecision*, albeit ironically, suggests?

4.3 Consumer Cycles, Obsolescence, and (Im)Mortality

According to some age scholars, economic practices and discourses profoundly influence the ways in which people internalize the meanings of aging and old age. Apocalyptic news reports in the media, for instance, contribute to the idea that "graying means paying" and that due to the demographic changes and the super-aging of many societies around the world, we are facing a "Gray Dawn" that has global repercussions (Peterson 46). The elderly are imagined as unproductive and selfish burdens that make future societies crumble under the financial weight they impose on younger generations (cf. Peterson 1999, Gullette 2004). The age critic Margaret

Morganroth Gullette criticizes, for instance, how the Baby Boomer generation is constructed as an enemy through "Boomer-bashing," in which Boomers are presented as a selfish and overly powerful generation that obstruct the younger generations' access to the job market and to social security (cf. *Aged by Culture* 47). Gullette also links life crises with economic crises and suggests that the definition of the quarterlife- or midlife-crisis might be understood as a cultural response to much larger apprehensions, such as financial or economic crises. For example, Gullette juxtaposes the "Bush recession that left young people without jobs" with "the construction of the 'slacker' stereotype" ("Age Studies as Cultural Studies" 226). The media supported this view, albeit with different connotations: They insinuated that slackers just did not work hard enough and were therefore unemployed; it was thus their own fault (cf. 226). For Gullette, the construction of the slacker figure represents a particular way of rationalizing fears about economic instability and decline.

In an autobiographically shaped essay called "The Other End of the Fashion Cycle: Practicing Loss, Learning Decline" (1999), Gullette discusses the processes of internalizing age-as-decline and the drastic semantics that accompany the connection between age and consumer culture. More precisely, Gullette traces how (female) consumers internalize the meanings of aging through their consumption practices (cf. 36). Gullette argues that the fashion industry teaches consumers that clothes can age, like human beings, and that old shirts or pants – regardless of the degree of their wear – are waste and must be discarded and replaced by the new season's apparel. This cycle of purchase and discard functions so well because consumer products are linked with emotions (cf. 48). Consumers feel good when they purchase a new product, which bestows them with some reputation (of youthfulness, for instance). They 'love' a new gadget or fabric (cf. 41). And they feel ashamed when they realize what they used to wear or used to like in the past, which helps them to discard products and continue the cycle (cf. 46, 48). Consumers have learned to welcome the new and mock the old (cf. 46); therefore, they have internalized "what befalls the self in time" (36). "Discarding teaches us that the self can expect to lose from living in time – lose selfhood" (36). Since the cycles of fashion become shorter and shorter, the experience of loss becomes routine.

The same vicious cycle of "human discard" (37), as Gullette calls it, applies to the reputation of film stars, pop icons, or politicians because they "depend on characteristics of youth for their livelihood" and "may become 'old' long before they reach middle age" (Neikrug 327). According to Gullette, the built-in, "mandatory obsolescence" forms the basis of capitalism and is easily transferable to the life course and to concepts of identity formation (41).

[W]e have been taught from childhood on through everyday practices and celebratory occasions that we relinquish a past self only to come into a same-but-better one. We happily give up the self that carried a blanket and sucked its thumb, that didn't know how to gargle, skip, or read, and in that process we learned to look forward to growing older in order to get better attributes. In other words, in the early crucial decades we learn, without benefit of purchases, one way to see the life course as progress. Suddenly, not much farther along, through a kind of enforced progress march symbolized by relinquishing objects, we have to begin to unlearn that, and learn that it's a decline. (50)

According to Gullette, these micro-narratives of the self are "master narratives of aging" (49). They constitute age autobiographies because it is through these narratives of the self that one learns to accept that living in time invariably entails losses to previous achievements or conditions. Hence, via such narratives, age knowledge is subtly and continually diffused x(cf. 51).

With her observations on consumer culture, Gullette positions herself as an activist who makes a case for the central theme that permeates her oeuvre: the pervasiveness and omnipresence of decline metaphors and decline narratives. The conclusions Gullette draws from the ideologies that constitute consumer cycles are particularly intriguing in light of the aged young adults in this study. One might argue that a character like Dwight, who comes from a wealthy family and is used to getting anything he wants, instinctively senses a connection between consumer culture and age or aging, and, to some extent, he realizes the paradoxical nature of the decline ideology when he encounters the world of Bolivian men his age, for whom age and aging have entirely different meanings. Nevertheless, Dwight seems to have internalized the decline ideologies of consumer culture and, therefore, it makes sense that he indirectly expresses his feelings of being meaningless, worthless, and failed through references to age.

Apart from Gullette, further cultural critics see a similar connection between age, aging, and consumer culture. The Polish-British sociologist and philosopher Zygmunt Bauman, for instance, describes the phenomena of built-in obsolescence and social death in *Mortality, Immortality and Other Life Strategies* (1992). Seven years prior to Gullette's article,[19] Bauman took his cue from an observation by Wolfgang Fritz Haug:[20]

Things do not die because of old age, metal fatigue, disintegrating beyond repair – not of 'natural causes'; not because death is inescapable. They disappear long before they reach the point of 'natural death'; indeed, well before they begin to show signs of 'senility'. Their removal from the life-world at such a trouble-free age would not undermine their 'principal' timelessness. They could be infinitely durable, nay immortal, if we wished them to be. But we do not wish them to be immortal. (*Mortality* 188)

Bauman contextualizes Haug's ideas by arguing that "pre-designed obsolescence" is an integral part of a commodity and essentially defines its value: Objects must become waste soon so that new products can be purchased.[21] The crucial point is, however, that built-in obsolescence entails

---

19 Gullette does not refer to any of Bauman's theories in her essay from 1999, and her claims are part of a different argument. In contrast to Bauman, Gullette – as a resident scholar at the Women's Studies Research Center at Brandeis University – argues from a gender perspective. She primarily focuses on the fashion industry and only makes short excursions to corporate capitalism. Gullette uses her observations on the fashion cycle to prove that people are aged by culture in subtle ways and unconsciously learn and internalize the decline narrative of aging. Bauman's interest lies in investigating how people deal with mortality and immortality.

20 The German philosopher Haug coined the concept of "commodity aesthetics" in the 1970s, arguing that the appearance of a commodity is more important than its real utility value.

21 In a speech at Stanford University in 2005, Steve Jobs spoke to students about his cancer diagnosis and his apprehension of death. In his speech, Jobs applied the concept of built-in obsolescence to his own life: "Death is very likely the single best invention of Life. It is Life's change agent. It clears out the old to make way for the new. Right now the new is you, but someday not too long

moral aging and not physical aging (cf. 86). Hence, similar to Gullette, Bauman understands aging or obsolescence as a socio-economically shaped phenomenon.[22]

According to Bauman, built-in or mandatory obsolescence is closely connected with the threat of social death. Referring to Germaine Greer and the importance of social networks and media, Bauman argues that invisibility is tantamount to death (cf. 13). Invisibility goes together with slowness, which also "portends social death," as Bauman argues elsewhere when he reflects upon the ways in which consumer culture heralds progress, development, movement, and speed: The biggest concern for consumer economy is stagnation; therefore, people are coerced to keep up and to not let themselves be overtaken by others (84). Staying put implies falling behind (cf. 84). Apathy, doubts, or passivity thus decelerate the accelerated race for progress. "'To consume' therefore means to invest in one's own social membership," which is, however, an endless and laborious endeavor (56).

This never-ending requirement to consume and to postpone social death as well as one's looming obsolescence appears in Gullette's article on the fashion cycle in the form of symbolic capital. Gullette adapts Bourdieu's definition of symbolic capital to the idea of age and considers youthfulness a component of symbolic capital,[23] arguing that, in Western cultures, age – and here she means youthfulness – has turned into a symbolic capital. This capital is

> a possession only of the chronologically young – and then only briefly. After that, dominant culture soon exposes the aging to the various kinds of identity stripping

---

from now, you will gradually become the old and be cleared away" ("Stay Hungry" n. pag.).

22 For more information on the concept of "planned obsolescence," its relation to the American Great Depression, and its use in the advertisement industry in the 1950s, consider Micah White (2008) and Giles Slade (2006).

23 Pierre Bourdieu defines symbolic capital as "a legitimate possession grounded in the nature of its possessor" (*Logic* 129) and as a form of recognition and prestige: "[F]or those who, like the professionals, live on a sale of cultural services to a clientele, the accumulation of economic capital merges with the accumulation of symbolic capital, that is, with the acquisition of a reputation for competence and an image of respectability and honourability" (*Distinction* 291).

that come related to the category of age. As more people are known to be undergoing cosmetic surgery to avoid looking 'older' [...] and as people submit to the knife earlier ('preventive' facial surgery before forty, men in their thirties getting calf implants), and as the procedures become less stigmatized, the more deeply even the rest of us internalize the meaning of passing time as the loss of our capital. (*Aged* 22).

According to Gullette's appropriation of Bourdieu's concept, symbolic capital is continually in danger of disappearing or becoming waste. The efforts of each individual thus consist in continually monitoring and investing in one's symbolic capital, that is one's youthfulness, and to delay its inevitable decline as long as possible. This endeavor is, of course, an attack on windmills. Nevertheless, decline and death – whether social, moral, or physical – are considered to represent threats to the integrity of the consuming individual, which – to quote Susan Sontag – are "never really used up" and which, like the "territory of aging," have "no fixed boundaries" ("Double Standard" 33).

Mortality and Immortality

How do individuals deal with the permanent threat of decline and death? Bauman claims in *Mortality, Immortality and Other Life Strategies* (1992) that Western cultures have developed two distinct strategies of dealing with this predicament: (1) a modern strategy that deconstructs mortality and (2) a postmodern strategy that deconstructs immortality. This differentiation into seemingly historical and successive periods of modernity and postmodernity can be misleading because it suggests a chronological separateness of the two strategies. Bauman maintains, however, that they are "deployed *simultaneously*" in contemporary society, even though, he admits, they are inherently contradictory (10; original emphasis).

The first strategy concerns the ways in which people have learned to deal (or rather not deal) with death or mortality. Bauman argues that death has been shunned from public attention and pushed to the private arena. It has become difficult to talk about death because people have been trained to speak a "language of survival," which "spurs into action" and promises that people can fight death through reasonable, health-promoting behavior (130, 139). The language of survival reduces the finality of death into "manageable problems" and slices death into "curable afflictions" (130, 140). In addition, the increasing medicalization brings about "surrogate solutions to the existential predicament that allows no solution. They [the medical practices] merely avert attention from big things which cannot be done to other, smaller things that can" (159-60). As a consequence, individuals begin to believe that "each *particular* case of death [...] can be resisted, postponed, or avoided altogether" (137-8). Mortality thus becomes deconstructed and turns into a matter of personal effort and permanent labor. The consequences for the individual are similar to those described by Ehrenreich, Ehrenberg, and McGee: an awareness about one's absolute self-responsibility, a willingness to perpetual (emotional) work, and a shared knowledge about illness as a sign of personal failure (cf. 146). Thus, individuals carry with them an "impending" doom (153), which is a surprisingly similar wording compared to Susan Sontag's idea of age or aging as a "moveable doom," which disseminates a "poignant apprehension of unremitting loss" ("Double Standard" 31, 33).

For Bauman, the life strategy of deconstructing mortality has moved death "from the remote horizon to the center of daily life" (*Mortality* 10), thereby transforming it into a "daily nightmare" (140). This fear and "permanent horror" is counteracted with a "near-hysterical busyness" and a "bustle of 'doing something about it'" (140). Age scholars, like Katz or Powell, describe similar strategies when they talk about "busy bodies" (see Chapters 2.2 and 4.1). According to Bauman, this nervous commotion for the sake of being active and busy is welcomed by an orientation towards projects in Western societies, which represents a strategy of breaking down the inevitability of death into smaller, more manageable units – either in terms of units of illness or units of labor (cf. 163-4). The modern way of "living-with-the-project, in-the-shadow-of-the-project, toward-a-project" not only characterizes the fight against diseases but also describes how an unmanageable and unknown future is broken down into short and controllable present moments which can be influenced actively via economic reasoning (163):

One can carefully set the means against the end, search for the resources necessary for the means to be implemented, calculate the cost of the resources and draw the cost-and-effects balance sheet of the whole operation. One can, in other words, be a rational agent in the fact of (in spite of) the predicament that bars rationality. (153)

Entrepreneurial reasoning in terms of self-monitoring, or time management thus contributes to Bauman's deconstruction of mortality.

The second strategy – the deconstruction of immortality – is a strategy that Bauman associates with postmodernity. Interestingly, Bauman illustrates the differences between the modern and postmodern strategies by referring to life course imaginaries: The first strategy, he argues, envisions human development – either in terms of identity or biography – as a gradual development, "built level by level, storey by storey" (164). People thus follow a planned life-itinerary or life-project, which gives them a sense of security and a goal to work towards (cf. 167). Individual identity is "plotted along the line of rising knowledge and know-how" in terms of a "continuous, unbroken path" (165). The *Bildungsroman*, typically considered a modernist literary genre (cf. Rishoi 60), fits Bauman's description of the modern strategy and its underlying assumptions of a gradual development and growing through time.

Bauman's second strategy is characterized by a different notion of time, namely "pointillist time," which is characterized by ruptures and discontinuities (*Consuming Life* 32). Pointillist time freezes individuals in the eternal present moment because it is "broken up, or even pulverized, into a multitude of 'eternal instants' – events, incidents, accidents, adventures, episodes" (32). The future is not imagined as a linear, uninterrupted path but has "holes in time" and "holes in space" (*Mortality* 165). People move like flexible, uprooted nomads who wander through space, time, and various identities, exchanging one momentary place or identity for the next (cf. 167). Projects, let alone life-projects, lose their meaning entirely because the future is now; and the here and now is all that counts. Dwight Wilmerding's notion of short term and long term, his frequent mental leaps, his aimlessness, and his focus on the present moment are reminiscent of Bauman's postmodern strategy.

Necessarily, such a conception of the world and time entails a different understanding of mortality. Mortality has been transferred into the present and has become a matter of daily negotiation:

In a life composed of equal moments, speaking of directions, projects and fulfillments makes no sense [...] Every state is as momentary and passing as any other, and each one is – potentially – the gate opening into eternity. Thus the distinction between the mundane and the eternal, the transient and durable, mortal and immortal, is all but effaced. Daily life is a constant rehearsal of both mortality and immortality. (168)

In a world in which eternity (or the future) is dissolved in the present, immortality becomes meaningless. Nothing is truly immortal, and, as a consequence, "nothing seems mortal either" (170). As in the Buddhist philosophy, no loss is truly everlasting.[24] People (and objects) "disappear from view for a time only" and can reappear anytime; loss is no longer irretrievable (173). Disappearance has thus replaced mortality and can be repeated endlessly. Daily repetition then turns into a rehearsal of mortality, which constitutes, as Bauman calls it, a deconstruction of immortality.

As a result, when people no longer strive for (or believe in) immortality, other aspects of human life change their meaning: "Skills, jobs, occupations, residences, marriage partners" – nothing is for life, "nothing is truly irreplaceable" (188-9). The rehearsal of death is accompanied by a rehearsal of the inconsequentiality of things and events, which are only one-off happenings without any significance, durability, or impact (cf. 186ff.). Instead, durability is proclaimed to be boredom and "age to be obsolescence" (189). Permanence is turned "into a world of ridicule," and attention, concentration, and focus are lost entirely (189). Beneath these practices of the here and now, a vacuum appears: Individuals become "free-floating nomads of the post-linear-time, post-life-project universe" (195).

---

24 The historian John R. Gillis makes a related observation in an article on families and the modern culture of aging. Gillis uses the notion of linear and cyclical time: "While linear time is irreversible and is forever lost to us, cyclical time can be slowed, stopped, and even reversed" (109). Gillis, however, sees advantages in the cyclical time model (which he relates to the wheel of life imaginary) because it enables people to imagine themselves beyond their individual life courses and thus as part of a larger, eternal community of mankind. In industrial days with linear time imaginaries, however, life and death become matters of numerical reasoning and predictable life courses. Time turns into capital: "Age, like time, was no longer seen as a gift of God, but now both time and age were seen as a kind of private property, capital which, when used well and invested correctly, would produce more time and better aging, but when used badly could bring failure and humiliation" (114-5). Time thus becomes scarce and people have a constant sense of "time famine" (115).

Bauman's analyses and interpretations of contemporary life appear drastic. Still, his suggestions are surprisingly congruent with the opinions and observations voiced by a character like Dwight Wilmerding, who seems to suffer from exactly the concurrence of the "rehearsal of both mortality and immortality" that creates such contradictory reactions as panic and carelessness, frantic busyness and depressive apathy, delusions of grandeur, and a sense of powerlessness (168). The synchronicity of Bauman's strategies presents an enormous and seemingly unsolvable challenge because it both demands specific life plans and projects and, at the same time, questions the meaningfulness of such endeavors; it advocates hard work for achieving permanence and, simultaneously, denies all durability. Despite these contradictory consequences, there is a corollary that exists in both strategies, namely the significance of human agency and the emphasis on self-responsibility. Confronted with the contradictory and serious consequences that Bauman's life strategies entail, a crisis, as the one that Dwight experiences, seems highly likely.

In Benjamin Kunkel's *Indecision*, we encounter a character who takes an ironic distance and positions himself as a remote observer of the challenges of contemporary American culture. Dwight is acutely aware of the link between identity and consumer culture but he refuses to (or cannot) see himself as an entrepreneur of the self. The hero of Don DeLillo's *Cosmopolis*, Eric Packer, who is the same age as Dwight, assumes a completely different role: He is entirely immersed in consumer culture and has adopted the ideal of the entrepreneurial self. He believes that he can fight mortality, but, when he becomes aware of his own obsolescence, he is confronted with the synchronicity of Bauman's strategies, which deeply unsettles him and triggers a crisis. In *Cosmopolis*, DeLillo paints a quite bleak portrait of a character who tries to negotiate the cultural imaginaries associated with age, living in time, and consumer culture.

4.4 DON DELILLO'S *COSMOPOLIS*

Cosmopolis (2003) is the story of 28-year-old Eric Packer, a ruthless, multi-million currency trader and the head of Packer Capital, whom the reader follows for an unspecified day in April 2000 on his ride across New York

City. Eric instinctively knows that his lifetime is running out, and two interpolated confessions in which Eric's assassin Benno Levin describes his plans and motivations confirm his "[i]ntuition of early death" (191).²⁵

DeLillo's thirteenth novel has received predominantly "hostile" reviews (Campbell n. pag.). Michiko Kakutani describes *Cosmopolis* as a "major dud," "dated," "heavy-handed" and "oddly generic," with descriptive passages that read "like mannered parodies of avant-garde writing" (n. pag.). Her colleague at *The New York Times,* Walter Kirn, criticizes the "fossilized academic futurism," which lacks "surprise or spontaneity" (n. pag.). Others wondered how the reader can care for a character as unsympathetic and bizarre as Eric Packer (cf. Updike n. pag.). In one of his rare interviews, DeLillo defends his protagonist and describes him as an extraordinary fellow who consumes "what's around him and then, it's almost a cultural process of white hot consumption followed by instantaneous waste" (qtd. in Brockes n. pag.). The difficulties of envisioning a future around the time of the terrorist attacks of 9/11, a future that is shaped by dread not by hope, old religions, and technology are topics that DeLillo discusses in his essay "In the Ruins of the Future" and that reverberate in *Cosmopolis,* even though the novel is set in the year 2000. Brockes argues that "*Cosmopolis* presents a version of the world that is already obsolete" (n. pag.). Obsolescence and the passing of time are, indeed, central themes in the novel (cf. Noble 2008). Other major topics are "chaos and asymmetry" (Kakutani n. pag.), "the behavior of crowds [...] the way modern culture is so inured to trauma [...] and what the endless repetition of TV images does to encourage this" (Brockes n. pag.). Similarly, the moral consequences of rogue capitalism (cf. Varsava 2005) and "the alleged insanity of Nasdaq-era hypercapitalism" (Kirn n. pag.) are identified as key themes in the novel.

Peter Boxall juxtaposes *Cosmopolis* with *The Body Artist* and argues that DeLillo's novels of the new millennium are concerned with describing and trying to understand the paradoxes of present time: The novels "take place in the time of mourning, in a kind of evacuated time which has lost its narrative quality, which can neither inherit the legacy of the past, nor move towards the possibility of a new and undiscovered future. It is a time which has lost its sense of identity" (216). Boxall also highlights the significance

---

25 The novel was adapted to the screen by David Cronenberg in 2012, starring Robert Pattinson as Eric Packer and Paul Giamatti as Benno Levin.

of death in DeLillo's work, arguing that "DeLillo's oeuvre catalogues [...] a kind of acceleration towards the end" (11). With neither past nor future and with death looming, Eric Packer embodies many of the concepts discussed in Chapters 4.1 and 4.3, such as Bauman's concepts of the eternal present of pointillist time, obsolescence, short-termed consumer cycles and the entrepreneur of the self.

In my reading of the novel, I want to investigate how *Cosmopolis* weaves together the topics of death, obsolescence, and decline. At first glance, the story seems to be exclusively concerned with laissez-faire capitalism and cybercapital, representing a "chilling portrait of a rogue capitalist running amok in the dying days of the stock-market bubble" (Varsava 80). After all, Eric is the perfect embodiment of neoliberal rationality, self-governance, and endless self-examination. His excessive sense of entitlement, which is coupled with his enormous financial success, makes Eric emerge as a cold-blooded, self-concerned, and egotistical character. Yet, over the course of the novel, this rather unappealing protagonist realizes his corporality and mortality. Eric is confronted with a sense of ambivalence that he was not aware of earlier in his life: He always strove for utmost control, a pursuit of excellence, and physical flawlessness. Being superseded by a younger generation of hackers and investors, Eric gradually becomes aware of an alternative view of life by gaining insight into the creative potential that lies in imperfection and deficiency. References to age accompany Eric's changing state of mind and indicate a semantic duplicity in the notions of obsolescence and aging: While Eric's immersion in the capitalist worldview has made him believe in the notion of obsolescence as a loss of value and a (physical and symbolic) decline, Eric is now confronted with an alternative vision of his body and its mortality, in which a loss of control provides a new source of meaning, which promises wholeness or connectedness. The metaphors of age suggest Eric's sense of being different and of having failed, and thus of age as a (temporary) status marker of otherness. Eric is, however, also searching for alternative meanings of age, aging, and living in time, and during this quest, references to age assume more hopeful meanings than merely decline and death.

Aging as Obsolescence: Eric's Sense of Decline

Age plays a crucial role in Eric Packer's universe. Whenever a new character is introduced, a comment about the character's chronological age is made: Eric's wife Elise Shifrin is "in her mid-twenties" (16), his currency analyst Michael Chin is twenty-two (23), his art dealer Didi Fancher is forty-seven (26), his security guard Danko is "a man about forty" (125). Brutha Fez, the Sufi rapper, died in his mid-thirties (134) and Benno Levin, Eric's assassin, is forty-one (189). Levin relativizes the importance of his age when he wonders: "Or did I turn forty-two, which is possible, because I don't keep track, because why should I?" (189). To Levin, chronological age is not important and neither are age stages endowed with any particular relevance when Levin maintains that "I never felt a distinction over time between child and man, boy and man. I was never consciously a child as the term is usually applied. I feel like the same thing I always was" (59). Levin's indifferent attitude towards age and age stages greatly contrasts with Eric's hyper-sensitivity about his own as well as other people's ages.

In some cases, Eric does not know the age of his employees, but he speculates about their age. Regarding Vija Kinski, for example, his chief of theory, Eric wonders "why he didn't know how old she was" (78). He then judges her by her appearance and observes that she has "smoky gray" hair, which looks "withered and singed" (78). Her face is, however, "barely marked" (78). Jane Melman, Eric's chief of finance, is also not given an exact age, but Eric describes her as aged.

> Here, she was a single running mother in a foldout seat, knock-kneed and touchingly, somehow, gaunt. A splash of hair lay moist and flat on her forehead, showing first faint veining of gray. The water bottle dangled from a lank hand. (47)

(Seemingly) middle-aged Jane Melman lacks youthful stamina and physical vigor in contrast to younger employees such as Shiner or Chin. In Eric's eyes, she appears frail and worn out and this fact arouses Eric, who admits that he is more excited than he's been "since the first burning nights of adolescent frenzy" (49). This recourse to a sense of youthful enthusiasm and vitality is juxtaposed with Eric's simultaneous medical examination in the limousine. Death can occur everyday, Eric argues to justify his exaggerated preventive measures (a doctor examines him everyday). Eric is driven by a fear of dying and wants to control his body by all means in order to prevent illness and death. It seems that Eric has internalized what Bauman calls the modern strategy of deconstructing mortality.

Over the course of the novel, the reasons for Eric's premonition of death become clearer: He realizes that he is no longer "younger than anyone else" (24). His youthfulness, on which his earlier sense of self was grounded, is waning. To Chin, for instance, Eric admits that "I was always younger than anyone around me. One day it began to change" (23). This change, Eric fears, might soon depose him from the legend he is accustomed to being: "We're all young and smart and were raised by wolves. But the phenomenon of reputation is a delicate thing. A person rises on a word and falls on a syllable" (12). Eric's symbolic capital of reputation, intelligence, and youthfulness is thus in danger. The fear of being outrun is imminent. When Eric realizes that his employees begin to be younger than he is, Eric cannot help but notice, for example, that Shiner, his chief of technology, is "small and boy-faced" (11). And 22-year-old Chin is described in the following way: "Chin had advanced degrees in mathematics and economics and was only a kid, still, with a gutterpunk stripe in his hair, a moody beet-root red" (21-2). In these examples, references to being young and kid-like do not indicate degradation or social deviance (as in *Away We Go* or *Little Children*). On the contrary, in the fictional world of *Cosmopolis*, Chin's unprofessional, youthful appearance is an asset in the financial world because it promises "stamina," "single-mindedness," and "relentless will" (12). These features are the measurements by which Eric evaluates his staff and himself.

Later in the novel, DeLillo makes clear that it is not only Eric who assesses and categorizes how valuable people are on the basis of their age. When Eric sees a man on the streets who sets himself on fire in an act of a protest, we are told:

He [the man on fire] was young or not. He'd made the judgment out of lucid conviction. They wanted him young and driven by conviction. Eric believed even the police wanted this. No one wanted a deranged man. (98)

The age of this suicide victim seems to determine the value of his deeds: If he were young, his act would be is judged as determined and inspired (and thus as positive and admirable). If he were old, his actions would be devalued and sanctioned as deranged. Youth thus seems to function like a symbolic refuge for a person like Eric because it allows him to justify his relentlessness and lack of scruples and morals.

Eric's sense of being aged is voiced explicitly when he goes into a theater in which a rave is taking place. "Kids" is the first word that comes to Eric's mind when he describes the dancing crowd to his security guard Danko (125). When Danko talks about a new drug, which he supposes the "kids" have taken, Danko shows himself uncomprehending because the drug eliminates pain and he wonders: "But what pain do they feel too young to buy beer?" Eric responds: "There's pain enough for everybody now" (125). Eric can relate to these "American teenagers" and feels infected by the spectacle. He admits that he is "beginning to like it," that is the music, yet shortly after this sense of connectedness, Eric realizes that he is not part of the crowd: "But he felt old, watching them dance. An era had come and gone without him" (127). Even though he feels a connection with the young dancers and realizes that the spectacle of music and drugs makes him feel "a little less himself, a little more the others, down there, raving," he is only a bystander, observing the crowd from a remote place (127).

Immediately after this realization, the topic of death surfaces. First, Eric asks Danko if he has killed people in his job as a security guard (which Danko affirms). Next, the narrator pronounces the rave quasi-dead: "It was the last techno-rave, the end of whatever it was the end of" (127). With this feeling of finitude, Eric leaves the theater and notices some of the drugged ravers in the dressing room, concluding that "it was tender and moving, to know them in their frailty, their wistfulness of being, because kids is all they were, trying not to scatter in the air" (128). It seems as if this moment somewhat reconciles Eric, but the discrepancy between him and the kids remains.

Back in his limousine, riding across Manhattan, Eric shows an astute sense for the inkling of oldness, which he notices in the neighborhood he is passing through: "the old brawl, the old seethe and heat of Hell's Kitchen, the rake of fire escapes on old brick buildings" (129). Descriptions of the obsolescence of objects and language occur repeatedly throughout the novel, mirroring Eric's acute sense of the practices of being aged. Aging, as it seems, not only affects people but objects and language alike. In the first half of the novel, Eric keeps mentioning objects, technologies, or businesses that he considers to be outdated. These include skyscrapers, hand organizers, ear buds, scan retrievals, the lowering of windows, stethoscopes, ATMs, the diamond business, cash registers, phones, walkie-talkies, and computers. The word skyscraper, for instance, is ascribed an "anachronistic quality [...] No recent structure ought to bear this word. It belonged to the olden soul of awe, to the arrowed towers that were a narrative long before he was born" (9). Similarly, his hand organizer is "an object whose original culture had just about disappeared. He knew he'd have to junk it" (9). For a man like Eric who works in his limousine, the word 'office' is "outdated" and has "zero saturation" (15). As a visionary in terms of future progress who predicts the development of currencies via charts and patterns, Eric has a sharp eye for the material world around him. It seems that everything with a history, whether of decades or years, is prone to expire and turn into 'junk' as soon as the material reality changes and a new product enters the market. Therefore, ear buds are "vestigial" and "degenerate structures" (19); a handgun might become obsolete soon because the word 'handgun' is "lost in blowing mist" (19). Even language itself is outrun by the speed of change in social reality: The material world changes so quickly that language cannot keep up and words become obsolete. The expression 'automated teller machine,' for example, is

aged and burdened by its own historical memory. It worked at cross-purposes, unable to escape the inference of fuddled human personnel and jerky moving parts. The term was part of the process that the device was meant to replace. It was antifuturistic, so cumbrous and mechanical that even the acronym seemed dated. (54)

Similarly, words such as 'computer' "sound backward and dumb" (104) and Eric is no longer sure if "vestibule [...] is still a word" (182). All these references to age and obsolescence clearly indicate decline and loss of value or relevance – the stereotypical meanings of old age in Western cultures. In doing so, the references contribute to the bleak atmosphere of the novel and hint at Eric's emotional state of mind, which is marked by his fear of physical decline, his (self-)destructiveness and forlornness, as the following instances illustrate.

When Eric talks about the obsolescence of ATMs, he sees Benno Levin, his assassin, for the first time (not yet realizing that Levin's appearance foreshadows his death). Shortly after Eric's reflections on ATMs, Dr. Ingram confirms that Eric's prostate is asymmetrical. This medical condition is normal and – as it turns out later – of no greater importance. Still, the diagnosis deeply unsettles Eric because it goes beyond his means of control and his aesthetic sense of symmetry. The asymmetrical prostrate also links Eric with his assassin Benno, who – as we learn at the end of the novel – has the same condition.

A similar correlation between the obsolescence of objects and threats on Eric's life occurs when Eric mentions the obsolescence of walkie talkies – "a contraption [...] carrying the nitwit rhyme out of the age of industrial glut" (102). Eric is confronted with a credible threat on his life before and right after he reflects upon walkie talkies. Or, when Eric mocks the use of scan retrievals – again, a dated technology according to Eric –, his observations are framed by the death of Arthur Rapp and an attempt on the president's life (cf. 101-3). The obsolescence of commodities thus correlates directly with physical mortality in the narrative alignment of events. DeLillo further emphasizes this connection when he links objects with institutionalized practices that usually apply to human beings: "It is time to retire the word phone," Eric muses at some point, echoing Gullette's notion that accelerated product life cycles are comparable to (and maybe influencing our perception of) institutionalized human life cycles (88). Eric moves within a zone of all-pervasive obsolescence and death, both literally and metaphorically. When Eric thus claims that he feels old, he expresses a sensitivity towards a loss of value and decline, that affects both objects and human beings.

DeLillo also connects different kinds of life cycles when he links natural cycles to market cycles in order to predict currency movements (cf. 200). As a currency analyst, Eric taught Benno Levin "the cross-harmonies between nature and data" and how "market cycles can be interchangeable with the time cycles of grasshopper breeding, wheat harvesting" (200). The logical consequence of this kind of reasoning is that not only natural cycles but also human life cycles become congruent with economic cycles.

Hence, these instances of obsolescence are not only forebodings of Eric's death at the end of the novel; they also stand for a fast-paced world, in which objects rapidly become obsolescent and a man can rise on a word and fall on a syllable (cf. 12). Eric is aged by the culture in which he used to thrive. His sense of being obsolescent is not his own fault but seems to be a consequence of the consumer culture he is part of and which devalues objects (and people) as soon as a new product line (or generation in the form of Eric's younger colleagues) enters the market. This ruthless world "junks" Eric, just as he is about to junk his hand organizer. This devaluation is a short and quick process. Time has accelerated and Eric is very much aware that "[e]verything is barely weeks. Everything is days. We have minutes to live [...] Time is a thing that grows scarcer everyday" (69). Fittingly, the temporal frame of *Cosmopolis*, which tells Eric's story within only one day, amplifies this feeling of distorted and accelerated time (cf. Bertodano n. pag.).

New Time Cycles

Time is an ambivalent issue for Eric. He is thrilled when he thinks in zeptoseconds (cf. 106). At the same time, Eric is deeply disturbed when he realizes that time not only grows scarcer but is also no longer predictable. Eric experiences leaps in time, which means that he sees things that have not happened yet. In his limousine, for instance, he watches himself touching his chin on one of the screens, when he realizes that he has just actually placed his thumb on his chinline, "a second or two after he'd seen it onscreen" (22). A similar phenomenon happens with Vija Kinski as a witness (cf. 93). And then, at the end of the novel, Eric sees his own corpse on his crystal watch, a mysterious gadget that operates inside "the watch body" and collects images in the vicinity of the person wearing the watch, in this case Eric (205). Through this crystal watch, Eric realizes at the end of the novel "O shit I'm dead" when he sees a dead body with an identification tag "Male Z" on his watch and assumes that it is his own, future dead body (206). These leaps in time emphasize the acceleration but also the instability and volatility of time. And they show that Eric is losing (or has lost) control over time. This circumstance makes it impossible for Eric to project himself into the future and to imagine a future or alternative life beyond his career.

The persistent imminence of obsolescence and accelerated time showcased in *Cosmopolis* seems to suggest that a major socio-cultural change has occurred. Life course imaginaries in the fictional world of *Cosmopolis* are no longer what they used to be. The extended rise and decline trajectories of a nineteenth century stair case of life (see Chapter 3.3) no longer adequately describe contemporary life courses that are shaped by capitalist business practices. The symmetrical ascending and descending shape of the staircase is replaced by a life course, in which the downfall is shortened and the point of death – whether physical or social – is pushed to an earlier moment in life. The balanced division of the life course into equal phases of rise and fall has become asymmetrical. In this sense, Eric's death does not appear as premature or untimely, nor is his age awareness inadequate. Rather, the references to age, obsolescence, and death stand for a sense of imminent decline and loss that is symptomatic of the world he lives in, which affects not only identities and values but also the cultural imaginaries of people's lives. From this perspective, Benno's death sentence is telling: When Benno says to Eric "you're already dead. You're like someone already dead. Like someone dead a hundred years" (203), he not only voices his long-standing wish to kill Eric. He also points to the fact that Eric has already become obsolete. According to the new cycles and patterns of capitalist consumer culture, Eric's (physical) death is long overdue.

During a philosophical discussion between Vija Kinski and Eric, both characters discuss changes in the concept of time. Like age or youthfulness, time has become a symbolic capital or corporate asset. Echoing Bauman and Chudacoff, Kinski maintains:

Money makes time. It used to be the other way around. Clock time accelerated the rise of capitalism. People stopped thinking about eternity. They began to concentrate on hours, measurable hours, man-hours, using labor more efficiently. (79)

The acceleration of time and the breaking down of time into zeptoseconds and nanoseconds complicates people's sense of the past, present, and future. This situation needs to be corrected, according to Kinski, in order to "[b]ring nature back to normal, more or less" (79). Eric is the perfect embodiment of Kinski's theories. He has always lived in the future and has enjoyed it, but now he realizes that it is exactly this lifestyle, which gives him a feeling of insubstantiality. "The present is harder to find," Kinski reasons. Eric, however, does not entirely agree with Kinski's nihilistic agenda. He realizes that his looming death gives him a new reason to live. With death close, he can now "begin the business of living," Eric maintains at the end of part one (107). This new insight, however, does not mean that Eric's hostile and misanthropic attitude towards life has softened. On the contrary. Eric kills his security guard Torval because he wants to expedite the moment when he meets his own killer Benno Levin. Eric's self-centeredness and lack of respect towards life prevail. By killing Torval, he believes to have made way "for deeper confrontation" (147).

Paradoxically, Eric does not struggle against the imminent threats on his life. Instead, he participates in accelerating his fall by losing all of his own and his wife's money. In a sense, Eric's self-destructive actions mirror the inexorable consequentiality with which he pursues the contemporary rules of life. His career was the paragon of a magnificent rise. Now Eric engineers a similarly spectacular downfall. Eric believes that his death is inevitable and obligatory and this realization does not really upset him. It is rather the possibility that he may *not* die, that there is no assassin out there waiting for him, which truly scares him: "This was the coldest possible prospect, that no one was out there. It left him in a suspended state, all that was worldly and consequential in blurry ruin behind him but no culminating moment ahead" (169). Eric is like a walking dead man, moving about in a world in which he sees his own decline mirrored in material objects, language, and social practices.

One important social practice that is also associated with references to age and time is doing business. Eric is defined by his cold-blooded business practices and his relentless orientation towards profit. When the limousine passes through the diamond district, Eric cannot help but marvel at this strange world, which stands in stark contrast to the cyber capital business.

Hundreds of millions of dollars a day moved back and forth behind the walls, a form of money so obsolete Eric didn't know how to think about it. It was hard, shiny, faceted. It was everything he'd left behind or never encountered, cut and polished, intensely three-dimensional. People wore it and flashed it. They took it off to go to bed or have sex and they put it on to have sex or die in. They wore it dead and buried. (64)

Clearly, Eric recognizes an "old" way of doing business and is torn between abhorrence and fascination: "The street was an offense to the truth of the future. But he responded to it. He felt it enter every receptor and vault electrically to his brain" (65). Eric's ambivalent feelings in this "huddle of old cultures" indicate that he moves in between two worlds (66). His own world of cyber capital, endless acceleration, and ruthless charting of bodies, minds, and currencies – a world which he used to rule dexterously – is increasingly juxtaposed with remnants of an older world, which surface in language, objects, or business practices. The rules of the new world, which have so long defined Eric's sense of self, are interspersed with the leftovers of former times. Despite their obsolescence and absurdity, the remnants emanate a fascination that subtly shakes Eric's convictions. References to age thus seem to indicate a threat and a fascination at the same time, suggesting the possibility that an alternative life exists, which is defined by legacy, history, and community.[26]

The Body In Between Mortality and Immortality

Besides the repeated references to obsolescence and age, instances of physical death abound: Arthur Rapp (32, 35) and Nikolai Kaganovich (81), two international businessmen, are assassinated in North Korea and Russia; a protester sets himself on fire (98); and Brutha Fez' funeral brings the city's traffic to a halt (130). Most of these public figures die while Eric is riding through Manhattan. Eventually, Eric's chief of security Torval is killed by Eric (146). And a friend of the family, the hairdresser Anthony Adubato, recalls the death of Eric's father long ago, when Eric was still a child (161).[27]

Eric's reaction to this accumulation of deaths is multi-faceted. He hates Rapp "with sizable violence of heart" and obsessively and repeatedly watches the TV-recording of Rapp being stabbed (33). Instead of feeling terrified or expressing a heightened desire for safety, Eric feels refreshed by Rapp's death (cf. 35). With Kaganovich, Eric shares a friendship and a seemingly remarkable hunting experience. It becomes clear, however, that Eric does not mourn the death of his friend, with whom he has much in common (they are both men of "swaggering wealth and shady reputation" 81). He is "glad to see the man dead in the mud" because it relaxes him (81-2). Kinski, Eric's chief of theory, explains these uncommon feelings in

---

26 A similarly ambivalent meaning of age references can be observed when Eric feels attracted to Jane Melman. She is described as a middle-aged woman who lacks the stamina of youth. Eric's reactions range from disgust to fascination and sexual arousal.

27 Besides these actual deaths, the life of the president who is also in the city on this day is threatened (cf. 35). And André Petrescu, the so-called pastry assassin, manages to successfully ambush and assault Eric (cf. 142).

the following way: "He was a rival in some sense, yes? [...] He died so you can live" (82).

The two following deaths, however, deeply affect Eric: He is both fascinated and shocked by the self-immolation of an unknown protester; and Brutha Fez's death profoundly upsets Eric. Fez, a famous rapper in his mid-thirties, dies of cardiac problems and thus of natural causes. Fez's premature death involves no spectacle, violence, or aggression, which makes Kozmo, Fez' manager, apologize to Eric: "Hope he didn't let you down," Kozmo says, believing apparently that Fez' trivial and petty cause of death might be a disappointment. Eric is deeply moved by the spectacle of the funeral, which he finds mystical and "well beyond the scan of human encompassment" (134). The spectacle also triggers thoughts about his own funeral, making Eric realize that he cannot compete with Fez' farewell because he does not have friends or worshippers. Those who would come to his funeral would be "[m]en he'd crushed" who would only gloat and mock him (136). Eric feels "unworthy and pathetic" and realizes that he has no control over Fez' funeral or over his own (136). Eventually, Eric even starts to cry and, after this emotional outburst, "Eric slowly grew still. In the leather and flesh of Kozmo's enveloping bulk, he felt the beginnings of thoughtful acceptance" (139). Apparently, Eric begins to realize that his downfall will not only be a financial spectacle. Instead, there is "no beauty in dying young" (138), Eric remarks when he listens to one of Fez' songs. He becomes aware of the fact that his own death as a young man cannot be solved or rendered more heroic by transforming it into a spectacle. It is going to be a petty matter.

The many cases of death within a single day convey a quite obvious message: The fact of physical death can be neither prevented nor controlled via medical examinations or security personnel. After all, Fez's death was not precipitated by external violence. He did not take drugs, nor is he responsible for his early death by some other carelessness. And even though Fez consulted specialists and faith healers, he could not fix his heart that "just wore out" (132). Eric, however, has long believed in the preventability of death. Or, in Bauman's words, he believed in the deconstruction of mortality. He has engaged in numerous efforts to shape his body and to eat healthily. He has hired a nurse and two armed guards who sit close to his office and monitor him constantly through cameras (cf. 15). Moreover, a doctor comes by his office to examine him everyday, even on weekends.

When Jane Melman mocks this exaggerated caution, Eric replies: "We die, Jane, on weekends [...] We die because it's the weekend [...] We die everyday" (45). Eric even goes so far as to worry about a blackhead, asking his doctor what he should do about it. Eric wants utmost control over his body and he enjoys feeling it scrutinized (during a rectal examination) or seeing his heart throbbing on a screen (during an echocardiogram).

One of Eric's prominent concerns is his asymmetrical prostate, which shakes his confidence in mastering his body. He mentions this medical condition very early in the novel (cf. 8) and keeps bringing it up through the final pages. It seems that his prostate troubles him for several interdependent reasons: There is an aesthetic motive because Eric treasures symmetry, order, and straightforwardness. He looks for "balance, beautiful balance, equal parts, equal sides" (200) and employs techniques of charting and forecasting that give him a feeling of beauty and precision (cf. 756). To Eric, charts and numbers are not cold data but "soulful and glowing, a dynamic aspect of the life process" (24). It is in the digital world with its "zero-oneness" that bodies are "knowable and whole" (24). Eric is somehow intrigued by the idea of asymmetry, considering it a "counterforce to balance and calm, the riddling little twist, subatomic, that made creation happen" (52). But when he applies these ideas to his body, he begins "to feel pale and spooked" because he associates "the shadow of pissed pants" and "limp-dick desolation" – two assumed consequences of an asymmetrical prostate that haunt him "to the point of superstitious silence" (53). Physical asymmetry signifies Eric's powerlessness to shape and control his body according to his own desires. This medical condition makes Eric aware of the imperfection, possible dysfunction, and frailty of his body. Despite all of the medical examinations and precautionary measures he endures, he might not be able to prevent incontinence, impotence, or some other form of dysfunction. Eric even believes that he might (slowly) die as a result of this dysfunction (cf. 120).

By acknowledging to some extent the possibility of asymmetry and his own lack of control – an acceptance that is emphasized by Eric's decision to leave his hairdresser with only one side trimmed – Eric opens himself up to a fundamental dimension of physical life and living in time: mortality. In doing so, *Cosmoplis* deals with a central topic in age discourses, namely the biological dimensions of age and aging. Certainly, 28-year-old Eric Packer is not confronted with the consequences of physical old age; nonetheless, his increasing age awareness opens him up to an understanding of his body that is malleable by and contingent on diseases and the passing of time. Eric's body thus becomes a major focus and source of knowledge in his attempt to better understand his current status in life. While he used to see his body as a chartable mass of information, which he controlled meticulously, he starts to give in to all kinds of bodily needs, desires, and cravings on the presumed last day of his life. He has several strong sensations of hunger, which he satisfies by devouring unhealthy food in unbridled portions (cf. 17, 114, 118, 140). "He could not stop tossing peanuts in his mouth" and gulps down food that contradicts his diet (114). "Today is different," he explains (114). Eric also gives in to his sexual desires and has sex with three women in the course of the novel – with his art dealer Didi Fancher (cf. 26), with his security guard Kendra Hays (cf. 111), and with his wife Elise Shiffrin (cf. 177). To increase his bodily perception, he even inflicts physical pain on himself. He asks Kendra Hays, for example, to taser him with a shockgun (cf. 115). He insists on a rectal exam during Dr. Ingram's visit and enjoys the pain. And, eventually, in his confrontation with his assassin Benno Levin, Eric shoots himself in the palm of his hand to provoke Benno. In all of these instances, physical pain oddly exhilarates Eric. The shock gun makes him "feel freer than usual" and "strangely elated, deprived of his faculties for reason" (115).

During the rectal exam, Eric makes the following observation:

He felt the pain. It traveled the pathways. It informed the ganglion and spinal cord. He was here in his body, the structure he wanted to dismiss in theory even when he was shaping it under the measured effect of barbells and weights. He wanted to judge it redundant and transferable. It was convertible to wave arrays of information. It was the thing he watched on the oval screen when he wasn't watching Jane. (48)

In Eric's eyes, his body used to be a shapeable but also negligible mass of information and he believed that he could render his body immortal by transferring it into data. "He always wanted to become quantum dust, transcending his body mass, the soft tissue over his bones, the muscle and fat. The idea was to live outside the given limits, in a chip, on a disk, as data, in whirl, in radiant spin, a consciousness saved from void" (206). Immortality is thus not a technological fantasy to Eric but the logical consequence of his belief in progress and control. Therefore, he reasons that "[i]t would be the master thrust of cyber-capital, to extend the human experience toward infinity as a medium for corporate growth and investment, for the accumulation of profits and vigorous reinvestment" (207). The merger of technology and human beings would render "never-ending life" possible (105). People would not die but become "streams of information" (104). "Why die when you can live on disk? A disk, not a tomb. An idea beyond the body" (105). Eric slowly realizes, however, that this vision is faulty: His sleeplessness and his feelings of insubstantiality indicate that something is wrong with the idea of dismissing the body.

By afflicting pain to his body, Eric realizes that his vision of comfort in immortality is an error in reasoning. Eric's sense of corporeality, triggered by his bleeding hand, sends him through a set of emotions and crucial insights. His pain is a "counter-consciousness," just as much as asymmetry is a "counterforce" (50, 52), which he learns to accept. "The pain was crushing him, making him smaller [...] reducing him in size, person and value [...] The hand felt necrotic. He thought he could smell a million cells dying" (198). Physical pain lifts Eric to a new level of comprehension and awareness: "The pain was the world. [...] He could feel himself contained in the dark but also beyond it, on the lighted outer surface, the other side, belonged to both, feeling both, being himself and seeing himself" (201). This near-death-experience makes Eric realize the self-delusion inherent in believing in immortality:

[H]is pain interfered with his immortality. It was crucial to his distinctiveness, too vital to be bypassed and not susceptible, he didn't think, to computer emulation. The things that made him who he was could hardly be identified much less converted to data [...] He'd come to know himself, untranslatably, through his pain. He felt so tired now. (207)

Eric realizes that his body is non-transferable, "not convertible to some high sublime, the technology of mind-without-end" (207-8). On the contrary, his body is "all him" (207).

This grounding in the body and acceptance of physical mortality is correlated with another lesson that Eric has to learn. The asymmetrical prostate that has plagued him so long turns out to be irrelevant. Benno has the same condition and maintains that "It means nothing [...] It's harmless. A harmless variation. Nothing to worry about. Your age, why worry?" (199). This revelation trivializes Eric's panic scenarios when he imagined a loss of control, incontinence, impotence, and even death. Benno's disclosure also reveals that Eric has failed on two levels: He has misinterpreted and over-dramatized the meaning of his condition, and he has missed the simplest lesson that it could have taught him, as Benno argues, namely,

> [t]he importance of the lopsided, the thing that's skewed a little. You were looking for balance, beautiful balance, equal parts, equal sides [...] But you should have been tracking the yen in its tics and quirks. The little quirk. The misshape [...] That's were the answer was, in your body, in your prostate. (200)

In other words, the answer to Eric's doubts and fears, as Benno suggests, might lie in accepting a loss of control, in letting go and accepting dysfunction and decline. (Or it might lie in questioning the severity of this supposed decline and in investigating into the meanings and consequences of such a condition.)

Cosmopolis illustrates how deeply Eric is involved in the ideological agenda of his world, in which decline of value over time, acceleration of time, and shortening life cycles shape his worldview. Eric cannot imagine an alternative view of life because, in his world, in which time is measured in zeptoseconds, he does not have any time left for deeper knowledge and wisdom – skills that are often attributed to the processes of aging and old age. Instead, Eric rigidly follows the path to decline that he has internalized. He even contributes actively to making it impossible for himself to accept the possibility of survival.

Survival in a Neoliberal World

In Eric's world, it seems, aging has become altogether impossible. Death is unavoidable, of course, but in the novel it has become imminent and excludes a prior time span of adjustment, learning, and maturing. Eric is stricken doubly by mortality: He is confronted with ideational mortality through obsolescence and a loss of value as well as physical mortality, which is embodied in his assassin Benno Levin. The alternative to premature death, namely the possibility for survival, is also present in the novel but it remains an unintelligible option to Eric.

Survival is mentioned several times in the novel. It surfaces in a sense of wholeness and connectedness to a larger collective spirit or in otherworldly mysticism. Eric is stunned, for instance, by Fez' funeral where he finds "something mystical about this [funeral spectacle], well beyond the scan of human encompassment, the half-crazed passion of a desert saint" (134). And, shortly before he encounters Benno Levin, when Eric stumbles upon a movie set and becomes part of a mass of naked bodies, he realizes that he wants to be part of this group (of rather imperfect people).

He wanted to be here among them, all-body, the tattooed, the hairy-assed, those who stank. He wanted to set himself in the middle of the intersection, among the old with their raised veins and body blotches and next to the dwarf with a bump on his head [...] There were the young and the strong. He was one of them. He was one of the morbidly obese, the tanned and fit and middle-aged. He thought of the children in the scrupulous beauty of their pretending, so formal and fire-boned. He was one. (176)

For Eric, however, there is no long-lasting comfort in the above-mentioned spectacles and rituals. While Eric is fascinated with Fez' funeral, he also feels dispirited when he realizes that his own funeral would be rather dreary in comparison because no one would actually mourn him. After Eric experiences the connectedness on the movie set, he has sex with his wife. But "[t]he instant he knew he loved her, she slipped down his body and out of his arms" (178). Hence, even though Eric tries to unite himself with others, he is left alone and finds no comfort in connectedness or community with other people. Moreover, Eric senses that, when he dies, he will not live on in the minds of a loving wife or other mourners.

Eric's attempt to connect himself to some legacy, history, or tradition through his marriage with Elise Shifrin fails in the end. He is intrigued by the history of her money, "piling up over generations, through world wars. This is not something I need but a little history is nice. The family retainers. The vintage cellars [...] This is stupid but nice" (120). Shortly after Eric has explained his reasons for marrying Elise, she declares their marriage to be over. In the passages before the novel ends, Eric comes back to his motivations for marrying Elise, connecting her reaction to his death with archaic forms of mourning:

[H]e'd married when he'd married in order have a widow to leave behind. He imagined his wife, his widow, shaving her head, perhaps, in response to his death, and choosing to wear black for a year, and watching the burial in isolated desert terrain, from a distance, with her mother and the media. (208)

Similarly, he imagines his bodyguard and lover Kendra Hays washing his viscera in palm wine, evoking associations with ancient mortuary practices (cf. 208). These imaginations attest to Eric's wish to be mourned and remembered and to become part of a legacy. At the same time, Eric's mourning fantasy seems strangely exaggerated and eccentric.

Eventually, Eric finds a way of leaving such a trace in the world by imagining how he wants his funeral to take place: It is – typical of Eric – both spectacular and marked by economic reasoning. Eric wants to be cremated and buried in "his nuclear bomber" (208).

He wanted to be solarized. He wanted the plane flown by remote control with his embalmed body aboard [...] reaching maximum altitude and leveling at supersonic dash speed and the sent plunging into the sand, fireballed one and all, leaving a work of land art [...] that would [...] be held in perpetual trust under the auspices of his dealer and executor, Didi Fancher, [...] for pre-approved groups and enlightened individuals under exempt-status section 501(c)(3) of the U.S. Internal Revenue Code. (209)

Besides the megalomania Eric displays here, it seems as if he is so deeply engrained in capitalist reasoning that he cannot even think outside of economic regimes when it comes to imagining his own death. His monumental tomb of land art is strangely reminiscent of a museum exhibit or a cultural site in terms of the pyramidal dimensions in which Eric seems to imagine his own tomb. Such a monumental tomb is, however, not only a scientific or cultural object of interest but also a commodity on the tourist market – hence the reference to the Internal Revenue Code which rules that charitable organizations, for instance, are tax-exempt. Museum exhibits – whether in terms of pieces that speak of a monumental historical past or items that represent commodities that are reminiscent of an earlier time – render older cultures somewhat immortal and ensure access for younger generations.

Once more, Eric's funeral fantasies indicate this character's eccentricity and immersion in economic rationality.[28]

Eric's hope for immortality is, however, destroyed by the grim, cold, and disillusioned world he inhabits. This loss of hope is also of Eric's own making: Eric has orchestrated his financial downfall; he has killed a man and destroyed his marriage. There seems to be no alternative to Eric's death, no possibility of reversal or change of mind. These prospects eventually even eradicate Eric's zest for life.

Maybe he didn't want that life after all, starting over broke, hailing a cab in a busy intersection filled with jock-eying junior executives, arms aloft, bodies smartly spinning to cover every compass point. What did he want that was not posthumous? He stared into space. He understood what was missing, the predatory impulse, the sense of larger excitation that drove him through his days, the sheer and reeling need to be. (209)

With no vital energy left at twenty-eight, Eric Packer is doomed to die. Eric has been aged by the cybercapitalist world but has been denied the experience of aging in a temporal and physical dimension, which encompasses the possibility of change across time in terms of a dignified and enriching development or as a form of personal growth. In Eric's world, there is no gain in being aged – let alone aging – but a cold and merciless disillusionment and submissive acceptance of one's fate.

When the age critic like Gullette reflects upon the lethal consequences of the "new regimes of ageism," she argues that they "can cause even relatively young people to think that perhaps they should make an exit before they become a 'burden'" (*Agewise* 43). While Gullette refers to people in midlife when she speaks of "relatively young people," her claim seems to match 28-year-old Eric Packer. According to Gullette, the duty-to-die ide-

---

[28] One might also interpret Eric's vision of his tomb as a form of resistance to the commodity cycle – just as Margaret Morganroth Gullette speaks of her wardrobe of old clothes as a form of resistance against the relentless fashion cycle. A person like Eric, who has lived fervently and uncompromisingly within the economic life cycle, could thus find an exit from this cycle via his stubbornness in persisting.

ology is a common phenomenon in American culture, triggered by an anti-aging ideology which purports that "[t]he only way to be truly anti-aging is to die younger" (100). *Cosmopolis* pushes this anti-aging idea to the extreme: Eric, who is so immersed in the particular ideology of his world, does not see any other way out but *not* to age. He readily accepts a premature and predetermined exit.

In *Cosmopolis*, Eric Packer's anti-aging disposition is counteracted with an alternative prospect. References to age not only insinuate decline and a loss of value, they also suggest alternatives to Eric's pessimistic worldview in that they indicate an opportunity for survival and aging-past-youth. This alternative vision, however, goes beyond Eric's strategies of rationalization, measurement, and control because it values the skewed, the unexplainable, and the uncontrollable (cf. 200). To Eric, however, this approach to aging – as attractive as it may appear to him occasionally – is unfeasible. Instead, Eric clings to the idea that aging only leads to decline, imperfection, and a loss of control. Survival in this lethal, ageist world seems impossible.

In *The Future* (2011), filmmaker Miranda July also sends her characters to the borderland of (symbolic) death and has them negotiate accelerated and frozen time, their future aged selves, and life course imaginaries. In contrast to Don DeLillo, however, July creates a more hopeful fictional world by using the devices of cinematography in creative and inspiring ways to suggest an alternative to the decline imaginaries. Her characters Sophie and Jason experience acute age awareness and anticipate their looming deaths; but they persist, and they take on the challenge of aging-past-youth.

5 Positive Age Metaphors: Miranda July's *The Future* and *It Chooses You*

Miranda July, born in 1974, is an American filmmaker, writer, and performance artist, who became known to a wider, international public with her first feature film *Me and You and Everyone We Know* (2005), which won the Caméra d'Or in Cannes. Since then, she has received much public attention and praise as a new voice of the independent American art scene. She published her short stories in the *Paris Review, Harvard Review, Harper's Magazine,* and *The New Yorker* and she is well known for an online collaborate public art project (with Harrell Fletcher) called "Learning to Love You More," which gave out assignments to amateur artists and asked them for artistic and partly autobiographical contributions to the online platform.[1] The project ran for seven years and, in 2010, the San Francisco Museum of Modern Art acquired the homepage and archived the collected material.[2]

---

1 See Nassim W. Balestrini's essay on photography as a form of online life writing in "Learning to Love You More" (2013).
2 July's work as well as her personality polarize her critics (cf. Scott, "Is That All" n. pag.). She is adored by a considerable fan base, who praises her peculiar attention to the details of everyday life. Her critics are annoyed by "her neurotic, painfully honest persona," her "twee, stylized, pseudo-existential films," and "the Etsy-shopping, Wes Anderson-quoting, McSweeney's-reading, coastal-living category of upscale urban bohemia" (Wheatley n. pag., Onstad 26).

July's work does not respect boundaries regarding fact and fiction, genres and formats, or her role as an artist. This blending of boundaries becomes particularly apparent in her second feature film, *The Future*, which she developed from an avant-garde performance piece (cf. Stout n. pag.). The piece was called "Things We Don't Understand and Definitely Aren't Going To Talk About" and featured many ideas and features that later found their way into the movie, such as the talking cat and moon, the basic storyline of Jason and Sophie, and the dance in the shirt (cf. Stout n. pag.). Because of these elements in the film, Catherine Wheatley categorizes *The Future* as a surrealist film with elements of "magical realism" (n. pag.) and Ebert defines the movie as "one that inhabits no known genre" (n. pag.). While the magical elements emphasize the fictional quality of the movie, July's book *It Chooses You* (2001), which is a sort of companion book to the film, reveals how much of the material used in *The Future* is autobiographical and documentary. In the book, July describes the production process of *The Future*, particularly her writer's block, and she provides background information on the characters, their story, and her personal motivation for the movie. It becomes clear that Sophie's and Jason's conflicts originated in July's personal life experiences. This particular combination of material catapults the film into a twilight zone between fact and fiction.

The Future features the couple Sophie and Jason, both aged 35, who live together in Los Angeles. Sophie is a dance teacher for children, and Jason works at home as a tech support. Jason and Sophie seem to spend most of their free time online, which is particularly debilitating for Sophie, who keeps watching a colleague's dance video instead of taking heart and initiating a dance project of her own. In this sense, Sophie and Jason are typical perpetual adolescents: Instead of facing the realities of adult life, they withdraw from the world into their sheltered togetherness. But then, Sophie and Jason decide to adopt a cat from the shelter, assuming that the cat will only live another month. When they come to the clinic to pick up the cat, they learn (to their horror) that the cat may live another five years if they treat him well.[3] The cat has to stay in the clinic for another four weeks before he can be released into their care. At home, Jason and Sophie have an epipha-

---

3   The cat's gender is unclear. Even though July uses her own voice for the cat's off text, I decided to use the male form because July does so as well in *It Chooses You*.

ny: They realize that they only have one more month to figure out their lives because the cat will be just as big a commitment for them as a child. As a consequence, Sophie decides to start a dance project while Jason quits his job and starts to work for a small environmental organization, selling trees from door to door. Sophie's project fails, she becomes frustrated and begins an affair with Marshall, a forty-something suburban father of one daughter. When she confesses her betrayal to Jason, Jason is so upset that he magically stops time. Meanwhile – in what seems to be a different time continuum – Sophie has moved in with Marshall and becomes involved in the everyday routine of suburban life. But something is wrong, and Sophie eventually leaves Marshall. At this point, a month has passed and both Jason and Sophie remember individually the cat they wanted to adopt. When they go to the shelter, they learn that their cat was euthanized because they came one day late. Jason allows Sophie to stay one more night in their apartment. The movie ends at this point, and the future of their relationship remains open.[4]

It Chooses You, which is partly July's strategy to overcome her writer's block while working on the screenplay of *The Future*, features thirteen interviews July conducted with people who wanted to sell their belongings through the LA *PennySaver*. July interweaves the life stories of her interviewees with her own situation in life. She provides an interpretation of the movie and offers a glimpse into her own crises, which are quite similar to those of her fictional characters Sophie and Jason. July stresses several times that her own emotional landscape had a profound impact on the storyline: "I didn't set out planning to write a script about time, but the longer I took to write it and get it made, the more time became a protagonist in my life," revealing an astute awareness of the passing of time and mortality (112). July goes on reflecting upon her recent marriage: "And now that I had vowed to hang out with this man until I died, I also thought a lot about dying. It seemed I had not only married him but also married my eventual death" (112). In *The Future,* July interweaves these autobiographical experiences with fictional elements and, in doing so, she transgresses the

---

4   The plotline of *The Future* is interspersed with short sequences, in which the cat Paw Paw, waiting for Jason and Sophie to pick him up, speaks about his thoughts and fears. Paw Paw functions like a "guide and narrator throughout the film" (Wheatley n. pag.).

boundaries of words and visuals, book and film (also see page 16). From the perspective of an age reading, July's work, both fiction and non-fiction, resembles an age narrative because – following Gullette's definition – it organizes cultural knowledge about aging, regardless of genres of media forms (cf. pages 12-3). Therefore, I will read the film and the book next to each other.

As a jack-of-all-trades, July acts as the writer and director and she also plays the lead role. In interviews, she often equates the fictional character Sophie with herself or describes Sophie and Jason as two sides of her personality: "If Sophie was all my doubts and the nightmare of who I would be if I succumbed to them, then Jason could be the curiosity and faith that repel that fear" (*It Chooses Me* 201). In addition, July draws on many of her individual idiosyncrasies in her story about Sophie and Jason. Shirty, the old T-shirt that Sophie uses for comfort, exists in a similar form in July's life. Moreover, *The Future* features documentary scenes, which originated from the *PennySaver* project she worked on while experiencing writer's block. Joe Putterlik was one of the people July interviewed and he turned out to be a true gift and inspiration for the scriptwriting process. Fascinated by his life story and personal charm, July wrote Joe Putterlik into the screenplay and had him play himself during the shooting. July reveals in *It Chooses You* that the scenes, in which Joe Putterlik appeared, "were 80 percent improvisation and 20 percent scripted" (203). It is this blurring of boundaries that is typical of Miranda July's art and that is part of what Richard Brody calls her "freely imaginative stylization" (n. pag.).[5]

Summarizing the themes of the movie, some critics acknowledge the topics of impending adulthood, the finitude of time, and mortality. Hoberman, for instance, defines the central themes as "the inability to stop time, the finality of unborn children, the failure to protect posterity, the end of

---

5 Brody describes the genre of the book in the following way: It "is less a work of nonfiction or a memoir than it is a documentary film in book form. In effect, it's a making-of regarding several key elements of *The Future*" (n. pag.). Brody goes on summarizing the book as "a blend of confession and reporting, of raw data and confected response" which "traces the artist's own journey outside her own imagination, and proves the irresistible power of sensibility to make pretty much anything in the artist's purview, however haphazard or remote, an aspect of her own universe" (n. pag.).

romantic love, the limitations of memory, the routine of carelessness, and the futility of expectations" (n. pag.). And Wheatley finds that the film is "concerned with endings not beginnings, steeped in depression and death, and with little room for redemption or reconciliation" (n. pag.). For Scott, it is the title of *The Future* that points to the complexity of the movie, "which refers simultaneously to a terrifying abstraction – an unknowable territory bounded by death, eternity, the end of time" (n. pag.). Some critics mention Sophie's and Jason's age-inappropriate behavior and their delayed adulthood: "Though they are well into their 30s and measure the span of their relationship in years, they seem as shy and unworldly as children, passive-aggressively resisting the demands and enticements of adulthood" (Scott n. pag.). Casati maintains that the characters are in an anteroom to adulthood ("Wartezimmer zum Erwachsenwerden" n. pag.). And Hoberman argues that *"The Future* is transparently a movie about having a child, as well as about being one" (n. pag.). Compared to the reviews of the earlier fictional narratives that I have analyzed, it seems that critics have become attuned to or have developed a sensitivity to the relationship between young adults and topics of temporality, age-inappropriate behavior, or mortality.

The Future uses all of the plot characteristics that seem to be typical of stories about aged young adults: Two characters in their thirties become aware of their age and of the passing of time, which triggers a feeling of panic and a sense of finitude, leading them to change their lives in various ways. With their decision to adopt the cat Paw Paw, Sophie's and Jason's age awareness is set off and they realize "their looming loss of freedom" (*It Chooses You* 7). As in the other fictional narratives discussed so far, references to age are accompanied with the characters' sense of being losers. Moreover, the age references indicate otherness, albeit in a positive sense and, similar to *Away We Go,* the characters in *The Future* cherish being different from those around them and show no inclination to change this situation. Like Dwight in *Indecision*, Sophie and Jason seem to be overwhelmed by their freedom to do and be anyone they want to be and to have a plethora of choices and opportunities. This freedom is experienced as paralyzing.

In contrast to the other fictional narratives within this study, *The Future* stands out because of its playful use of magical elements and because July's work provides a much more optimistic vision of the dreaded crises triggered by age and (looming) decline. This hopeful and unconventional perspective is remarkable because its message about aging is not ageist or pessimistic (in contrast to *My Big Fat Greek Wedding* and *Cosmopolis*), because it does not argue for a glorification of perpetual adolescence (in contrast to *Away We Go*), and because it does not accept generic solutions, such as an eventual coming of age (in contrast to *My Big Fat Greek Wedding* or *Indecision*).

No Future in *The Future*

The central conflict in *The Future* is triggered by Sophie's and Jason's sudden realization that time is finite. When the couple finds out that they might have to take care of Paw Paw for the next five years, they are shocked and start calculating:

Sophie: We'll be forty in five years.
Jason: Forty is almost fifty, and after fifty the rest is just loose change.
Sophie: Loose change?
Jason: Like not quite enough to get anything you really want.
Sophie: O God! So for all practical purposes, in a month, that's it for us.

In this projection of the characters' aging selves, the passage of time is accelerated and old age and even death seem to be just around the corner. With the comparison to loose change, Jason also evokes the idea of worthlessness – a typical ageist view of old age. This age awareness and sense of finitude triggers the characters' crisis, as they realize that they have not lived up to their expectations.

Jason: God, I always thought I'd be smarter. I had also thought eventually we'd be rich.
Sophie: I always want to follow the news, you know, but then I'm so far behind, and now it's just like, what's the point?
Jason: I always thought that I'd end up being a world leader.
Sophie: Oh, yeah, that's not gonna happen. It's too late for us.

Wisdom, wealth, and authority are the areas in which Jason considers himself as failed and which often come with time and experience – but also with hard work and commitment. Like Dwight in *Indecision*, Sophie and

Jason are not ambitious, focused, or particularly industrious. Instead, as the first shot of the film indicates, they spend most of their time on the couch of their apartment, browsing the internet and wasting time (see fig. 11).

Fig. 11: Jason and Sophie wasting time

When Sophie summarizes their failure claiming that "It's too late for us," she not only exaggerates the couple's apparently irretrievable delay in making their lives worthwhile. She also describes her impression of deficiency in matters of self-realization. Moreover, she indicates a reduction of opportunities, which July addresses more specifically in *It Chooses You*, where she comments on this crucial dialog between Jason and Sophie. July concedes that she knew that the association of old age with loose change was not really true. And yet, she wanted to show the couple's epiphany as "a paralyzing sensation," which would allow her to express the feeling that "[t]here wasn't time to make mistakes anymore, or to do things without knowing why" (76). In an interview, July links her characters' experiences with her own life and elaborates on a feeling of finitude that befell her in her thirties:

It's kind of about letting go of that feeling of my 20s, that feeling that I will do absolutely everything, I will have sex with everyone, I will go to every country [...]. In your 30s, it's obvious that a finite amount of things will happen. (Onstad 29)

In July's work (and in her personal universe), references to age and time do not simply indicate a breach with socio-cultural norms or some form of problematic, age-inappropriate behavior. July's references to age are triggered by personal experiences, such as her anticipation of a decrease in opportunities and the shrinking of a time window, which she connects with a loss of freedom and adventure. One could argue that July's references to age evoke a particularly negative vision of adulthood, which is certainly true. But it seems to me that it is not simply adulthood (and thus the entry into a new life stage) that is feared but aging in a larger sense and thus across several age stages.

July explains her particular sense of loss and decline in *It Chooses You* when she reflects upon a *PennySaver* incident. July recounts how she met a recently graduated high school student, Andrew, who sold tadpoles through the *PennySaver*. During the interview, they talked about his future plans and July realizes that

[f]or a moment, I could feel time the way he felt it – it was endless [...] there was time for multiple lives. Everything could still happen, so no decision could be very wrong.
That was exactly the opposite of how I was feeling, at thirty-five. I drove home from Paramount feeling ancient, like the characters in my script. (76)

In this account of her age awareness, July connects her chronological age of thirty-five with feeling "ancient." This association is not only triggered by her comparison to a much younger high school student, it also occurs in combination with a larger crisis that is connected to the writing of her script and to other major life decisions she feels coerced to make, such as marriage or motherhood. July's autobiographical experiences are the emotional background that informs Jason and Sophie, who are both thirty-five as well and who apparently function as direct incarnations of July's concerns and fears.

In feeling ancient, July evokes a specific correlation: Feeling or being young, like Andrew, means endlessness in terms of time, chances, and decisions. Being young also has a moral component because decisions are not judged yet and are not considered serious in their consequences. Feeling ancient, on the contrary, implies finitude and the limitedness of time, chances, and decisions. The consequences of a person's actions are more serious. According to this logic, aging thus comes with a sense of irretrievable loss or decline of opportunities.

Hence, references to age indicate the characters' (and July's) crisis and trigger the further action in the movie. After her dramatic verdict "It's too late for us," Sophie goes to a wall calendar in the apartment and remarks:

Sophie: At least we have a month.
Jason: You know, that's actually a long time when you think about it. Like, we thought we'd have him home today, but instead we have a whole month to...
Sophie: To what?
Jason: I don't know, but, I mean, if this is our last month ever, shouldn't we...
Sophie: Yeah. Right. I mean, if we were dying in a month, we would definitely reprioritize.

Clearly, Sophie and Jason overdramatize their situation. In equating their sense of scarcity of time with "our last month ever" and the idea of "dying in a month," they exaggerate to make their feelings appear more urgent.

When Jason and Sophie use a countdown for their last month, the counting down of days further amplifies their sense of losing time. The countdown is visualized through the calendar, which reappears a couple of times over the course of the movie. It symbolizes the characters' presumed last chance at self-realization. The calendar also signifies the day they are to adopt the cat as a symbolic death-day.[6] In *The Future*, a second countdown is used in Sophie's dance project "30 days-30 dances," which emerges as a rival project to one of her colleague's regular online posts of new dance routines that Sophie watches repeatedly. Again, the countdown indicates awareness of the passing of time and amplifies Sophie's emotional quandary of growing panic and despair. Sophie fails to record any dances,

---

6   In Eric Schaeffer's romantic comedy *If Lucy Fell* (1996), the protagonist Lucy also paints a calendar of her last month as a 29-year-old in a supersized version on a wall in order to count down the days before she turns thirty. She plans to kill herself if she has not found the man of her dreams by then. Also, Julie Powell's tremendously successful blog, novel, and Hollywood movie, *The Julie/Julia Project*, features a similar countdown triggered by age awareness. Also see my article on "Countdown Blogs" (2012).

which intensifies her crisis and gradually leads her towards an affair with another man, Marshall.

Jason uses the countdown differently. He decides to let his fate or project choose him and ends up working with an environmental initiative, selling trees at doorsteps in different neighborhoods. This new purpose leads him to Joe, who plays a central role in Jason's story because it is this old man who teaches Jason about love and relationships. Joe functions as Jason's future self. Contrary to the future feared selves of aging, as conceptualized by Cassie Phoenix and Andrew C. Sparkes (see page 91), Joe is a hopeful future vision of Jason: a serene and loving husband of many years.

Future Selves

Jason and Joe's connection is established through visual clues: Both possess an Escher painting, a similar couch, and hippo figurines. They meet three times over the course of the movie. First, Jason goes to Joe's house because he wants to buy a used hairdryer that Joe offered via the *Penny-Saver*. Joe appears as a talkative man when he describes the advantages of the old objects he repairs. It is a scene heavy with meaning in an age context, particularly in relation to Gullette's notions of consumer cycles and their implicit messages about aging (see Chapter 4.3). According to Gullette, the consumer cycle equates old objects (regardless of their functioning) as worthless objects that need to be discarded. In conjunction with Jason's earlier comment about old age as loose change and thus as something worthless and insufficient, Joe's handling of old objects offers a more positive interpretation: Even though the hairdryer is not worth much in a pecuniary sense (Joe is selling it for only three dollars), he indicates to Jason that its symbolic worth is ten times higher than he is charging Jason for it. The value of the hairdryer is thus not affected by its age. On the contrary, its symbolic value lies in its hopeful message about persistence and survival.[7] Thus, even though July uses stereotypical notions about age and aging as the emotional background of her characters' crisis, her work presents a way out of the predicament that haunts her characters (and herself). Fur-

---

7   Similarly, Gullette argues that she tries to resist the detrimental messages of the consumer cycle by clinging to her old clothes instead of discarding them once they are out of fashion.

thermore, in presenting a vision of (romantic) love, trust, and connectedness that grows with age (as in Joe's marriage – see below), the movie's message about aging defies the established imaginaries of decline, obsolescence, and worthlessness. The fact that Joe Putterlik is not a fictional character but an actual person increases the persuasiveness of his optimistic message.

When Jason leaves after having purchased the hairdryer, Joe says to him mysteriously "You can always come back when you're ready." Jason follows this invitation and visits Joe a second time. He then learns about Joe's life, his loving relationship to his wife, and his activities to keep his marriage alive. Joe has been happily married for sixty-two years and knows that a relationship can be hard in the beginning. When Jason says about his relationship with Sophie that they did not have any problems in the beginning, Joe insists that they are "just in the middle of the beginning right now." Obviously, Joe has a different and more expansive understanding of time than Jason, for whom four years in a relationship is a long time. Joe teaches Jason that he is mistaken in his shortsightedness regarding the finitude of opportunities. In other words, Jason's relationship (and his future) may not be coming to an end; he is just in the middle of the beginning. During their third meeting, Jason and Joe have a sandwich together and Joe gives him a toy for Paw Paw that swings back and forth (see fig. 12). Paw Paw, as July explains in *It Chooses You*, is a "symbol of the couple's love" (198) and, in this sense, the toy's property of rocking back and forth becomes symbolic of the ways in which Jason and Sophie's love might change like a pendulum.

Fig. 12: Joe gives Jason a toy for Paw Paw

Sophie has a more complicated relationship with her future self. July associates Sophie with an aged woman across the street who might function as a symbolic future self, but Sophie gets no comfort or advice from her because she is a woman whom Sophie only observes from a distance and never actually speaks to. Sophie watches this woman twice and says admiringly during her meltdown (after realizing the failure of her dance project):

Sophie: This woman has her shit together. You can tell she's just totally 'carpe diem.'
Jason: She's a lonely spinster.
Sophie: (huffs) No, that is one tough cookie.

It seems that this "tough cookie" is a projection of the kind of person Sophie would like to be, namely someone who pulls herself together, who is strong and is able to seize the day. All of these qualities seem very appealing to Sophie, who has just wasted another day of her countdown project. Jason's labeling of this unknown woman as a lonely spinster is countered by Sophie's perception of a woman who is straightforward and tough – characteristics that Sophie seems to lack.

Sophie's second future self is a version of herself in the different life that she attempts to lead when she moves in with Marshall. The suburban, middle-class life that Marshall leads appears to be Sophie's escapist attempt to come to terms with her own life and her discontentment with her relationship with Jason. Sophie virtually becomes a housewife with a child, namely Marshall's daughter Gabriella, leading a life in a nice house in a suburban neighborhood. Sophie, however, does not belong in this house or family, and her inappropriateness is symbolically reinforced when Gabriella digs a grave for herself in the garden. Sophie asks her what she is doing and, when they notice that Marshall is watching them, Gabriella advises Sophie to wave and to "act naturally." The fakeness that is indicated in this scene reflects the artificiality of Sophie's situation. Gabriella's grave, into which she climbs one night to be buried by her father with her head barely sticking out of the ground, functions like a visualization of Sophie's emotional state – a grave-like feeling of being buried alive. Symbolically speaking, one might even argue that Gabriella represents the child in Sophie or the 'child life' that she used to live with Jason. Sophie buries this child and exchanges it for an 'adult life' with Marshall; however, this adult life, contrary to the coming-of-age story, means death not growth.

The wrongness of the situation is reversed when Shirtie appears. Shirtie is an animated T-shirt that moves magically and haunts Sophie while she is living in Marshall's house. Shirtie alludes to Sophie's child-like inclination for comfort.[8] In what looks like an avant-garde dance with Shirtie (see fig. 13), Sophie becomes herself again, breaks up with Marshall, and goes back to her old life (and self).

Fig. 13: Sophie and her dance

In her portrait of Miranda July, Onstad offers an intriguing interpretation of this scene:

The midlife crisis is usually a male response to mortality terror, but in *The Future*, it's July's character, Sophie, who takes up with a single dad, leaving her bohemian surroundings for an affair in a nice house in the suburbs. For July, the story of a woman fleeing her life was a personal purging. "I think I was afraid; I was committing to someone forever," she says.[9] "That [idea] that you might just defect from your life, I've been carrying around for so long. You don't want that to be a constant threat. So I think I was like: O.K., what would happen? So you leave. Then what

---

8   In an earlier scene, when Sophie and Jason are sitting on their couch (see fig. 12), Sophie has Shirtie in her hands and caresses it absent-mindedly.

9   July refers here to a decisive turning point in her own life, namely her marriage to Mike Mills, who is also a filmmaker.

happens? Then I realized: You're probably haunted by yourself. Your soul follows you." In the film, the soul takes the shape of a yellow T-shirt, which literally creeps out to the suburbs and back to Sophie. Then Sophie climbs inside the shirt for a kind of dance of suffocation and rebirth. (29)

The allusions to mortality terror that Onstad evokes here match the symbolic burial of Gabriella that I mentioned earlier and, besides the burial, references to mortality occur repeatedly in *The Future*.

The Imminence of Death

July's movie is suffused with references to death on different levels. Most obviously, Sophie's exclamation "That's it for us" insinuates that she sees herself in an anteroom to death. Likewise, the death of Paw Paw at the end of the movie can be interpreted as an indication of the end of Sophie and Jason's relationship. After all, July defines the cat as a symbol of the couple's love (cf. *It Chooses You* 198). On a less conspicuous level, death permeates the movie through the circumstances in which it was produced. Joe Putterlik, Jason's mentor, learned shortly before the shooting that he only had a few more weeks to live. He died before he could see the finished film.

In *It Chooses You*, death also plays a central role and points to a conflict in July's life. July describes how her reflections on mortality influenced the writing of the film. Interestingly, she was not directly concerned with death as such, but she describes her sense of looming mortality as a consequence of her apprehensions about marriage and children. Like her characters Sophie and Jason, July found herself at a turning point in her life: She was about to leave her youthful state as an unmarried, childless woman behind in order to become a responsible adult with many commitments. This watershed moment triggered fears of mortality in July – as does the adoption of Paw Paw for Jason and Sophie. July describes her associations in the following way:

And now that I had vowed to hang out with this man until I died, I also thought a lot about dying. It seemed I had not only married him but also married my eventual death. Before the vows, I might have lived alone, but forever; now I would definitely not be alone and I would definitely die. I had agreed to die, in front of all my family

and friends. Brigitte had taken a picture of the very moment: I was smiling and, understandably, crying. The only thing between me and death was this child. If I delayed having the child, then I could also delay death, sort of. So I was in a hurry to step across the void so I could make the movie so I could have a child before it was too late – and I was also secretly, not in a hurry.
I had shortened my life in another way too, by marrying a man who was eight years older than me, meaning he would die exactly eight years before me, rendering the last eight years of my life useless. I would just spend it crying. (112-3)

References to death work on two different levels here: On the one hand, they emphasize July's fears about the enormity of certain life decisions, indicating an emotional conflict and discomfort. Death implies an assumed inevitable and inescapable life path, an expected massive reduction of opportunities and choices, an acceleration of time, and an irretrievable finality. (Interestingly, neither July nor her characters seem to be afraid of aging as such, and thus of being or getting older.) On the other hand, references to death are also responsible for a great deal of exaggeration and irony. Most probably, July is not actually convinced that marriage is synonymous with death, nor can she be serious about the notion that her life would be shortened because she married an older man. Rather, (and similar to Eric Packer in *Cosmopolis*), the references to death indicate a relation to time that seems to skip aging altogether by artificially accelerating time to such an extreme that death appears as the next exit. References to aging and death thus function as affective amplifiers that also radiate a sense of irony and humor, depending on how serious one wants to take July's trepidations.

Controlling Accelerated Time

July presents different options for her characters to deal with their sense of accelerated time. On the one hand, due to the uncontrollability brought about by this acceleration that overwhelms Sophie and Jason, Sophie starts a countdown project in an effort to better seize the day. She fails, however, and escapes into an affair with Marshall. When Sophie returns to her old job in the dance studio, July invents an ingenious sequence that visualizes her character's fears: Sophie is sitting at the reception desk of the dance studio, when two of her friends, Tammy and Sasha, come in (see fig. 14). They are far advanced in their respective pregnancies and Sophie is visibly shocked to not have known about their pregnancies, realizing disconcertedly that a significant amount of time must have passed without her noticing. In the next shot, Tammy and Sasha are carrying their toddler-age children in their arms and we see Sophie's bewildered face. In the following shot, these children are preschoolers and again, we see Sophie who is speechless in view of the mystery that is unfolding before her eyes. Next, the children have become teenagers and are almost as tall as their mothers; hence, Sophie's bewilderment increases. Finally, these "children" are grown-ups and have a daughter of their own, whom they want to enroll in pre-ballet class. Using very simple means, the shot-and-reverse-shot montage visualizes how Sophie senses an acceleration of time. There are no special effects and the aging characters are kept recognizable because they appear in identical clothing throughout the montage. During the entire sequence, Sophie stays the same in terms of clothes and age. She literally sees time passing before her eyes, and this effect emphasizes her state of desperation. At the same time, the sequence is humorous in its absurdity and exaggeration. The dialog further accentuates and ridicules the superficiality that Sophie's friends express when they compare the joys of their pregnancies with Sophie's unrewarding job: "It's a drag but it's also amazing."[10]

It is no coincidence that July chooses the topics of maternity, family life, and the succession of generations in her visualization of Sophie's fears. In *It Chooses You*, July describes her own apprehensions about her future as well as her feelings of distress by repeatedly referring to 'time:'

I didn't set out planning to write a script about time, but the longer I took to write it and get it made, the more time became a protagonist in my life. At first my boyfriend and I thought we'd get married after our movies were made, but after about six months of trying to get the films financed we thought better of this plan and set a date, come what may. Nothing came, we got married. And then, right around the time I started blindly meeting *PennySaver* sellers, it began to dawn on me that not only was I now old enough to have a baby, I was almost old enough to be too old to have a baby. Five years left. Which is not very long if an independent movie takes at least one year to finance, one year to make, and throw in a year or two for unfore-

---

10 Sasha's and Tammy's lack of originality is also expressed in the rhyming names of their children, Barry and Carrie.

seen disasters. (And I couldn't make the movie while pregnant, even if I wanted to, because I was in it.)
So all my time was spent measuring time. While I listened to strangers and tried to patiently have faith in the unknown, I was also wondering how long this would take, and if any of it really mattered compared to having a baby. Word on the street was that it did not. Nothing mattered compared to having a baby. (112)

The parallels between Sophie and July are striking: Not only does Sophie use her countdown project of "30 days-30 dances" as a means of measuring time, Sophie and Jason's decision to adopt a cat is preceded in the movie by a short, suggestive conversation, in which the couple cautiously checks out each other's readiness to have a child. The symbolism of the cat thus expands beyond July's own interpretation of Paw Paw as "a symbol of this couple's love" (198). Onstad, for instance, believes that the cat is a "symbol of impending adulthood" (26). For Scott, Paw Paw "represents their long-deferred acceptance of adult responsibility, and a chance to break out of the malaise of waiting around for something to happen" (n. pag.). In connection with July's background information, one might also see the cat as a form of child-substitute for Sophie and Jason and thus as a test of their relationship and of their willingness to give up their own childishness.

Fig. 14: Accelerated time

Jason's strategy of dealing with the acceleration of time is also visualized through a cinematographic effect, though it is more 'magical' and sophisticated than Sophie's shot-and-reverse-shot montage: When Sophie confesses her affair to Jason, Jason magically stops time because he feels that his life changes too fast and he needs more time to digest the situation. July introduces the idea of stopping time in the very first scene of the movie, when it still has a playful tone and shows the couple pretending that Jason had actually stopped time. The idea of being able to stop time is also symbolic of Jason's and Sophie's lives: They have lived a timeless life in an everlasting present, and it is only when they realize that time is actually passing that their sense of time accelerates in a terrifying dimension. In the break-up scene, the pretense of being able to stop time becomes 'reality' and Jason literally stops time. While Sophie's life continues in a parallel universe, Jason's life stops that night at 3.14 a.m. Only the moon talks to Jason now (with the voice of Joe Putterlik), giving him advice about life. The moon eventually convinces Jason to embrace the difficulties of life and to allow time to run on. It is in this scene that Jason learns an important lesson about life, which is also an important message of the film: Have faith in the future.

The Hopefulness that Lies in Aging

When July describes how she came up with the title for her movie, she presents herself as a matter-of-fact person, at least to some extent.

> I'd been waiting for the perfect movie title, but finally I decided to just name it. It had to be short, a very familiar, short word. I looked up the most commonly used nouns. The number one most common noun was *time*. Which made me feel less alone; everyone else was thinking about it too. Number two was *person*. Number three was *year*. Number 320 was *future*. The Future. (*It Chooses You* 111)

July's selection process for the title starts out with a wish to capture the common concerns that people have and thus to relate her film to a larger audience. The fact that she ends up choosing word number 320 is further evidence of July's caprices. Nevertheless, the title makes sense because the inconceivability of the future and the many negative associations that are connected with the future, are central topics in the movie. Futurity has two very different connotations in *The Future*: On the one hand, it inspires fear because it is semantically equated with death. On the other hand, and this is the lesson that Sophie and Jason learn, it can also inspire faith and confidence because the movie envisions the possibility of a fulfilled and optimistic way of aging through time. For Sophie, this message is expressed in the figure of the woman next door: The seemingly "lonely spinster" is actually a woman of strength and inspiration. For Jason, it is Joe who teaches him about the beauty and worthiness that lies in aging and old age. If old objects like a hairdryer stay valuable, love can subsist as well.

July mentions the positive connotations of aging through time when she reflects upon the influence that Joe had on her own life:

Maybe I had miscalculated what was left of my life. Maybe it wasn't loose change. Or, actually, the whole thing was loose change, from start to finish—many, many little moments, each holiday, each Valentine, each year unbearably repetitive and yet somehow always new. You could never buy anything with it, you could never cash it in for something more valuable or more whole. It was just all these days, held together only by the fragile memory of one person—or, if you were lucky, two. And because of this, this lack of inherent meaning or value, it was stunning. Like the most intricate, radical piece of art, the kind of art I was always trying to make. It dared to mean nothing and so demanded everything of you. (199)

In *The Future*, July reevaluates the notions of time, the future, and age or aging and exchanges the connotations of alleged inevitable loss, decline, and death for attributions of value, magic, and faith. With this renegotiation, July's film carries a message that age scholars would certainly endorse: *The Future* offers hope and promises value and beauty in old age, despite the fact that Joe Putterlik passed away and that her characters' relationship might be over. The metaphoric practice involved in references to age, time, and mortality that are associated with young characters who are far from biological old age and decline, let alone death, reveals an affective and playful notion regarding the topics of age and aging which seem to resonate more strongly in *The Future* than the themes of delayed adulthood and coming of age. Therefore, to see *The Future* as a story about a (failed) coming of age might lead us to misunderstand the hopeful message of the movie, which goes beyond achieving maturity or entering a new life stage: July's message literally and metaphorically encompasses the entire life course, including old age and death. Similarly, to understand *The Future* as a movie about delayed adulthood might risk overlooking the playfulness and subtle irony inherent in July's movie, which puts a new twist on Sophie's and Jason's status of stagnation and sense of failure: Their lingering and indecisiveness appears as a necessary requirement for an attentive and delicate look at the subtleties of life and as a departure point for a more creative approach to what it means to live through time.

Conclusion

This study began with two questions: What does it mean when young adult characters feel old? And what functions do references to age have in fictional narratives? I suggested that references to age be understood as metaphors and thus as figures of speech which are not literal descriptions but indicators of other meanings or emotional connotations. By using the methodological approach of an age reading, which looks specifically at references to age (as well as aging, temporality, mortality, and the like), which tries to understand them within the narrative context, and juxtaposes them with socio-cultural discourses, I set out to achieve an understanding of age and aging that respects the complexities of fictional narratives and their narrative conventions and that acknowledges that the metaphoric practices of age and aging are anchored in North American and Western cultures.

Methodologically speaking, an age reading has many advantages because it helps to identify cultural age narratives about time, death, and decline which are alluded to in the novels and movies discussed in this book and which otherwise risk being overlooked. While other categories of difference, such as ethnicity, gender, or class, have influenced established academic approaches to narratives, a focus on age is equally important because, as Gullette argues, "[a]ge is becoming a Superfact at all ages" and can "in certain contexts trump other identities" ("Age Studies" 215). At the same time, age does not exist within a vacuum but is interwoven with cultural discourses and thus needs to be understood from an interdisciplinary perspective.

A focus on age, therefore, does not automatically help us understand novels and films better or differently. Rather, it is a social category that is easily mistaken for a natural fact of life and that can carry diverse narrative functions and cultural meanings. In speaking of age as a metaphor, I use concepts introduced by Laz, Sontag and Woodward and suggest that age is a flexible marker and can function like a proxy in that it helps address issues that are otherwise too complex and disparate to put into words, such as feelings of worthlessness, inadequacy, shame, or anxieties about the present and future. Consequently, references to age function as a metaphoric practice, presupposing that they are not simply a factual part of a character portrait but flexible elements of a text or dialog, which may point to the psychology of a character or to a particular (social or cultural) atmosphere or setting. Within the plot structure, references to age often accompany or precede crisis situations. The references to age add emotional urgency and thus intensify affective conflicts. At the same time, references to age may also be used to exaggerate a particular situation and to introduce a sense of irony and humor.

When metaphors of age are used, they often evoke feelings of failure and otherness or a looming sense of decline and loss of value. The metaphors can also insinuate inappropriateness with generally accepted norms and be juxtaposed with more severe social breaches. In some cases, they indicate oppressiveness, and a character's age-inappropriate behavior becomes a matter of defiance or rebellion. References to age, however, do not always involve negative meanings. Otherness or age-inappropriateness, for instance, is also used in a positive sense and can indicate that a character wants to be different from the rest. Age metaphors can also imply hopeful messages of growth, trust, and togetherness. Hence, while the fictional narratives in this study depart from binary and cliché notions of age, the functions and meanings of age and aging over the course of the fictional narratives are not necessarily determined by a binary division into 'positive' youth and 'negative' old age. Rather, we are dealing with a spectrum of meanings, within which age functions like a flexible slider that moves between different registers of functions and meanings. The appeal of age metaphors lies in this semantic flexibility and in the fact that people can access these meanings intuitively – either because they have internalized the cultural meanings of age and aging or because the narrative context of an age metaphor indicates its meaning.

When a young person or character thus says "I feel old" or is said to look old, we are not dealing with a literal meaning of "old" but with a claim of feeling (or appearing) different, failed, worthless, or inappropriate. Age as a category of difference thus functions as a temporary status report for young adult characters and is not a description of a factual process of actual aging into old age. Or, in an appropriation of Kunkel's words, age metaphors are about the 'short term' and not the 'long term' (cf. *Indecision* 141-2). While age metaphors do indeed evoke a sense of temporality and an awareness of the passing of time, their usage primarily focuses on *age* awareness and not on experiences of *aging*. A differentiation between "temporal" and "temporary," as Kunow and Hartung suggest in a different context (see Hartung "The Limits" 49), seems to be helpful in this respect. Unlike the traditional coming-of-age story, which focuses on *temporal* and processual development, the age references used in relation to the aged young adults of this study seem to function as a *temporary* marker that indicates a psychological state or describes a conflictual situation. In an era of anti-aging, the perpetual adolescents of this study have no interest in coming of age. And yet the characters seem to be overexposed to the cultural semantics of age and aging and they make use of the flexible semantic repertoire of age and aging to voice their current situations and feelings.

Thus, if age metaphors function as temporary status markers, references to age or the passing of time do not necessarily involve progress or a teleological dimension. Coming of age, however, presupposes such a processual development from one life stage into the next, which has become a precarious issue for young adults today, as the studies by Arnett, Blatterer, Burnett, Côté, or Settersten suggest and as the fictional narratives in this study prove as well. Since adulthood has become liminal (cf. Raby, "Theorizing" 2012), the possibility of making successful transitions has become uncertain. With this uncertainty, the teleological and linear structure of the coming-of-age story seems to be incongruous. Gullette suggests a different term and speaks of "aging past youth" when she describes the "assumption of our culture [...] that bodily decline starts not in old age but ever younger: for women and even some men, as early as thirty" (*Agewise* 33). For Gullette, however, "aging past youth" is not necessarily a message about decline, as it can imply solidarity and feelings of pleasure with one's aging body (cf. 32-3). "Aging-past-youth" may thus be an interesting alternative to coming-of-age because it acknowledges the (current) centrality of youth as a cultural ideal while recognizing youthfulness as a temporary phase in life. From the perspective of Gullette's activist call for age criticism, "aging-past-youth" may invite more age-conscious attitudes as well as more creative and hopeful meanings of age and aging.

An intriguing aspect of the coming-of-age story, a descendent of the *Bildungsroman*, is the middle-class background, which seems to be vital to the fictional narratives discussed here. It is striking that the characters of this book are all middle- to upper-class white Americans. With Toula as a Greek-American woman, one might also wonder in how far race or ethnicity is a factor in age or aging. After all, age is an intersectional category correlating with gender, class, and race (cf. Gullette, *Agewise* 82). There are two films that I would like to mention in this respect, which suggest that race or ethnicity may be secondary to my particular approach: The films feature non-white young adult characters who are embedded in narratives with numerous references to age, particularly to age thirty as a feared transitional moment. In Alankrita Shrivastav's Bollywood movie *Turning Thirty!!!* (2011), for instance, a young Indian woman associates her approaching thirtieth birthday with a crisis and is confronted with implicit and explicit references to age throughout the movie. In the American context, the movie *Thirty Years to Life* by Vanessa Middleton (2001) is noteworthy for its African-American-only cast. The problems, crises, functions, and meanings associated with age and aging are quite similar to those that the heroes of *Away We Go* or *Indecision* face. Apart from the similarities regarding the fact that both Shrivastav's and Middleton's characters are approaching their thirtieth birthday, which serves as a feared turning point, the two films share another parallel: Their characters belong to the middle class. It seems, therefore, that ethnicity might be less of an issue and that, instead, age seems to be a matter of class, particularly of middle-class characters who are presented as highly susceptible to the semantics of impending decline, inadequacy, or failure.[1]

With regard to gender as another social category, scholars such as Susan Sontag, Betty Friedan, or Margaret Morganroth Gullette have argued convincingly that age and aging affect women differently than men. And indeed, in some respects, the young adult women in the corpus of this study fear different issues than their male counterparts. While Toula, Verona, and Sophie are concerned with being belated, which also involves a fear of a

---

1   Also see Susan Sontag's comments on class in "The Double Standard of Aging" (31-2).

closing time window in terms of reproductive opportunities, Burt, Dwight, Brad, Eric, and Jason worry about limited opportunities with regard to professional careers, financial success, or authority. However, the meanings of age cannot be easily separated along a gender divide: Sarah, for instance, is also unhappy with her professional career, which she fears to have jeopardized when she escaped into a presumably easier life as a housewife and mother. Similarly, for Sophie, it is her lacking success (and maybe talent) as a dancer that accompanies her age crisis. Further research into these gendered contingencies would be an important pursuit that this study, with its equal distribution of male and female characters and its aim to make a case for the inclusion of male *and* female young characters into age studies, did not set out to cover.

When it comes to the contemporary focus of this study on fictional narratives from the new millennium, I want to point to two examples that indicate that the topic of age awareness goes beyond the temporal frame of this study and that speak for the pertinence of age readings. The American novelist Richard Yates published his debut novel *Revolutionary Road* in 1961, in which he describes the story of Frank and April Wheeler, a married couple in their late twenties who have two children and live in a Connecticut suburb in the 1950s. *Revolutionary Road* is a story about relationships, self-fulfillment, and hypocrisy that unfolds between the couple's big dreams, their simultaneous faintheartedness and the stifling conventions in which they find themselves. On Frank's thirtieth birthday, the topic of age figures prominently and his birthday is set at a crucial moment in the plot: The night before, Frank realizes that his marriage is failing. He also humiliates himself in front of his friends. On his birthday, he starts an affair with a coworker at his firm. When he commutes to the city on the morning of his birthday, Yates describes Frank's feelings in the following way: "And riding to work, one of the youngest and healthiest passengers on the train, he sat with the look of a man condemned to a very slow, painless death. He felt middle-aged" (68). The age references in this short passage alone provide ample opportunities for an age reading. Frank feels prematurely aged, mortality is looming, and there is a recognizable split between his subjective and his physical age. Frank's birthday and the references to age and aging allude to the character's (moral) decline that is about to take place.

Similarly, the short story "The Thirtieth Year" ("Das dreißigste Jahr" 1961) by the Austrian writer Ingeborg Bachmann expands the scope of an age reading to pre-millennial mentalities. In her story, a nameless young man reviews his life on the eve of his twenty-ninth birthday and maintains: "When a person enters his thirtieth year people will not stop calling him young. But he himself, although he can discover no changes in himself, becomes unsure; he feels as though he were no longer entitled to claim to be young" (Bachmann 12). This split between a subjective age and an exterior, biological, or chronological age indicates the character's life crisis, which is described in the following way:

> For up to now he has simply lived from one day to another, has tried something else each day and has been without guile. He has seen so many possibilities for himself and has thought, for example, that he can become absolutely anything: A great man, a beacon, a philosopher. (12)

These words are reminiscent of Kunkel's character Dwight Wilmerding or July's protagonists Sophie and Jason. The two examples from the 1960s suggest that the topic of age and aging and the metaphoric practice of age might be a recurring theme in stories about young adult characters across decades and national borders.

In the field of American studies, in which the current trends in academic research explore transnational and ecological avenues or focus on mobility studies, women's studies, or race studies, the age-old issue of age and aging, as this study suggests, continues to warrant attention. The greater value and maybe the future of an age reading may lie in providing a means by which to acknowledge the demographic changes we face both in Western cultures as well as on a global level. In the United States, for example, the percentage of people who are 65 or older will rise from 13% in 2010 to 20% in 2050 (cf. United States Census Bureau). With one fifth of the American population chronologically considered old, the topic of age and aging is not likely to lose momentum.[2] On the contrary, awareness of age and aging seems to be a "Supertopic" (following Gullette's notion of age as a Superfact). In the media landscape of the United States, for instance, age is a fascinating topic. On the one hand, *AARP The Magazine*, a bi-monthly

---

2   Worldwide, the projected world population of people 65 or older will increase from 8% in 2011 to 17% in 2050 (cf. United States Census Bureau).

publication of the American Association of Retired Persons, is the largest circulation magazine in the United States, which suggests that old people have a strong voice and lobby (cf. Lulofs n. pag.). On the other hand, it is still young people between 20 and 34 years of age, who have the highest representation in prime-time television with 40% compared to less than 5% of people 65 or older (cf. Harwood & Anderson 88). The question is how long this misrepresentation can be upheld in view of the demographic changes. And, how will an increase in older people on prime-time television affect the notions of youthfulness as an ideal? Moreover, with increasing youth unemployment rates, the socio-economic position of young people will become problematic and it is quite probable that these circumstances will affect the ways in which young people define their roles in society or, more generally, how youthfulness will be defined in the years to come. Of course, these developments need not be negative. Intergenerational exchange and support may become stronger and, presumably, an increasing media representation of active and healthy elderly people will alter the negative connotations of old age. Nevertheless, the financial burden of the demographic changes will be shouldered by the younger generations. Hence, age and aging will be relevant topics for the elderly and for younger generations alike, and the meanings of youth and old age will remain important in terms of their socio-economic and cultural dimensions as well as for individual experiences of identity, living in time and the good life. How young people in particular are aged by culture is thus of great interest to the field of age studies.

List of Figures

Fig. 1: 'Old' Toula in the family restaurant. Source: Screenshot from *My Big Fat Greek Wedding*, director: Joel Zwick, 2002.

Fig. 2: 'Young' Toula on a date with Ian. Source: Screenshot from *My Big Fat Greek Wedding*, director: Joel Zwick, 2002.

Fig. 3: The Portokalos family from Toula's point of view. Source: Screenshot from *My Big Fat Greek Wedding*, director: Joel Zwick, 2002.

Fig. 4: 'Old' Toula is singled out. Source: Screenshot from *My Big Fat Greek Wedding*, director: Joel Zwick, 2002.

Fig. 5: 'Young' Toula is part of the family. Source: Screenshot from *My Big Fat Greek Wedding*, director: Joel Zwick, 2002.

Fig. 6: 'Old' Toula at work in the family restaurant. Source: Screenshot from *My Big Fat Greek Wedding*, director: Joel Zwick, 2002.

Fig. 7: 'Young' Toula at work in the travel agency. Source: Screenshot from *My Big Fat Greek Wedding*, director: Joel Zwick, 2002.

Fig. 8: Burt and Verona in their future home. Source: Screenshot from *Away We Go*, director: Sam Mendes, 2009.

Fig. 9: Die Lebenstreppe. Source: "Das Stufenalter des Mannes," Verlag Gustav May Söhne, Painter: Fridolin Leiber (Draft), 1900. <http://commons.wikimedia.org/wiki/File:Das_Stufenalter_des_Mannes_c1900.gif>

Fig. 10: Visualization of the U-bend from *The Economist*. Source: Screenshot from *The Economist*, Illustrator: Marie-Helene Jeeves, 2010. <http://www.economist.com/node/17722567>

Fig. 11: Jason and Sophie wasting time. Source: Screenshot from *The Future*, director: Miranda July, 2011.

Fig. 12: Joe gives Jason a toy for Paw Paw. Source: Screenshot from *The Future*, director: Miranda July, 2011.

Fig. 13: Sophie and her dance. Source: Screenshot from *The Future*, director: Miranda July, 2011.

Fig. 14: Accelerated time. Source: Screenshots from *The Future*, director: Miranda July, 2011.

List of Works Cited

Aapola, Sinikka. "Exploring Dimensions of Age in Young People's Lives: A Discourse Analytical Approach." *Time and Society* 11.2/3 (2002): 295-314. *Sage.* Web. 31 Mar. 2011.

Acland, Charles R. *Youth, Murder, Spectacle: The Cultural Politics of Youth in Crisis.* Boulder: Western, 1995. Print.

Alden, Patricia. *Social Mobility in the English Bildungsroman: Gissing, Hardy, Bennett, and Lawrence.* Ann Arbor, Michigan: UMI Research Press, 1986. Print.

Alsop, Ron. "The 'Trophy Kids' Go to Work." *The Wall Street Journal.* Dow Jones & Company, 21 Oct. 2008. Web. 19 July 2010. <http://online.wsj.com/article/SB122455219391652725.html> Excerpt from *The Trophy Kids Grow Up: How the Millennial Generation Is Shaking Up the Workplace.* San Francisco: Jossey-Bass, 2008. Print.

Anguera, J.A., J. Boccanfuso, J.L. Rintoul, O. Al-Hashimi, F. Faraji, J. Janowich, E. Kong, Y. Larraburo, C. Rolle, E. Jonston and A. Gazzaley. "Video Game Training Enhances Cognitive Control in Older Adults." *Nature* 501 (Sept. 2013): 97-101. *ProQuest.* Web. 12 Sept. 2013.

Arnett, Jeffrey J. *Emerging Adulthood: The Winding Road from the Late Teens through the Twenties.* Oxford: Oxford University Press, 2007. Web. 25 April 2012. <http://www.oxfordscholarship.com/oso/public/content/psychology/9780195309379/toc.html>.

- - -. "Emerging Adulthood: A Theory of Development From the Late Teens Through the Twenties." *American Psychologist* 55.5 (2000): 469-80. Web. 4 Oct. 2010.

Away We Go. Dir. Sam Mendes. Screenwr. Dave Eggers, Vendela Vida. Focus Features, 2009. DVD.

Bachmann, Ingeborg. "The Thirtieth Year." *The Thirtieth Year: Stories*. Trans. Michael Bullock. New York: Holmes & Meier, 1987. 12-55. Print.

Balestrini, Nassim W. „Photography as Online Life Writing: Miranda July's and Harrell Fletcher's *Learning to Love You More* (2002-09). *American Lives*. Ed. Alfred Hornung. Heidelberg: Winter, 2013: 341-54. Print.

Bandura, Albert. *Self-Efficacy in Changing Societies*. Cambridge: Cambridge University Press, 1995. Print.

- - -. "Self-Efficacy: Toward a Unifying Theory of Behavioral Change." *Psychological Review* 84 (1977): 191-215. Print.

Baron, Zach. "The Decade's Best Books." *The Village Voice*. Village Voice Media, 23-29 Dec. 2009. Web. 25 July 2011.

Bauman, Zygmunt. *Consuming Life*. Cambridge: Polity, 2007. Print.

- - -. *Mortality, Immortality and Other Life Strategies*. Cambridge: Polity, 1992. Print.

Bearon, Lucille B. *Little Old Ladies and Grumpy Old Men: How Language Shapes Our Views about Aging*. North Carolina Cooperative Extension Service, n.d. Web. 15 Apr. 2011. <http://www.ces.ncsu.edu/depts/fcs/pdfs/fcs492.pdf>

de Beauvoir, Simone. *La Vieillesse*. Paris: Gallimard, 1970. Print.

Beck, Ulrich. *Risk Society: Towards a New Modernity*. London: Sage, 1992. Print.

- - - and Elisabeth Beck-Gernsheim. *Individualization: Institutionalized Individualism and Its Social and Political Consequences*. London: Sage, 2002. Print.

Bender, Justus. "Bin ich schon zu alt?" *Zeit Online*. Die Zeit, 22 Feb. 2011. Web. 24 May 2012.

Berntsen, Dorthe and David C. Rubin. "Cultural Life Scripts Structure Recall from Autobiographical Memory." *Memory and Cognition* 32.3 (2004): 427-442. Print.

- - -. "Emotionally Charged Autobiographical Memories Across the Life Span: The Recall of Happy, Sad, Traumatic, and Involuntary Memories." *Psychology and Aging* 17 (2002): 636–652. Print.

- - - . "Life Scripts help to Maintain Autobiographical Memories of Highly Positive, But not Highly Negative, Events." *Memory and Cognition* 31.1 (2003): 1-14. Print.
de Bertodano, Helena. "And Quiet Goes the Don." *The Telegraph*. The Telegraph, 13 May 2003. Web. 25 Oct. 2011.
Biggs, Simon. "Age, Gender, Narratives, and Masquerades." *Journal of Aging Studies* 18 (2004): 45-58. Web. 23 Mar. 2011.
- - - and Jason L. Powell. "A Foucauldian Analysis of Old Age and the Power of Social Welfare." *Journal of Aging and Social Policy* 12 (2001): 93-111. Print.
Blasberg, Anita. "Die schon wieder!" *Zeit Online*. Die Zeit, 18 April 2013. Web. 30 April 2013.
Blatterer, Harry. *Coming of Age in Times of Uncertainty*. New York: Berghahn, 2007. Print.
- - -. "Adulthood: The Contemporary Redefinition of a Social Category." *Sociological Research Online* 12.4 (2007): n. pag. Web. 22 Sept. 2011.
Blythe, Will. "All the Children Are Above Average." *The New York Times*. New York Times, 14 Mar. 2004. Web. 1 June 2011.
Booth, Frances. "When I Grow Up, I Want to be ... Childhood Dream Jobs." *Guardian.co.uk*. The Guardian, 10 Oct. 2009. Web. 5 June 2011.
Bourdieu, Pierre. *Distinction: A Social Critique of the Judgment of Taste*. Cambridge: Harvard University Press, 1984. Print.
- - -. *The Logic of Practice*. Stanford: Stanford University Press, 1990. Print.
Boxall, Peter. *Don DeLillo: The Possibility of Fiction*. New York: Routledge, 2006. Print.
Bradshaw, Peter. "*Away We Go*: Sam Mendes and Dave Eggers Team Up for a Sketchy but Likable Road-Trip Comedy." *Guardian.co.uk*. The Guardian, 17 Sept. 2009. Web. 18 July 2011.
Brockes, Emma. "Profile: Don DeLillo." *Guardian.co.uk*. The Guardian, 24 May 2003. Web. 25 Oct. 2011.
Brody, Richard. "Miranda July's Random Harvest." *The New Yorker*. Condé Nast, 21 Oct. 2011. Web. 10 Nov. 2011.
Burnett, Judith. "Thirtysomething and Contemporary Adulthood." *Contemporary Adulthood: Calendars, Cartographies and Constructions*. Ed. Judith Burnett. Houndmills: Palgrave Macmillan, 2010. 71-87. Print.

Butler, Robert N. "Age-ism: Another Form of Bigotry." *Gerontologist* 9 (1969): 243-5. Web. 17 Feb. 2011.

Bytheway, Bill. "Ageism and Age Categorization." *Journal of Social Issues* 61.2 (2005): 361-374. Web. 31 Mar. 2011.

Cain, Leonard D., Jr. "Life Course and Social Structure." *Handbook of Modern Sociology*. Ed. Robert E.L. Faris. Chicago: Rand McNally, 1964. 272-309. Print.

Campbell, Duncan. "Notes from New York." *Guardian.co.uk*. The Guardian, 4 May 2003. Web. 25 Oct. 2011.

Carmichael, Thomas. "Evanescence, Language, and Dread: Reading Don DeLillo." *Contemporary Literature* 44.1 (Spring 2003): 176-180. Web. 25 Oct. 2011.

Casati, Rebecca. "Generation Facebook: Im Wartezimmer zum Erwachsenwerden." *Süddeutsche*. Süddeutsche Zeitung, 6 Nov. 2011. Web. 7 Nov. 2011.

Charteris-Black, Jonathan. *Corpus Approaches to Critical Metaphor Analysis*. Basingstoke: Palgrave Macmillan, 2004. Print.

Chudacoff, Howard P. *How Old Are You? Age Consciousness in American Culture*. Oxford: Princeton University Press, 1989. Print.

Classen, Albrecht. "Old Age in the Middle Ages and the Renaissance: Also an Introduction." *Old Age in the Middle Ages and the Renaissance: Interdisciplinary Approaches to a Neglected Topic*. Ed. Albrecht Classen. Berlin: Walter de Gruyter, 2007. 1-84. Print.

Clausen, John A. *American Lives: Looking Back at the Children of the Great Depression*. Berkeley: University of California Press, 1993. Print.

Clow, Barbara. "Who's Afraid of Susan Sontag? Or, the Myths and Metaphors of Cancer Reconsidered." *Social History of Medicine* 14.2 (2001): 293-312. Web. 8 March 2013.

Cole, Thomas R. *The Journey of Life: A Cultural History of Aging in America*. Cambridge: Cambridge UP, 2006. Print.

- - -, Robert Kastenbaum and Ruth E. Ray, eds. *Handbook of the Humanities and Aging*. 2nd ed. New York: Springer, 2000. Print.

Combe, Kirk and Kenneth Schmader. "Naturalizing Myths of Aging: Reading Popular Culture." *Journal of Aging and Identity* 4.2 (1999): 79-109. Web. 16 Feb. 2011.

Côté, James E. *Arrested Adulthood: The Changing Nature of Maturity and Identity*. New York: New York University Press, 2000. Print.

Cross, Gary. *Men to Boys: The Making of Modern Immaturity.* New York: Columbia University Press, 2008. Print.

Curnutt, Kirk. „Teenage Wasteland: Coming-of-Age Novels in the 1980s and 1990s." *Critique* 43.1 (Fall 2001): 93-111. *ProQuest.* Web. 2 May 2013.

Cuzzocrea, Valentina and Sveva Magaraggia. "Blurred Transitions: Revisiting the Significance of Work and Parenthood for Young Adults in Italy." *Times of Our Lives: Making Sense of Ageing.* Eds. Harry Blatterer and Julia Glahn. Oxford: Inter-Disciplinary Press, 2012. 79-90. Web. 17 April 2012.

Dannefer, Dale. "Adult Development and Social Theory: A Paradigmatic Reappraisal." *American Sociological Review.* 49.1 (1984): 100-16. *JSTOR.* Web. 30 Sept. 2010.

Davidson, Kate. "Sociological Perspectives on Ageing." *An Introduction to Gerontology.* Ed. Ian Stuart-Hamilton. Cambridge: Cambridge University Press, 2011. 226-50. Print.

Davis, Alan. "Family Fictions." *The Hudson Review* 55.1 (Spring 2002): 161-6. *ProQuest.* 30 May 2013.

Deats, Sara Munson and Lagretta Tallent Lenker, eds. *Aging and Identity: A Humanities Perspective.* Westport: Praeger, 1999. Print.

DeLillo, Don. *Cosmopolis.* London: Picador, 2003. Print.

- - -. "In the Ruins of the Future." *Guardian.co.uk.* The Guardian, 22 Dec. 2001. Web. 06 June 2013.

Donoghue, Denis. Rev. of *Illness as Metaphor*, by Susan Sontag. *The New York Times.* The New York Times, 18 July 1978. Web. 1 May 2012.

Eakin, Emily. "Jonathan Franzen's Big Book." *The New York Times.* The New York Times, 2 Sept. 2001. Web. 25 July 2011.

Ebert, Roger. "*Away We Go*: They're Young, Sane, and in Love. So Okay, What Do They Do Now?" *rogerebert.com.* Roger Ebert, 10 June 2009. Web. 18 July 2011.

- - -. "My Big Fat Greek Wedding." *rogerebert.com.* Roger Ebert, 19 Apr. 2002. Web. 11 Feb. 2012.

- - -. "*The Future*: Fluffy Whimsy And A Core of Steel." *rogerebert.com.* Roger Ebert, 3 Aug. 2011. Web. 14 Feb. 2012.

Ehrenberg, Alain. *The Weariness of the Self: Diagnosing the History of Depression in the Contemporary Age.* Montreal: McGill-Queen's University Press, 2010. Print.

Ehrenreich, Barbara. *Smile or Die: How Positive Thinking Fooled America and the World.* London: Granta, 2010. Print.

Ekerdt, David J. "The Busy Ethic: Moral Continuity Between Work and Retirement." *The Gerontologist* 26.3 (1986): 239-244. Web. 2 Apr. 2011.

Elder, Glen H., Jr. "Perspectives on the Life Course." *Life-Course Dynamics. Trajectories and Transitions.* Ed. Glen H. Elder, Jr. Ithaca: Cornell University Press, 1985. 23-49. Print.

- - -. "Time, Human Agency, and Social Change: Perspectives on the Life Course." *Social Psychology Quarterly.* 57.1 (1994): 4-15. *JSTOR.* Web. 28 Sept. 2010.

- - -, Monica Kirkpatrick Johnson and Robert Crosnoe. "The Emergence and Development of Life Course Theory." *Handbook of the Life Course.* Eds. Jeylan T. Mortimer and Michael J. Shanahan. New York: Kluwer Academic/Plenum, 2003. 3-19. Print.

Erikson, Erik H. *Identität und Lebenszyklus: Drei Aufsätze.* Frankfurt: Suhrkamp, 1966. Print.

Featherstone, Mike and Andrew Wernick, eds. "Introduction." *Images of Aging: Cultural Representations of Later Life.* New York: Routledge, 2003. 1-18. Print.

Featherstone, Mike. "Post-Bodies, Aging, and Virtual Reality." *Images of Aging: Cultural Representations of Later Life.* Eds. Mike Featherstone and Andrew Wernick. New York: Routledge, 2003. 227-44. Print.

Foucault, Michel. *The Birth of Biopolitics: Lectures at the Collège de France, 1978-79.* Ed. Michel Senellart. New York: Palgrave Macmillan, 2008. Print.

- - -. "Genealogy of Ethics." *Michel Foucault: Beyond Structuralism and Hermeneutics.* Eds. Hubert L. Dreyfus and Paul Rabinow. Chicago: University of Chicago Press, 1983. Print.

- - -. *Naissance de la Biopolitique: Cours au Collège de France, 1978-1979.* Paris: Seuil/Gallimard, 2004. Print.

Franzen, Jonathan. "Perchance to Dream in the Age of Images: A Reason to Write Novels." *Harper's Magazine* (April 1996): 35-54. *ProQuest.* Web. 8 Aug. 2011.

- - -. *The Corrections.* New York: Farrar, Straus and Giroux, 2002. Print.

Freese, Peter. *Die Initiationsreise: Studien zum jugendlichen Helden im modernen amerikanischen Roman.* Neumünster: Karl Wachholtz, 1971.

Furman, Elina. *Boomerang Nation: How to Survive Living with Your Parents... the Second Time Around.* New York, Touchstone, 2005. Print.

The Future. Dir. Miranda July. Screenwr. Miranda July. Roadside Attractions, 2011. DVD.

Giddens, Anthony. *Modernity and Self-Identity: Self and Society in the Late Modern Age.* Stanford: Stanford University Press, 1991. Print.

- - -. *The Constitution of Society.* Berkeley: University of California Press, 1986. Print.

Gillis, John R. "A World of Their Own Making: Families and the Modern Culture of Aging." *Childhood and Old Age – Equals or Opposites?* Eds. Jørgen Povlsen, Signe Mellemgaard and Ning de Coninck-Smith. Odense: Odense University Press, 1999. 109-23. Print.

Greer, Germaine. *The Change. Women, Aging and the Menopause.* New York: Knopf, 1992. Print.

Gullette, Margaret Morganroth. "Age (Aging)." *Encyclopedia of Feminist Literary Theory.* Ed. Elizabeth Kowaleski Wallace. New York: Routledge, 2009. 11-4. Print.

- - -. *Aged by Culture.* Chicago: University of Chicago Press, 2004. Print.

- - -. "Age Studies as Cultural Studies." *Handbook of the Humanities and Aging.* 2nd ed. Eds. Thomas R. Cole, Robert Kastenbaum and Ruth E. Ray. New York: Springer, 2000. 214-34. Print.

- - -. *Agewise: Fighting the New Ageism in America.* Chicago: University of Chicago Press, 2011. Print.

- - -. "Creativity, Gender, Aging." *Aging and Gender in Literature: Studies in Creativity.* Eds. Anne M. Wyatt-Brown and Janice Rossen. Charlottesville: University Press of Virginia, 1993. 19-48. Print.

- - -. *Declining to Decline: Cultural Combat and the Politics of the Midlife.* Charlottesville: University of Virginia Press, 1997. Print.

- - -. "From Life Storytelling to Age Autobiography." *Journal of Aging Studies* 17 (2003): 101-11. Web. 18 Oct. 2011.

- - -. "The Other End of the Fashion Cycle: Practicing Loss, Learning Decline." *Figuring Age: Women Bodies, Generations.* Ed. Kathleen Woodward. Bloomington: Indiana University Press, 1999. 34-58. Print.

- - -. *Safe at Last in the Middle Years: The Invention of the Midlife Progress Novel.* Berkeley: University of California Press, 1988. Print.

- - -. "Taking a Stand Against Ageism at All Ages: A Powerful Coalition." *On the Issues Magazine*. Choices Women's Medical Center, Fall 2011. Web. 8 Oct. 2011.

- - -. "What Exactly Has Age Got to Do with It? My Life in Critical Age Studies." *Journal of Aging Studies* 22 (2008): 189-195. Web. 3 Mar. 2011.

Haller, Miriam. "'Unwürdige Greisinnen:' 'Ageing trouble' im literarischen Text." *Alter und Geschlecht: Repräsentationen, Geschichten und Theorien des Alter(n)s*. Ed. Heike Hartung. Bielefeld: transcript, 2005. 45-63. Print.

Halverson, Deborah. *Writing Young Adult Fiction for Dummies*. Hoboken: Wiley, 2011. Print.

Hartung, Heike. "The Limits of Development? Narratives of Growing Up / Growing Old in Narrative. *Amerikastudien/American Studies* 56.1 (2011). 45-66. Print.

- - -, and Rüdiger Kunow, eds. "Introduction: Age Studies." *Amerikastudien/American Studies* 56.1 (2011): 15-22. Print.

Harvey, Dennis. "*Away We Go* Reps a Digression into Loose, Anecdotal Amerindie-style Terrain." *Variety*. Variety, 22 May 2009. Web. 18 July 2011.

Harwood, Jake and Karen Anderson. "The Presence and Portrayal of Social Groups on Prime-Time Television." *Communication Reports* 15.2 (Summer 2002): 81-97. Web. 13 June 2013.

Havighurst, Robert J. *Developmental Tasks and Education*. 3rd ed. New York: David McKay, 1974. Print.

Hazan, Haim. *Old Age: Constructions and Deconstructions*. Cambridge: Cambridge University Press, 1994. Print.

Heinz, Walter R., ed. *Institutions and Gatekeeping in the Life Course*. Weinheim: Deutscher Studien Verlag, 1992. Print.

- - -. "Selbstsozialisation im Lebenslauf: Umrisse einer Theorie biographischen Handelns." *Biographische Sozialisation*. Eds. Erika M. Hoerning and Peter Alheit. Stuttgart: Lucius & Lucius, 2000. 165-86. Print.

- - -. "Self-Socialization and Post Traditional Society." *Advances in Life Course Research* 7 (2002): 41-64. Web. 29 Oct. 2010.

Henig, Robin Marantz. "What Is It About 20-Somethings?" *The New York Times*. The New York Times, 18 Aug. 2010. Web. 14 Nov. 2011.

Hepworth, Mike. "Positive Ageing: What Is the Message?" *The Sociology of Health Promotion: Critical Analyses of Consumption, Lifestyle and Risk.* Eds. Robin Bunton, Sarah Nettleton and Roger Burrows. London: Routledge, 1995. 176-90. Print.

Hermanson, Tove. "Grey Hair as Fleeting Trend, or Social Statement [sic]?" *Huffpost Style.* The Huffington Post, 6 Aug. 2010. Web. 13 Mar. 2013.

Hoberman, J. "In *The Future*, Miranda July Grows Up." *The Village Voice.* Village Voice Media, 27 July 2011. Web. 2 Feb. 2012.

Hochschild, Arlie Russell. *The Managed Heart: Commercialization of Human Feeling.* Berkeley: University of California Press, 2003. Print.

Hodgetts, Darrin, Kerry Chamberlain and Graeme Bassett. "Between Television and Audience: Negotiating Representations of Ageing." *Health* 7 (2003): 417-38. *Sage.* Web. 15 Feb. 2011.

Hunter, James Davison. "Wither Adulthood?" *The Hedgehog Review* (Spring 2009): 7-17. Web. 5 Oct. 2011.

Illouz, Eva. *Warum Liebe weh tut: Eine soziologische Erklärung.* Berlin: Suhrkamp, 2011. Print.

Jessen, Jens. "Warum so verzagt? Eine Antwort auf Anita Blasbergs Essay über die Macht der Alten." *Zeit Online.* Die Zeit, 25 April 2013. Web. 30 April 2013.

Jobs, Steve. "Stay Hungry. Stay Foolish: Steve Jobs' Speech at Stanford." *Hindustan Times.* Hindustan Times, 6 Oct. 2011. Web. 25 May 2012.

July, Miranda. *It Chooses You.* San Francisco: McSweeney's, 2011. Print.

Kahn, Robert L. "On 'Successful Aging and Well-Being: Self-Rated Compared with Rowe and Kahn.'" *The Gerontologist* 42.6 (2002): 725-6. Web. 30 Mar. 2011.

Kakutani, Michiko. "A Family Portrait As Metaphor For the 90's." *The New York Times.* The New York Times, 4 Sept. 2001. Web. 25 July 2011.

- - -. "Headed Towards a Crash, Of Sorts, in a Stretch Limo." *The New York Times.* New York Times, 24 Mar. 2003. Web. 12 Oct. 2011.

- - -. "Who's Afraid of Holden Caulfield?" *The New York Times.* The New York Times, 23 Aug. 2005. Web. 9 Aug. 2011.

Katz, Stephen. *Cultural Aging: Life Course, Lifestyle, and Senior Worlds.* Peterborough: Broadview, 2005. Print.

- - -. *Disciplining Old Age: The Formation of Gerontological Knowledge.* Charlottesville: University of Virginia Press, 1996. Print.

- - -. "Fashioning Agehood: Lifestyle Imagery and the Commercial Spirit of Seniors Culture." *Childhood and Old Age – Equals or Opposites?* Eds. Jørgen Povlsen, Signe Mellemgaard and Ning de Coninck-Smith. Odense: Odense University Press, 1999. 75-92. Print.

- - -. "Old Age as Lifestyle in an Active Society." *The Doreen B. Townsend Center Occasional Papers* 19 (1999): 1-21. Web. 22 Feb. 2011.

Kehr, Dave. "Film in Review: *My Big Fat Greek Wedding.*" *New York Times.* New York Times, 19 Apr. 2002. Web. 17 Apr. 2011.

Kirn, Walter. "Long Day's Journey Into Haircut." *New York Times.* New York Times, 13 Apr. 2003. Web. 12 Oct. 2011.

Kohl, Martina. *The Wilhelm Meister Pebble.* Würzburg: Königshausen & Neumann, 1994. Print.

Koll-Stobbe, Amei. "Forever young? Sprachliche Kodierungen von Jugend und Alter." *Alter und Geschlecht.* Ed. Heike Hartung. Bielefeld: transcript, 2005. 237-252. Print.

Kramer, Undine. "Sprachwissenschaftliche Aspekte zur Altersdiskriminierung: sprachliche Diskriminierung des Alters – *alt* und *Alter* in Wörterbüchern, Kollokationen und Idiomen." *Forum Seniorenarbeit NRW.* Kuratorium Deutsche Altershilfe, n. d. Web. 18 May 2011.

Kohli, Martin. „Gesellschaftszeit und Lebenszeit – Der Lebenslauf im Strukturwandel der Moderne." *Die Moderne – Kontinuitäten und Zäsuren.* Ed. Johannes Berger. Göttingen: Otto Schwartz, 1986. 183-208. Print.

- - -. "The Institutionalization of the Life Course: Looking Back to Look Ahead." *Research in Human Development* 43.3-4 (2007): 253-71. Web. 22. Feb. 2011.

Krekula, Clary. "Age Coding – On Age-Based Practices of Distinction." *International Journal of Ageing and Later Life* 4.2 (2009): 7-31. Web. 11 Feb. 2012.

Kunkel, Benjamin. *Indecision.* New York: Random, 2005. Print.

- - -. "Treatment for Therapy." *In These Times.* Institute for Public Affairs, 21 Nov. 2001. Web. 25 July 2011.

Kunow, Rüdiger. "Chronologically Gifted? 'Old Age' in American Culture." Eds. Heike Hartung and Rüdiger Kunow. *Amerikastudien/ American Studies* 56.1 (2011): 23-44. Print.

- - -. "The Coming of Age: The Descriptive Organization of Later Life." *Representation and Decoration in a Postmodern Age*. Eds. Alfred Hornung and Rüdiger Kunow. Heidelberg: Winter, 2009. 295-309. Print.
- - -. "Ins Graue: Zur kulturellen Konstruktion von Altern und Alter." *Alter und Geschlecht: Repräsentationen, Geschichten und Theorien des Alter(n)s*. Ed. Heike Hartung. Bielefeld: transcript, 2005. 21-44. Print.
Küpper, Thomas. *Filmreif: Das Alter in Kino und Fernsehen*. Berlin: Bertz und Fischer, 2010. Print.
La Ferla, Ruth. "Young Trendsetters Streak Their Hair With Gray." *The New York Times*. New York Times, 1 Apr. 2010. Web. 13 Mar. 2013.
Lakoff, George and Mark Johnson. *Metaphors We Live By*. Chicago and London: University of Chicago Press, 1980. Print.
Laslett, Peter. *A Fresh Map of Life: The Emergence of the Third Age*. Cambridge: Harvard University Press, 1991. Print
Laz, Cheryl. "Act Your Age." *Sociological Forum* 13.1 (1998): 85-113. Web. 28 Mar. 2011.
- - -. "Age Embodied." *Journal of Aging Studies* 17 (2003): 503-19. Web. 16 Mar. 2011.
Lesko, Nancy. "Denaturalizing Adolescence: The Politics of Contemporary Representations." *Youth and Society* 28.2 (1996): 139-61. *Sage*. Web. 20 Dec. 2012.
Levinson, Daniel J. *The Seasons of a Man's Life*. New York: Knopf, 1978. Print.
- - -. *The Seasons of a Woman's Life*. New York: Knopf, 1996. Print.
Lim, Dennis. "Much Better Than That Thing With Kevin What's-His-Name." *The Village Voice*. Village Voice Media, 14-20 Apr. 2004. Web. 17 May 2011.
- - -. "A Generation Finds Its Mumble." *The New York Times*. The New York Times, 19 Aug. 2007. Web. 9 Aug. 2011.
Little Children. Dir. Todd Fields. Screenwr. Todd Field, Tom Perrotta. New Line Cinema, 2006. DVD.
Lucke, C., M. Lucke and M. Gogol. "Lebenstreppen – oder wie man den Alternsprozess über die Jahrhunderte gesehen hat." *European Journal of Geriatrics* 11.3-4 (2009): 132-40. Web. 21 May 2012. <http://d-nb.info/999634798/34>

Lulofs, Neal. "Top 25 U.S. Consumer Magazines for the Second Half of 2012." *Alliance for Audited Media.* Alliance for Audited Media, 7 Feb. 2013. Web. 30 Sept. 2013.

Lyman, Rick. "A Big Fat (And Profitable) Cinderella Story: 'Greek Wedding' Courts a Prince Named Oscar." *New York Times.* New York Times, 28 Nov. 2002. Web. 11 Feb. 2012.

Maierhofer, Roberta. *Salty Old Women: Eine anokritische Untersuchung zu Frauen, Altern und Identität in der amerikanischen Literatur.* Essen: Die Blaue Eule, 2003. Print.

Marchetti, Christian. *Dreißig werden: Ethnographische Erkundungen an einer Altersschwelle.* Tübingen: Tübinger Verein für Volkskunde, 2005. Print.

Marshall Victor W. and Philippa J. Clarke. "Agency and Social Structure in Aging and Life Course Research." *The Sage Handbook of Social Gerontology.* Eds. Dale Dannefer and Chris Phillipson. London: Sage, 2010. 294-305. Print.

Maslin, Janet. "The Disappointed Mothers of Suburbia." *The New York Times.* The New York Times, 8 Mar. 2004. Web. 17 May 2011.

Mayer, Karl Ulrich. "The Sociology of the Life Course and Lifespan Psychology – Diverging or Converging Pathways?" *Understanding Human Development: Dialogues with Lifespan Psychology.* Eds. Ursula M. Staudinger and Ulman Lindenberger. Boston: Kluwer Academic, 2003. 463-481. Web. 27 Sept. 2010.

McGee, Micki. *Self-Help, Inc.: Makeover Culture in American Life.* Oxford: Oxford University Press, 2005. Print.

McInerney, Jay. "*Indecision*: Getting It Together." *New York Times.* New York Times, 28 Aug. 2005. Web. 9 Aug. 2011.

McNally, John. "I Want a New Drug: The Ultimate Slacker Dude Finds a Cure for His Wasted Life." *The Washington Post* (11 Sept. 2005): n. pag. *Pro Quest.* Web. 9 Aug. 2011.

Meyer, John W. "Self and the Life Course: Institutionalization and Its Effects." *Institutional Structure: Constituting State, Society, and the Individual.* Eds. George M. Thomas, John W. Meyer, Francisco O. Ramirez, and John Boli. Newbury Park: Sage, 1987. 242-60. Print.

--- and Ronald Jepperson. "The 'Actors' of Modern Society: The Cultural Construction of Social Agency." *Sociological Theory* 18.1 (2000): 100-20. *JSTOR.* Web. 20 Oct. 2010.

Millard, Kenneth. *Coming of Age in Contemporary American Fiction.* Edinburgh: Edinburgh University Press, 2007. Print.
Miller, Peter and Nicolas Rose. "Governing Economic Life." *Economy and Society* 19.1 (February 1990): 1-31. Print.
Minkler, Meredith. "Gold in Gray: Reflections on Business' Discovery of the Elderly Market." *The Gerontologist* 29.1 (1989): 17-23. Web. 1 Apr. 2011.
Montepare, Joann M. "Variations in Adult's Subjective Ages in Relation to Birthday Nearness, Age Awareness, and Attitudes Toward Aging." *Journal of Adult Development* 3.4 (1996): 193-203. Web. 15 Feb. 2011.
Moody, Harry R. *Abundance of Life: Human Development Policies for an Aging Society.* New York: Columbia University Press, 1988. Print.
My Big Fat Greek Wedding. Dir. Joel Zwick. Screenwr. Nia Vardalos. IFC Films, 2002. DVD.
Neikrug. Shimshon M. "Worrying about Frightening Old Age." *Aging and Mental Health* 7.5 (2003): 326-33. Web. 23 Mar. 2011.
Neugarten, Bernice L. "Age Groups in American Society and the Rise of the Young-Old." *Annals of the American Academy of Political and Social Science* 415 (1974): 187-98. *JSTOR.* Web. 15 June 2012.
- - -, Joan W. Moore and John C. Lowe. "Age Norms, Age Constraints, and Adult Socialization." *The American Journal of Sociology* 70.6 (1965): 710-7. *JSTOR.* Web. 22 Dec. 2009.
Niles, Lisa. "Owning 'the dreadful truth'; Or, Is Thirty-Five Too Old?: Age and the Marriageable Body in Wilkie Collins's *Armadale.*" *Nineteenth-Century Literature* 65.1 (2010): 65-92. Web. 27 Mar. 2012.
Noble, Stuart. "Don DeLillo and Society's Reorientation to Time and Space: An Interpretation of *Cosmopolis.*" *aspeers* 1 (2008): 57-70. Web. 25 Oct. 2011.
Nuessel, Frank H. Jr. "The Language of Ageism." *The Gerontologist* 22.3 (1982): 273-6. Web. 20 Oct. 2010.
Nussbaum, Jon F. and James D. Robinson. "Attitudes Toward Aging." *Communication Research Reports* 1.1 (1984): 21-7. Web. 10 Nov. 2010.
Preminger, Alex (Ed.), Frank J. Warnke and O.B. Hardison, Jr. (Associated Editors). *The Princeton Handbook of Poetic Terms.* Princeton, N.J.: Princeton University Press: 1986. Print.

O'Connor, Michael. Rev. of *Little Children*, by Tom Perrotta. *About.com*. New York Times Company, n. d. Web. 5 June 2011.

Onstad, Katrina. "The Make-Believer." *New York Times Magazine*. New York Times, 17 July 2011. Web. 2 Feb. 2012.

Oswald, Andrew and David G. Blanchflower. "Is Well-being U-Shaped over the Life Cycle?" *Warwick Economic Research Papers*. The University of Warwick, 29 Oct. 2007. Web. 22 Mar. 2011.

Oxford English Dictionary. Oxford University Press, 2001. Web. 15 Aug. 2010.

Palmore, Erdman. "Three Decades of Research on Ageism." *Generations* 29.3 (2005): 87-90. Web. 16 Feb. 2011.

Payne, Monica A. "Teen Brain Science and the Contemporary Storying of Psychological (Im)maturity." *Times of Our Lives: Making Sense of Ageing*. Eds. Harry Blatterer and Julia Glahn. Oxford: Inter-Disciplinary Press, 2010. 55-68. Web. 17 Apr. 2012.

Penning, Abby. "The Next Generation of Anti-Aging." *GCI Magazine*. Allured Business Media, 1 Feb. 2012. Web. 5 Feb. 2012.

Perrotta, Tom. *Little Children*. London: Allison and Busby, 2006. Print.

Peters, Tom. "The Brand Called You." *Fast Company*. Fast Company, 31 Aug. 1997. Web. 15. Aug. 2010.

Peterson, Peter G. "Gray Dawn: The Global Aging Crisis." *Foreign Affairs* (Jan./Feb. 1999): n. pag. *Pro Quest*. Web. 27 Apr. 2012.

Phoenix, Cassie, Guy Faulkner and Andrew C. Sparkes. "Athletic Identity and Self-Ageing: The Dilemma of Exclusivity." *Psychology of Sport and Exercise* 6 (2005): 335-47. Web. 21 Mar. 2011.

--- and Andrew C. Sparkes. "Young Athletic Bodies and Narrative Maps of Aging." *Journal of Aging Studies* 20 (2006): 107-21. Web. 20 Apr. 2011.

Powell, Jason L. *Social Theory and Aging*. Lanham: Rowman and Littlefield, 2006. Print.

--- and Azrini Wahidin. *Foucault and Aging*. New York: Nova Science, 2006. Print.

Quinn, Edward. *A Dictionary of Literary and Thematic Terms*. 2nd ed. New York: Facts On File, 2006. Print.

Raby, Rebecca. "Age: Decentering Adulthood." *Power and Everyday Practices*. Eds. Deborah Brock, Rebecca Raby and Mark P. Thomas. Toronto: Nelson, 2012. 133-56. Print.

- - -. "Theorizing Liminal Adulthood and Its Consequences for Youth" *Times of Our Lives: Making Sense of Ageing*. Eds. Harry Blatterer and Julia Glahn. Oxford: Inter-Disciplinary Press, 2012. 69-78. Web. 17 Apr. 2012.

Rambo, Carol [Carol Rambo Ronai]. "Managing Aging in Young Adulthood: The 'Aging' Table Dancer." *Journal of Aging Studies* 6.4 (1992): 307-17. Web. 19 Apr. 2011.

"Retailer Launches Beauty Line Aimed at 8-Year-Olds." *The Independent*. Independent Print Limited, 28 Jan. 2011. Web. 5 Feb. 2012.

Richards, Ivor A. *The Philosophy of Rhetoric*. Oxford: Oxford UP, 1967. Print.

Riemann, Gerhard. "An Introduction to 'Doing Biographical Research.'" *Historical Social Research* 31.3 (2006): 6-28. Web. 21 Oct. 2010.

- - - and Fritz Schütze. "'Trajectories' as a Basic Theoretical Concept For Analyzing Suffering and Disorderly Social Processes." *Social Organization and Social Process: Essays in Honor of Anselm Strauss*. Ed. David R. Maines. New York: Gruyter, 1991. 333-57. Web. 21 Oct. 2010.

Rishoi, Christy. *From Girl to Woman: American Women's Coming-of-Age Narratives*. Albany: State University of New York, 2003. Print.

Rolle, Robert. *Homo Oeconomicus: Wirtschaftsanthropologie in philosophischer Perspective*. Würzburg: Königshausen & Neumann, 2005. Print.

Rook, Karen S., Ralph Catalano and David Dooley. "The Timing of Major Life Events: Effects of Departing From the Social Clock." *American Journal of Community Psychology* 17.2 (April 1989): 233-258. *ProQuest*. Web. 17 Jan. 2012.

Rooke, Constance. "Old Age in Contemporary Fiction: A New Paradigm of Hope." *Handbook of the Humanities and Aging*. Eds. Thomas R. Cole, Robert Kastenbaum and Ruth E. Ray. New York: Springer, 1992. 241-57. Print.

Rosa, Hartmut. "Social Acceleration: Ethical an Political Consequences of a Desynchronized High-Speed Society." *Constellations* 10.1 (2003): 3-33. Web. 27 Oct. 2010.

Rosenberg, Amy. "Benjamin Kunkel's *Indecision*." *Poets & Writers* 33.5 (2005). *ProQuest*. Web. 9 Aug. 2011.

Rosenbloom, Stephanie. "Generation Me vs. You Revisited." *New York Times*. New York Times, 17 Jan. 2008. Web. 6 Sept. 2011.

Rosenmayr, Leopold. "On Freedom and Aging: An Interpretation." *Journal of Aging Studies* 1.4 (Winter 1987): 299-316. Web. 9 Sept. 2013.

Rowe, John W. and Robert L. Kahn. "Human Aging: Usual and Successful." *Science* 237 (10 July 1987): 143-9. *JSTOR*. Web. 16 May 2012.

Sackmann, Reinhold and Matthias Wingens. "From Transitions to Trajectories: Sequence Types." *Social Dynamics of the Life Course: Transitions, Institutions, and Interrelations*. Eds. Walter R. Heinz and Victor W. Marshall. Hawthorne: Aldine de Gruyter, 2003. 93-116. Print.

Sandage, Scott A. *Born Losers: A History of Failure in America*. Cambridge: Harvard University Press, 2005. Print.

Schäfer, Stefanie. *'Just the Two of Us:' Self-Narration and Recognition in the Contemporary American Novel*. Trier: WVT, 2011. Print.

R. C. Schank and R.P. Abelson. "Scripts, Plan, and Knowledge." *Thinking: Readings in Cognitive Science*. Eds. P. N. Johnson-Laird and P. C. Wason. Cambridge: Cambridge University Press, 1977. 421-35. Print.

Scherger, Simone. *Destandardisierung, Differenzierung, Individualisierung: Westdeutsche Lebensläufe im Wandel*. Wiesbaden: Verlag für Sozialwissenschaften, 2007. Print.

- - - . "Cultural Practices, Age and the Life Course." *Cultural Trends* 18.1 (2009): 23-45. Web. 27 Apr. 2012.

Scott, A.O. "Among the Believers." *New York Times*. New York Times, 11 Sept. 2005. Web. 9 Aug. 2011.

- - -. "Is That All There Is? Milking Life For More." *New York Times*. New York Times, 28 July 2011. Web. 14 Feb. 2012.

- - -. "Practicing Virtue, and Proud of It." *New York Times*. New York Times, 5 June 2009. Web. 18 July 2011.

Settersten, Richard A. Jr. "Age Structuring and the Rhythm of the Life Course." *Handbook of the Life Course*. Eds. Jeylan T. Mortimer and Michael J. Shanahan. New York: Kluwer, 2003. 81-98. Print.

Settersten, Richard A. Jr. and Barbara E. Ray. *Not Quite Adults: Why 20-Somethings Are Choosing a Slower Path to Adulthood, and Why It's Good for Everyone*. New York: Bantam, 2010. Print.

Shakespeare, William. *As You Like It. Project Gutenberg*. Project Gutenberg, 26 Mar. 2011. Web. 27 Apr. 2012.

Shanahan, Michael J. and Ross Macmillan. *Biography and the Sociological Imagination: Contexts and Contingencies*. New York: Norton, 2008. Print.

Shanahan, Michael J. and Erik Porfelli. "Integrating the Life Course and Life-Span: Formulating Research Questions with Dual Points of Entry." *Journal of Vocational Behavior* 61 (2002): 398-406. Web. 17 Oct. 2010.

- - -. Rev. of *Arrested Adulthood: The Changing Nature of Maturity and Identity*, by James Côté. *Social Forces* 81.3. (2003): 1063-6. *ProQuest.* Web. 3 Oct. 2010.

Sheehy, Gail. *Passages: Predictable Crises of Adult Life*. New York: Dutton, 1976. Print.

Simon, Scott. "Interview: Benjamin Kunkel Discusses His New Novel *Indecision*." *National Public Radio*. National Pubic Radio, 17 Sept. 2005. Web. 9 Aug. 2011.

Slade, Giles. *Made to Break: Technology and Obsolescence in America*. Cambridge: Harvard University Press, 2006. Print.

Smith, Sidonie and Julia Watson: *Reading Autobiography: A Guide for Interpreting Life Narratives*. Minneapolis: University of Minnesota Press, 2001. Print.

Sokoloff, Janice. *The Margin That Remains: A Study of Aging in Literature*. New York: Peter Lang, 1987. Print.

Sommer, Elyse and Dorrie Weiss. *Metaphors Dictionary*. Detroit: Visible Ink, 2001. Print.

Sontag, Susan. "The Double Standard of Aging." *The Saturday Review*. 23 Sept. 1972: 29-38. Print.

- - -. *Illness as Metaphor & Aids and Its Metaphors*. London: Penguin, 2002. Print.

Spiewak, Martin. "Bitte schön spießig. Harmonische Familien: Die Generationen verstehen sich besser denn je." *Zeit Online. Die Zeit*, 31 Mar. 2013. Web. 9 Sept. 2013.

Steen, Gerard. "Literary and Nonliterary Aspects of Metaphor." *Poetics Today* 13.4 (Winter 1992): 687-704. *JSTOR*. Web. 14 Mar. 2013.

Stoddard, Karen M. *Saints and Shrews: Women and Aging in American Popular Film*. London: Greenwood, 1983. Print.

Strauss, Anselm L. and Barney G. Glaser. *Time for Dying*. Chicago: Aldine, 1968. Print.

Strawbridge, William J., Margaret I. Wallhagen and Richard D. Cohen. "Successful Aging and Well-Being: Self-Rated Compared with Rowe and Kahn." *The Gerontologist* 42.6 (2002): 727-33. Web. 30 Mar. 2011.

Strecker, Trey. Rev. of *The Corrections*, by Jonathan Franzen. *Review of Contemporary Fiction* 22.1 (Spring 2002): 122-3. *ProQuest*. 30 May 2013.

Stout, Andrew. "The Q&A: Miranda July, Filmmaker." *More Intelligent Life*. The Economist, 22 Mar. 2011. Web. 3 Feb. 2011.

Teuscher, Ursina and Christof Teuscher. "Reconsidering the Double Standard of Aging: Effects of Gender and Sexual Orientation on Facial Attractiveness Ratings." *Personality and Individual Differences* 42 (2007): 631-9. Web. 9 Feb. 2011.

Thomas, L. Eugene, Patricia A. Kraus and Kim O. Chambers. "Metaphoric Analysis of Meaning in the Lives of Elderly Men: A Cross-Cultural Investigation." *Journal of Aging Studies* 4.1 (1990): 1-15. *JSTOR*. Web. 15. Mar. 2013.

Tierney, John. "2004: In a Word; Adultescent." *The New York Times*. The New York Times, 26 Dec. 2004. Web. 6 Feb. 2012.

Turan, Kenneth. "*Away We Go*." *Los Angeles Times*. Los Angeles Times, 5 June 2009. Web. 18 July 2011.

Turner, Victor. *Dramas, Fields and Metaphors: Symbolic Action in Human Society*. Ithaca: Cornell University Press, 1974. Print.

- - - . *From Ritual to Theater: The Human Seriousness of Play*. New York: PAJ, 1982. Print.

- - - . *The Ritual Process: Structure and Anti-structure*. Chicago: Aldine, 1969. Print.

Twenge, Jean. *Generation Me: Why Today's Young Americans Are More Confident, Assertive, Entitled – and More Miserable Than Ever Before*. New York: Free Press, 2006. Print.

"The U-bend of Life: Why, Beyond Middle Age, People Get Happier As They Get Older." *The Economist*. The Economist Group, 16 Dec. 2010. Web. 21 Mar. 2011.

United States Census Bureau. "Older Americans Month: May 2012." N. p., 1 Mar. 2012. Web. 13 June 2013.

Updike, John. "One-Way Street." *The New Yorker*. The New Yorker, 31 Mar. 2003. Web. 25 Oct. 2011.

Varsava, Jerry A. "The 'Saturated Self:' Don DeLillo on the Problem of Rogue Capitalism." *Contemporary Literature* 46.1 (2005): 78-107. *JSTOR*. Web. 1 Nov. 2011.

Wainwright Steven P. and Bryan S. Turner. "'Just Crumbling to Bits'? An Exploration of the Body, Ageing, Injury and Career in Classical Ballet Dancers." *Sociology* 40.2 (2006): 237-55. *Sage*. Web. 19 Apr. 2011.

Walden, Celia. "Quintastic: 50 is the new 30." *The Telegraph*. Telegraph Media Group, 28 Jan. 2010. Web. 1 Feb. 2012.

Wallace, Diana. "Literary Portrayals of Ageing." *An Introduction to Gerontology*. Ed. Ian Stuart-Hamilton. Cambridge: Cambridge University Press, 2011. 389-415. Print.

Walther, Andreas. "Regimes of Youth Transitions: Choice, Flexibility and Security in Young People's Experiences Across Different European contexts." *Young* 14 (2006): 119-39. *Sage*. Web. 17 May 2012.

Waxman, Barbara Frey. *From the Hearth to the Open Road: A Feminist Study of Aging in Contemporary Literature*. New York: Greenwood, 1990. Print.

Wheatley, Catherine. "The Future." *Sight and Sound* 21.12 (2011). *ProQuest*. Web. 3 Feb. 2012.

White, Micah. "Consumer Society Is Made To Break." *Adbusters*. Adbusters Media Foundation, 20 Oct. 2008. Web. 16 Oct. 2011.

White, Roger M. *The Structure of Metaphor*. Oxford, Cambridge, MA: Blackwell, 1996. Print.

Whittock, Trevor. *Metaphor and Film*. Cambridge: Cambridge University Press, 2009. Print.

Wilinska, Monika and Elisabet Cedersund. "'Classic Ageism' or 'Brutal Economy'? Old Age and Older People in the Polish Media." *Journal of Aging Studies* 24 (2010): 335-43. Web. 9 Sept. 2013.

Wohlmann, Anita. "Depression and Aging in Jonathan Franzen's *The Corrections*." *The Health of a Nation*. Eds. Meldan Tanrisal and Tanfer Emin Tunc. (EAAS Izmir 2012 Conference Volume). Forthcoming in 2014.

- - -. „Junge Altersbilder in den Medien: Stereotype über das Alter(n) in zeitgenössischen romantischen Komödien." *Screening Age: Medienbilder – Stereotype – Altersdiskriminierung*. Eds. Dagmar Hoffmann, Clemens Schwender, Wolfgang Reißmann. München: kopaed, 2013. 137-48. Print.

- - -. "Let the Countdown Begin: Aging Experiences of Young Adults in Countdown Blogs." *The Journal of Aging Studies* 26 (2012): 90-101. Web. 12 Oct. 2012.

- - -. "Teenage Nostalgia: Perpetual Adolescents in *Little Children* and *Young Adult.*" *The Multiple Life Cycles of Children's Media: Childhood Nostalgia in Contemporary Convergence Culture.* Ed. Elisabeth Wesseling. Forthcoming in 2014.
Woodward, Kathleen. "Against Wisdom: The Social Politics of Anger and Aging." *Cultural Critique* 51 (2002): 186-218. *JSTOR*. Web. 10 Mar. 2011.
- - -. *Aging and Its Discontents: Freud and Other Fictions.* Bloomington: Indiana University Press, 1991. Print.
- - -. "Introduction." *Figuring Age: Women, Bodies, Generations.* Ed. Kathleen Woodward. Bloomington: Indiana University Press, 1999. ix-xxix. Print.
- - -. "Performing Age, Performing Gender." *NWSA Journal* 18.1 (Spring 2006): 162-187. *Project Muse*. Web. 6 Oct. 2011.
Wright, Rebecca. "Anti-Aging: Beauty & Beyond." *Nutraceuticals World.* Rodman Publishing, 1 Sept. 2008. Web. 5 Feb. 2012.
Wyatt-Brown, Anne M. "The Coming of Age of Literary Gerontology." *Journal of Aging Studies.* 4.3 (1990): 299-315. Web. 30 Nov. 2011.
- - -. "Late Style in the Novels of Barbara Pym and Penelope Mortimer." *The Gerontologist* 6 (1988): 835-9. Web. 27 Apr. 2012.
Yahnke, Robert E. "Intergeneration and Regeneration: The Meaning of Old Age in Films and Videos." *Handbook of the Humanities and Aging.* Eds. Thomas Cole, Robert Kastenbaum and Ruth E. Ray. 2nd ed. New York: Springer, 2000. 293-323. Print.
Yates, Richard. *Revolutionary Road.* London: Vintage, 2007. Print.
Zimmerman, Edith. "Dealing With Your Own Cultural Irrelevance (at Age 28)." *New York Times.* New York Times, 10 Nov. 2011. Web. 14 Nov. 2011.